AN ILLUSTRATED WORLD
HISTORY

IV

THE MODERN WORLD

Also available in this series:

I

Prehistory
and the Ancient World

II

The Middle Ages
and the Renaissance

III

Revolution and Empire

THE MODERN WORLD
was created and produced by
McRae Publishing Ltd, London
www.mcraepublishing.co.uk

Publishers: Anne McRae, Marco Nardi
Series Editor: Anne McRae
Authors: Lisa Isenman, Neil Morris,
Art Director: Marco Nardi
Layouts: Nick Leggett, Starry Dogs Books Ltd
Project Editor: Vicky Egan
Research: Vicky Egan
Repro: Litocolor, Florence

DISCLAIMER:

An Illustrated World History has previously been published in 24 volumes by McRae Books, now an imprint of McRae Publishing Ltd.

The Publishers of *An Illustrated World History* would like to thank all the authors and consultants who have participated in the elaboration of the text and the supervision of the illustrations created for this work.

Chapter I - **North America: Expansion, Civil War and Emergence**
Author: Lisa Isenman
Consultants: Dr. Ellen L. Berg, CAssoicate Fellow, Rothermere American Institute, University of Oxford

Chapter II - **Turn of the Century and the Great War**
Author: Neil Morris
Consultant: Professor Hew Strachan, MA, PhD, FRSE, FRHistA, Hon D. Univ (Paisely), Chichele Professor of the War, All Souls College, Oxford University, UK.

Chapter III - **From Versailles to World War II**
Author: Neil Morris
Consultant: Professor Hew Strachan, MA, PhD, FRSE, FRHistA, Hon D. Univ (Paisely), Chichele Professor of the War, All Souls College, Oxford University, UK.

Chapter IV - **From 1945 to the Cold War**
Author: Neil Morris
Consultant: Professor Willian Scott Lucas, Professor of American Studies, University of Birmingham, UK

Chapter V - **From 1991 to the 21st Century**
Author: Michael Kerrigan
Consultants: Consultant: Professor Willian Scott Lucas, Professor of American Studies, University of Birmingham, UK

Chapter VI - **Issues Today**
Author: Tony Allan
Consultants: Dr. Lawrence Black, Department of History, Durham University, UK

An Imprint of Sterling Publishing
387 Park Avenue South
New York, NY 10016

This 2014 edition published by Sandy Creek.

ISBN 978-1-4351-5438-4

Manufactured in Hong Kong
Lot #:
2 4 6 8 10 9 7 5 3 1
02/14

AN ILLUSTRATED WORLD
HISTORY

THE MODERN
WORLD

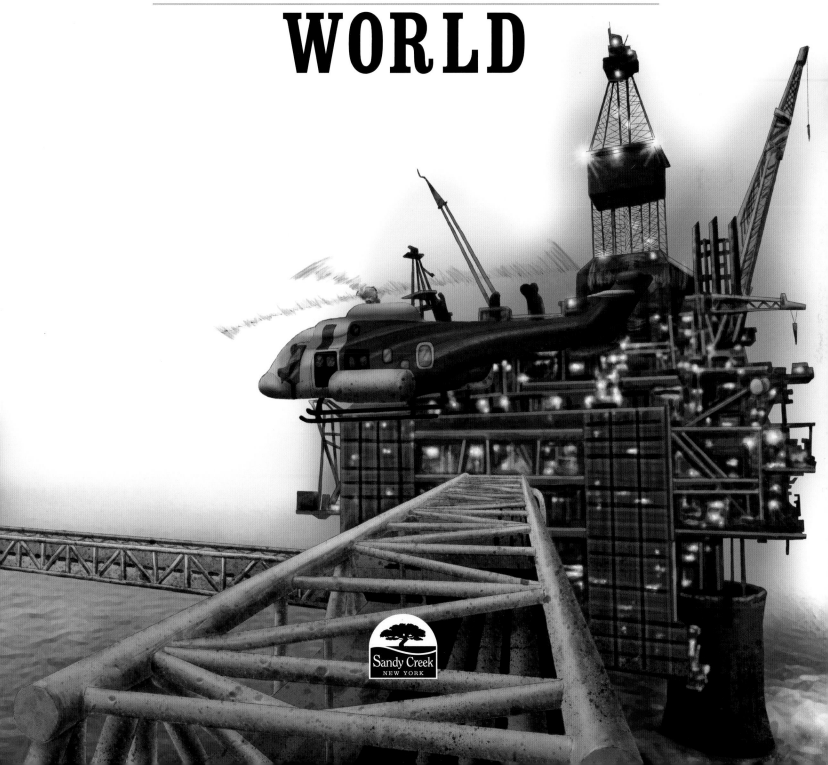

Sandy Creek
NEW YORK

Contents

The United States of America grew from a young republic to a powerful nation during the 19th century. The Louisiana Purchase in 1803 nearly doubled the size of the country, and victories in wars against Britain, Spain, and Mexico gave the Americans control of lands from the Atlantic to the Pacific coasts. As the country and its economy developed, the rifts deepened between the North and South, resulting in the Civil War (1861–65). The century ended with major developments in business, technology, and transportation.

In the north, Canada grew from a few colonies governed by the British to a nation that spanned the continent. Relations among its peoples, who included a large French population, were fairly peaceful, and by the end of the century self-rule was established.

This book tells the story of the two expanding nations, including the triumphs and the human costs, particularly to the Native Americans, the African Americans, and the soldiers and families affected by the Civil War.

Abraham Lincoln became president in 1861. He led the United States through the Civil War, and was able to preserve the Union, abolish slavery, strengthen government, and modernize the economy. He was assassinated in April 1865.

TIMELINE

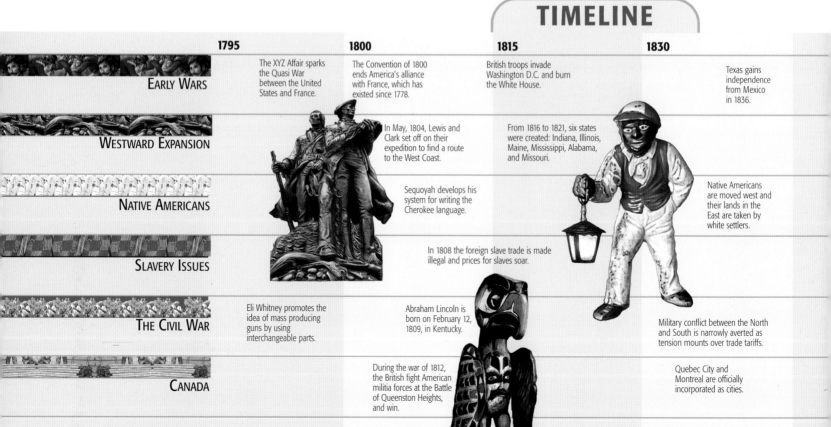

	1795	1800	1815	1830
EARLY WARS	The XYZ Affair sparks the Quasi War between the United States and France.	The Convention of 1800 ends America's alliance with France, which has existed since 1778.	British troops invade Washington D.C. and burn the White House.	Texas gains independence from Mexico in 1836.
WESTWARD EXPANSION		In May, 1804, Lewis and Clark set off on their expedition to find a route to the West Coast.	From 1816 to 1821, six states were created: Indiana, Illinois, Maine, Mississippi, Alabama, and Missouri.	
NATIVE AMERICANS		Sequoyah develops his system for writing the Cherokee language.		Native Americans are moved west and their lands in the East are taken by white settlers.
SLAVERY ISSUES		In 1808 the foreign slave trade is made illegal and prices for slaves soar.		
THE CIVIL WAR	Eli Whitney promotes the idea of mass producing guns by using interchangeable parts.	Abraham Lincoln is born on February 12, 1809, in Kentucky.		Military conflict between the North and South is narrowly averted as tension mounts over trade tariffs.
CANADA		During the war of 1812, the British fight American militia forces at the Battle of Queenston Heights, and win.		Quebec City and Montreal are officially incorporated as cities.

North America: Expansion, Civil War, and Emergence

In Canada, trappers and fur traders worked for the Hudson's Bay Company, traveling on foot through forests and across mountains, as well as by canoe along Canada's extensive rivers.

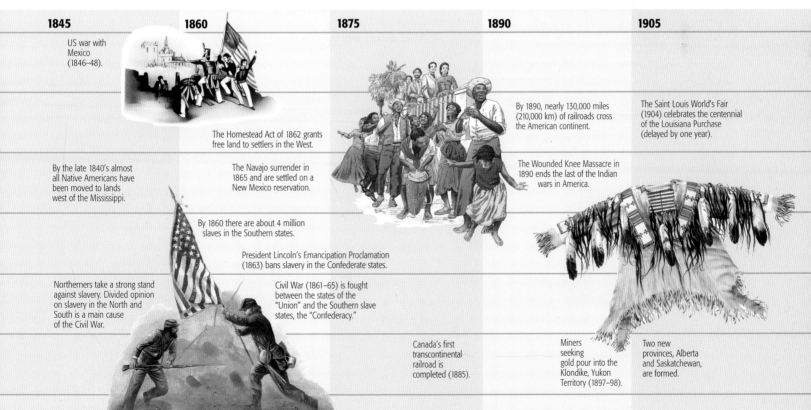

1845	1860	1875	1890	1905

US war with Mexico (1846–48).

The Homestead Act of 1862 grants free land to settlers in the West.

By 1890, nearly 130,000 miles (210,000 km) of railroads cross the American continent.

The Saint Louis World's Fair (1904) celebrates the centennial of the Louisiana Purchase (delayed by one year).

By the late 1840's almost all Native Americans have been moved to lands west of the Mississippi.

The Navajo surrender in 1865 and are settled on a New Mexico reservation.

The Wounded Knee Massacre in 1890 ends the last of the Indian wars in America.

By 1860 there are about 4 million slaves in the Southern states.

President Lincoln's Emancipation Proclamation (1863) bans slavery in the Confederate states.

Northerners take a strong stand against slavery. Divided opinion on slavery in the North and South is a main cause of the Civil War.

Civil War (1861–65) is fought between the states of the "Union" and the Southern slave states, the "Confederacy."

Canada's first transcontinental railroad is completed (1885).

Miners seeking gold pour into the Klondike, Yukon Territory (1897–98).

Two new provinces, Alberta and Saskatchewan, are formed.

Plains Indians, who lived on the Great Plains in the central part of North America, wore clothing and moccasins made of animal skins. Each tribe had its own unique culture.

A family and their animals outside their house, made of mud and grass, in Kansas, in about 1860. Pioneers settled across the Great Plains during the 19th century.

Growth of a Modern Nation

The United States began as thirteen colonies on the east coast, but by the end of the 1800s the nation extended all the way to the west coast. The Native Americans were forced into increasingly smaller pockets of land as white settlers spread west. Towns and cities grew up across the continent, and millions of immigrants swelled the work force. By the end of the century, America was no longer an underpopulated agricultural nation, but a leading industrial one.

Native Peoples

Native American peoples had strong cultures and traditions that had developed over the centuries. In the 19th century, white settlers wanted to take their lands. The native people tried hard to hold on to their lands and ways of life. Some adopted European ways and tried to fit in; others fought back. But eventually the American government forced them to give up their homes and move to reservations on less desirable land.

Pioneers Push Back the Frontier

The century began with the expansionist policy of President Thomas Jefferson, who in 1803 bought the Louisiana Territory from France, nearly doubling the size of the United States. Settlers were encouraged to claim land across the country, often pushing out native peoples. To start with, the settlers only possessions were those they had brought with them. Wars against Britain, Spain, and Mexico resulted in American control of land across the continent.

Opening up the West

"Go west, young man, and grow up with the country," wrote an Indiana journalist in 1851, encouraging young men to take advantage of the opportunities of the American frontier. Many thousands of Americans heeded his advice. From the early 1840s, explorers, pioneers, immigrants, and gold seekers traveled west in search of adventure, land, wealth, religious freedom, and a new life. The American government supported them in an effort to gain control of more land.

Pioneers traveled by covered wagon and stagecoach during the mid 1800s. By the end of the century most people traveled by train.

The Slavery Issue

Southerners relied on slaves for labor of all kinds, but especially for the hard work of planting and picking cotton, which was central to the Southern economy. By 1860 there were about 4 million slaves in the South. Northerners, who increasingly earned money through business and manufacturing, did not need slaves for their livelihood. Many of them were abolitionists, people who opposed slavery. They felt that slavery was cruel and violated the principal of freedom that was the basis of the US Constitution.

These slaves are planting sugar cane on a plantation estate in Antigua in 1823. Sugar cane was also an important Southern crop. Slaves were considered property by their slave owners, and were often treated very cruelly.

Right: This satirical death certificate for the Confederacy celebrates the Union victory in the Civil War in 1865.

A Union Divided

A rift grew between the northern and southern American colonies during the first half of the century. The northern colonies became more industrial, with the economy centered on big cities. The southern colonies were largely agricultural, worked by slaves on plantations. Southerners grew resentful of the US government, which wanted to abolish slavery in all the states. In 1860 the Southern states began withdrawing from the Union, and formed the Confederate States of America. Civil War broke out after abolitionist Abraham Lincoln became president in 1861.

Immigrants and Industrialization

Toward the end of the century, new developments in business, technology, and transportation began to create the modern nation. Farming was no longer the basis of the American economy, and industrial activity spread across the continent. People from all over the world were drawn to the United States seeking new opportunities for work; nearly 12 million immigrants arrived between 1870 and 1900. Although a few people made large fortunes, most people worked very hard to make a home for themselves and their families.

Left: The Wason Manufacturing Company, in Springfield, Massachusetts, made the railway carriages for the first transcontinental railway, completed in 1869.

Right: Jewish immigrants brought tailoring skills, among others, to the United States during the 19th century.

The French and Barbary Wars

During the 1790s, the war between Britain and France gave America the opportunity to trade with both sides as a neutral country. Its exports soared. France, however, declared that it would seize any neutral ships carrying British goods. America was held to ransom; France would only agree to stop attacking US ships in return for money. America responded by capturing 85 French ships, although war was never officially declared. In the Mediterranean, US ships came under attack from North African Barbary pirates. The conflict lasted until 1805.

Mass-Produced Guns
Eli Whitney (1765–1825) was an inventor. He promoted the idea of using interchangeable parts to make guns. Until 1798, guns had been made by hand; if one part broke, a new part had to be specially made. Whitney used power machinery and unskilled workers to make gun parts using molds. The identical parts could be assembled quickly, and any part would fit any gun.

In 1798, in preparation for war with France, the US government gave Whitney a contract to make 10,000 muskets like this one.

The XYZ Affair and the Quasi War
French attacks on US ships carrying British goods caused tension to mount between the two nations. In 1797, US President John Adams sent some delegates to France to negotiate peace terms. The delegates met three French agents (later known as X, Y, and Z), who demanded money in return for letting the delegates meet the French foreign minister. America was furious, and naval battles between America and France ensued. The conflict—which became known as the "Quasi" War, because no official declaration of war was made—was resolved by a treaty in 1800.

Right: In 1785, Thomas Jefferson (1743–1826) was the US ambassador to France. He strongly objected to his government's policy of paying money to the pirates of North Africa to stop them attacking US ships. Jefferson was elected president in 1801.

After Jefferson ended the foreign slave trade, slaves continued to be sold within the USA at public auctions like this one.

Ban on the Foreign Slave Trade
Thomas Jefferson believed strongly in personal freedom and he condemned the slave trade, which he blamed on England's King George III. In 1807 Jefferson signed a bill prohibiting the importation of slaves. The ban took effect on 1 January, 1808. Estimates vary, but some suggest the United States imported as many as 170,000 slaves between 1783 and 1808.

Founding Father Alexander Hamilton, the first Secretary of the Treasury, was a major-general in the army during the Quasi War.

THE BARBARY WARS

The Barbary Coast

The Barbary Wars were fought in the Mediterranean Sea off the coast of North Africa. The region was also known as the Barbary Coast (Barbary is derived from "Berber," the name of the region's original inhabitants). The main ports used by the Barbary pirates were Tripoli (in Tripolitania, the northwest region of Libya), Algiers, Salé, and other ports in Morocco.

The Barbary Wars

From the 17th century, Barbary pirates in North Africa had been demanding money from Britain and France in exchange for the safe passage of their ships across the Mediterranean. After 1783, the newly independent America also had to start paying tribute to protect its ships. For 18 years it paid out huge sums. But during this time, America's naval strength was growing. In 1801 the new president, Thomas Jefferson, refused to pay any more money to the Barbary rulers. War broke out with Tripolitania and lasted until 1805, when a treaty was signed that stopped payments to Tripoli and ended the First Barbary War.

Stephen Decatur's Night Raid

Stephen Decatur (1779–1820) became a national hero during the Barbary Wars. In 1804 he led a daring night raid into Tripoli harbor, where the captured US warship *Philadelphia* was at anchor. Lieutenant Decatur managed to destroy the ship, preventing its use by the enemy. He was made a captain at the age of 25, and later led troops against the British in the War of 1812.

Decatur's ship, the Intrepid, disguised to look like a Barbary ship, successfully sets fire to the USS Philadelphia in Tripoli harbor, February 1804.

THE LOUISIANA PURCHASE

SPANISH TERRITORY

LOUISIANA TERRITORY

UNITED STATES OF AMERICA

America Doubles in Size
President Thomas Jefferson's government bought the Louisiana Territory for about $15 million. The vast area covered more than 800,000 square miles (2 million sq km), and stretched from the Mississippi River west to the Rocky Mountains, and from the Gulf of Mexico north all the way to the border with Canada.

The French flag is lowered and the American flag raised in New Orleans' town square to mark the Louisiana Purchase in 1803.

A statue of Lewis and Clark was erected in Oregon, at the end of their trail to the West Coast. Clark wrote in his journal, "Ocean in view! O! the joy."

Lewis and Clark

In 1803 the United States bought a huge area of land, the Louisiana Territory, from France. This largely uncharted territory needed exploring. Led by US army captain Meriwether Lewis and lieutenant William Clark, a group of nearly 50 men set out in May 1804 on a journey of discovery that took more than two years. Starting near St. Louis, Missouri, they covered about 8,000 miles (12,800 km), traveling by boat, horse, and on foot all the way to the West Coast and back again. On the way they mapped the region and recorded valuable information about the native peoples, animals and plants.

LEWIS AND CLARK

1803
The United States buys the Louisiana Territory from France.

1804
Lewis and Clark set off on their expedition in May. In November, French Canadian fur trader Toussaint Charbonneau and his Shoshone Indian wife Sacagawea are hired as interpreters and guides.

1805
The expedition reaches the West Coast in November.

1806
The return journey begins in March. In July the group divides up to find shorter routes and explore more territory. The members of the expedition reunite in September and return to St. Louis.

The Expedition
The explorers, called "the Corps of Discovery," started their journey aboard a 55-foot (17-m) long keelboat, which they took up the Missouri River. The men kept detailed journals, and Lewis identified 178 new plant species and 122 animals. Although they had to navigate dangerous rivers, cross mountains, and face wild animals, as well as extreme hunger and cold, only one man died on the journey.

Right: Clark's notebook contained a sketch of the expedition's keelboat. His notes, and particularly his maps, provided valuable information about the northwest region of America.

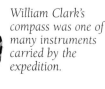

William Clark's compass was one of many instruments carried by the expedition.

THE ROUTE

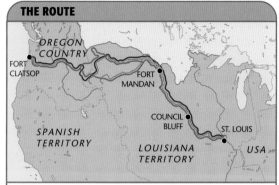

Following the Rivers

One purpose of the expedition was to find a river route across the northwest, for commercial reasons. After following the Missouri up river, Lewis and Clark crossed the Rocky Mountains and then followed the Clearwater, Snake, and Columbia rivers, which took them to the Pacific Ocean.

━━━━━ Outward journey   ━━━━━ Return journey and explorations

Fort Clatsop

The expedition built Fort Clatsop in what is now northern Oregon, in December, 1805. Finished on Christmas Day, it was their last camp before their return journey. They spent a wet and cold winter there before heading back up the Columbia River in March, 1806.

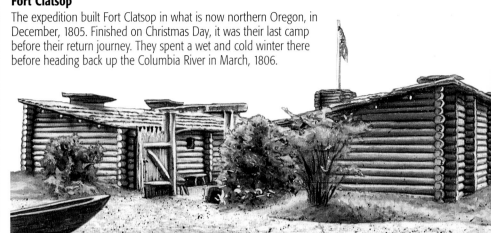

Lewis and Clark named their 1805–06 winter quarters Fort Clatsop, after the friendly Native Americans who lived in the region. This replica was built in the 1950s.

Sacagawea was born a Shoshone Indian, but was kidnapped as a girl by the Hidatsa Indians, so she spoke both languages. The expedition took her along as an interpreter. When they reached her Shoshone tribe, the chief turned out to be her long-lost brother. Sacagawea helped the expedition obtain horses from the Shoshone for crossing the mountains. Her baby son, Jean-Baptiste, was nicknamed "Pomp" by Clark.

The War of 1812

Relations were tense between the United States and Britain in the early 1800s. Britain's tight control on shipping—a consequence of the war between Britain and France—affected American trade. Britain also caused bitterness by stopping US merchant ships and searching them for British naval deserters. Thousands of suspected deserters were "pressed," or forced, into British service. Meanwhile, disputes continued over the border with Canada, where Britain was giving military aid to the Shawnee people to help them defend their lands from American settlers. War with Britain broke out in 1812 and ended in 1814, with no clear victor.

Jefferson's Embargo Act was issued partly in response to a British attack on the American warship the USS Chesapeake, seen here on the left.

The Battle of Tippecanoe

In 1811, General William Henry Harrison, governor of the Indiana Territory in the northwest of the United States, was intent on clearing the Shawnee people from the region so that American settlers could take over the land. Two Shawnee brothers, Tecumseh (see page 17) and Tenskwatawa, led a confederacy of tribes to resist the settlers. Harrison and the Shawnee came to blows at the Battle of Tippecanoe, in Indiana. Harrison's army fought off a Shawnee attack and burned their village.

General William Henry Harrison at the Battle of Tippecanoe. Although many of his men were killed, the battle was considered a US victory.

Naval Encounters in the Atlantic

The British had a much larger and more powerful navy than the United States at this time, but the Americans won some significant naval victories during the war. Only weeks after war was declared, the USS *Constitution* captured and burned HMS *Guerrière*. By June 1813, the British blockade of US ports was so tight that most US ships were unable to leave harbor. The USS *Chesapeake*, commanded by Captain James Lawrence, defied the blockade and engaged HMS *Shannon* off Boston harbor. The British won a fierce battle and captured the *Chesapeake*.

Captain James Lawrence (1781–1813) was mortally wounded defending the Chesapeake. His dying words, "Don't give up the ship," became legendary.

The Embargo Act of 1807

In an effort to prevent the British and French from interfering with US shipping, the US Congress passed the Embargo Act of 1807. The act made it illegal for American ships carrying export goods to land in any foreign port. It also set strict rules limiting British imports. The aim was to hurt Britain, which would lose food and supplies. But it was US farmers, who could no longer sell their produce, who were hit hardest. The act was later repealed.

The Battle of Queenston Heights

On June 18, 1812, the Americans declared war on the British. One of their aims was to drive the British out of Canada. In October 1812, a large American force crossed the Niagara River into Canada. For a while they held their position, but lacking reinforcements, they were surrounded and captured near the town of Queenston. The British commander, Major General Sir Isaac Brock—known as the "Hero of Upper Canada"—died in the battle.

THE NORTHERN FRONTIER

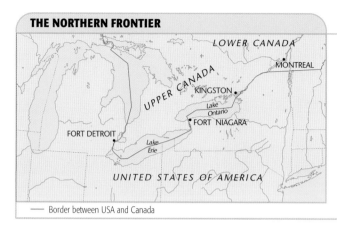

LOWER CANADA

MONTREAL

UPPER CANADA

KINGSTON

Lake
Ontario

FORT NIAGARA

FORT DETROIT

Lake
Erie

UNITED STATES OF AMERICA

—— Border between USA and Canada

US Invasion Plans

At the outbreak of the war, in 1812, the US army planned to march into the British colonies of Upper Canada (present-day southern Ontario) and Lower Canada (present-day Québec) and take control. They planned to invade at four strategic points: across from Detroit, in the Niagara area, at Kingston, and south of Montréal. From there they planned to march on and capture Québec City. Both sides won and lost some significant battles, but in the end the British held on to their colonies.

Laura Ingersoll Secord and the Battle of Beaverdams

After crossing into Canada, the US army occupied the Niagara Peninsula. Some of the officers took over the house of James and Laura Secord, and used it as their headquarters to plan an attack on the local Canadian militia, commanded by Lieutenant James FitzGibbon. Laura overheard their plans, and bravely walked 20 miles (32 km) across dangerous territory to warn FitzGibbon. Prepared for the attack, the militia and their Native American allies were able to defeat the Americans at the Battle of Beaverdams, on June 24, 1813.

Laura Ingersoll Secord (1775–1868) and her homestead in Queenston, Ontario. She kept quiet about what she had done and survived the war to live to an old age.

Sir Isaac Brock (1769–1812) was mortally wounded at the Battle of Queenston Heights. His final words were reported to be: "Push on, brave York Volunteers."

THE WAR OF 1812

1812
In August, Native Americans under Shawnee leader Tecumseh help the British capture Detroit. In October, the British win the Battle of Queenston Heights in Canada.

1813
In April, US forces capture York (now Toronto) in Upper Canada. More victories follow in September, when US forces led by Captain Oliver Perry win the Battle of Lake Erie, and in October, when US forces win the Battle of the Thames in Canada. Tecumseh is killed, and this leads to the collapse of the Native American Confederation.

1814
In August, British troops invade Washington, D.C., and burn the White House. They attack Fort McHenry in Baltimore in September, inspiring Francis Scott Key to write "The Star-Spangled Banner" (which Congress names the American National Anthem in 1931). The Treaty of Ghent officially ends the war on Christmas Eve.

1815
In January, US forces win the Battle of New Orleans, before hearing that the war is over.

An engraving by George Catlin (1796–1872) showing the Choctaw Ball-Play Dance. This ceremonial dance would take place before a game of stickball was played. Stickball later developed into the sport of lacrosse.

The Five Tribes

In the years following the American War of Independence, tension grew between white settlers and Native Americans over land ownership. The southeast was home to five large tribes: the Cherokee, Chickasaw, Choctaw, Creek, and Seminole peoples. Each tribe had its own towns and schools. When white settlers began claiming their land, the native peoples tried many things to keep their homes, including adopting European ways. The US government, however, forced almost all of them to move to a designated region called the Oklahoma Territory.

The Five "Civilized" Tribes
Europeans called the peoples of the southeast the five "civilized" tribes, because many of them adopted European styles of dress, farming, and education. The Seminole people (an offshoot of the Creeks) moved south to Florida and accepted other people, including runaway slaves, into their tribe. The Chickasaw and Choctaw languages, like the Seminole and Creek, are Muskogean, while the Cherokee language is Iroquoian.

Creek Way of Life
Creek towns consisted of mud houses with thatched roofs, surrounding a central plaza used for meetings and ceremonies. Sometimes the towns had a dome-shaped temple built on top of an earth mound. Creek women were mostly responsible for the farms, where they grew maize, beans, and squash. They also kept livestock and gathered wild plants. The men were hunters, fishermen, and warriors.

The Creek War
The Creek War started as a civil war between the Creek Indians. A group of Creek warriors called the "Red Sticks," after their red war clubs, clashed with other Creek chiefs over the encroachment by whites onto their land. They also attacked Creeks who had adopted white ways. In 1813, the US army was drawn into the conflict when a group of soldiers looted some Creek munitions that had been bought with British money. Various attacks followed, including the massacre of several hundred people at Fort Mims in Alabama by the Red Sticks. US troops retaliated at the Battle of Horseshoe Bend, where the Red Sticks were crushed in 1814.

Creek "Red Stick" chief William Weatherford (1780–1824), or "Red Eagle", surrendered to US general Andrew Jackson after the Battle of Horseshoe Bend. Jackson released him on the condition that he keep the peace.

Opposition to White Expansion

The Shawnee chief Tecumseh (see page 14) was the inspirational leader of Native American resistance to white encroachment at this time. Tecumseh believed that the only way to combat the threat was for all Native Americans to unite as a single political body, rather than as a loose confederation. In 1812, he visited the Five Tribes of the southeast on a mission to recruit allies. Although many of the southern nations rejected his appeals, he gained the support of the Creek "Red Sticks."

In this drawing, Chief Tecumseh (1768–1813) is shown wearing a British tunic and medal—a sign of his allegiance to Britain and opposition to the United States.

The Cherokee Language

Cherokee was only a spoken language until a Cherokee Indian named Sequoyah invented the written language. During the Creek War, Sequoyah realized how significant it was that he and his people could not write letters home, read military orders, or keep a diary of events. So after the war, he made up 86 different symbols to represent the sounds made in speech. Using this system, the Cherokee people were able to read and write in Cherokee, and books and newspapers could be published.

An illustration of the Cherokee writing system. Sequoyah (c.1770–1843), also known as George Guess, called his Cherokee language symbols "talking leaves."

Many southeastern tribes held an annual pre-harvest Green Corn festival, celebrating rebirth, thanksgiving, and forgiveness. People would clean and rebuild their villages, pray, fast, dance, and feast.

Texas and Mexico

In 1820, the United States stretched from the east coast westward only as far as present-day Louisiana. The whole of the southwest, including Mexico and Texas, was part of Spain's colonial empire. American settlers were not content with this. They wanted to own all the land between the Atlantic and the Pacific Oceans. Texan independence and victory in the war against Mexico added more than 500,000 sq miles (1,300,000 sq km) of land to the United States.

The Monroe Doctrine

In 1823, President James Monroe gave a famous speech outlining his foreign policy. He pledged that the United States would not interfere in any wars within Europe. He also said that he would not tolerate attempts by European powers to colonize any part of the Americas. Monroe adopted this policy, which later became known as the "Monroe Doctrine," partly because he was worried that Spain might try to reclaim some of its colonies (Argentina, Chile, and Peru, for example) in South America.

James Monroe (1758–1831) pledged that the Americas would "henceforth not to be considered as subjects for future colonization by any European Power."

Missions in Texas

Spanish Catholic missionaries were sent to Texas not just to convert the Native Americans to Christianity, but also to teach them Spanish ways of living and Spanish politics, and to integrate them into the Spanish empire. The missions were institutions, protected and controlled by the Spanish state—some had soldiers posted at them. Missionaries tried to oversee almost every aspect of the Native Americans' daily life, including work, prayer, and leisure activities. Many native peoples resisted their rigid ideals. There were 27 missions in Texas operating from the late 1600s to the early 1800s.

The San Jose mission in San Antonio, Texas, was completed in 1782. The church doorway is surrounded by typical Spanish baroque decoration.

Mexico Gains Independence from Spain

In 1810, in the small town of Dolores in central Mexico, the parish priest, Miguel Hidalgo y Costilla (1753–1811), joined a group of patriots and began promoting the idea of Mexican independence. Many native Mexicans were angry that they were so poor compared to their Spanish rulers. The uprising that Hidalgo and his patriot friends started developed into a war of independence that was to last more than 10 years. During the last year of the war, in 1821, Spanish army leader Agustin de Iturbide (1783–1824) changed sides, allying himself with the rebels against the Spanish government. The Spanish were defeated and Mexico gained its independence.

Agustin de Iturbide was a lieutenant in the Spanish army before joining the rebels. As Agustin I, he was emperor (1822–23) of the newly independent Mexico.

Texas Gains Independence from Mexico

In 1821, an American named Stephen Austin (1793–1836) gained permission from the newly formed Mexican government to establish an American colony in Texas (then a province of Mexico). Settlers were given land on condition that they became Mexican citizens and Catholics. Soon the settlers outnumbered the Mexicans, and they demanded independence from Mexico's oppressive regime. War broke out in 1835. The following year, Sam Houston (1793–1863), commander-in-chief of the Texan army, led his troops in a surprise attack on Mexican dictator Santa Anna's army. The Texans won the war and gained independence for Texas.

The "Lone Star" flag became Texas's national flag in 1839 and then its state flag when it joined the union in 1845.

Remember the Alamo!

The siege of the Alamo is one of the most legendary battles in American history. A force of 3,000 Mexican troops led by Santa Anna marched on San Antonio in 1836. There they were met by only 187 American men, defending themselves inside a mission called the Alamo. The Americans succeeded in holding the Alamo for 10 days, killing about half of the Mexicans, but eventually they were all killed. The following month, "Remember the Alamo!" became the American war cry at the battle of San Jacinto, the last battle in the war that won Texas its independence.

The Mexican War of 1846

Having gained its independence from Mexico, Texas remained independent for nine years. Then, in 1845, it was allowed to join the United States as the 28th state. Mexico, still bitter at having lost Texas and unwilling to relinquish its claim on the province, felt provoked by the annexation into attacking American soldiers on Texas's southern border. War broke out in 1846, and was won by the United States in 1848. As a result, the USA gained what are now the states of New Mexico, Arizona, Utah, Nevada, and California.

US forces under General Winfield Scott (1786–1866) captured Mexico City on September 13, 1847, effectively winning the Mexican War.

The Siege of the Alamo made heroes of Colonel William B. Travis (1808–1836) and frontiersmen Jim Bowie (1796–1836) and Davy Crockett (1786–1836). Crockett became a legendary folk hero in America.

TEXAS AND MEXICO

1819
By the Adams-Onís Treaty, Spain cedes Florida to the USA and the USA renounces claims to Texas. (The treaty takes effect in 1821).

1821
Agustin de Iturbide and rebel leader Vicente Guerrero declare Mexican independence.

1836
After a final, victorious battle, Sam Houston (wounded with a bullet in his leg) secures Texas's independence.

1846
The United States declares war on Mexico. US forces under General Zachary Taylor capture Monterrey, Mexico.

1847
US forces under General Winfield Scott capture Veracruz before traveling inland to take control of Mexico City.

1848
By the Treaty of Guadalupe Hidalgo, the Mexican War is ended.

The Trail of Tears

I n the early 1800s it seemed nothing would stop the United States from expanding its territory. Native Americans already living in the United States were forced north and west by the American settlers. In the northeast, many of the Iroquois people moved north to Canada. In the southeast, the five tribes (see pages 16–17) were relocated to "Indian Territory" in what is now Oklahoma. The Cherokee people of northwestern Georgia were among the last to go, and their journey across the Midwest to Oklahoma became known as the Trail of Tears.

To celebrate the harvest, the Iroquois wore masks made of corn.

INDIAN REMOVAL

1829
Gold is discovered on Cherokee lands in northwestern Georgia.

1830
The Indian Removal Act allows the US government to move Native Americans west in exchange for their lands in the east.

1832
The Supreme Court rules that the Cherokee have a right to their land, but the federal government refuses to enforce it.

1835
A small faction of Cherokee sign the Treaty of New Echota, agreeing to move. The Cherokee majority under Chief John Ross (1790–1866) protest, but the treaty is enforced by the Supreme Court.

1835–42
In the second Seminole War, the Seminole people fight alongside runaway slaves against US troops to keep their land in Florida.

1838–39
Martin van Buren, US president 1837–41, oversees the removal of Cherokees along the Trail of Tears.

Around 14,000 Cherokee were forcibly moved from Georgia to "Indian Territory" in Oklahoma. The name "Trail of Tears" comes from the Cherokee Nunna-da-ul-tsun-yi, which means "the place where they cried."

Removal of the Cherokee

For many years the Cherokee lived among the white settlers in Georgia. They adopted European style government, schools, churches, and even wore colonial dress. But the US government was determined to remove them. Most Cherokee refused go, so in 1838 the government sent 7,000 soldiers to force them out. They were taken from their homes, at gunpoint if they resisted, and rounded up into camps. The 1,000 mile (1,600 km) journey to Oklahoma took four months, and thousands of Cherokee people died of cold, illness, and starvation on the way. When they finally arrived, they were confronted by more angry settlers who did not want them there.

TRAIL OF TEARS

INDIAN
TERRITORY
(OKLAHOMA)

Arkansas River

Tennessee River

CHEROKEE
NATION

Two Routes Taken

The Cherokee were sent by one of two routes to Oklahoma. Some left Georgia on foot and horseback, traveling through Tennessee, Kentucky, Illinois, Missouri, and Arkansas before reaching Oklahoma. Others traveled by boat on the Tennessee, Ohio, Mississippi, and Arkansas rivers. Exhausted and sick people were not allowed to stop and rest during the journey, and many died.

◼ Cherokee Nation ▬ Overland route ▬ Water route

Removal Policy

In 1830, President Andrew Jackson signed the Indian Removal Act into law. It had been fiercely debated by Congress. Jackson believed that the Native Americans could never live peacefully among whites, and argued that moving them was in their best interests. Many Americans argued that the policy was unjust, immoral, and cruel.

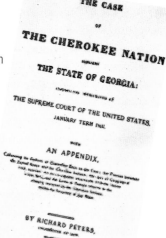

An anti-removal tract by the Cherokee nation, which tried to use legal means to prevent the US from taking its land.

Andrew Jackson (1767–1845), 7th US president, was a leading advocate of the removal of Native Americans.

Escaping Religious Persecution

The Mormons were another group who moved west during the mid 1800s. Facing religious persecution in Illinois, they began moving west in 1847. Led by Brigham Young (1801–77), they traveled to the Great Salt Lake Valley in what is now Utah. There they defended their right to practise their faith, and developed a strong community.

Mormons are members of the Church of Jesus Christ of Latter-Day Saints. The group's founder, Joseph Smith (1805–44) reported receiving golden plates from the angel Moroni, which he translated for publication as the Book of Mormon in 1830.

Gold and the Oregon Trail

During the mid 1800s, large numbers of Americans moved west. Pioneers, anxious to start a new life, were lured by reports from fur traders of fertile lands beyond the Rocky Mountains. The settlers traveled in covered wagons or by stagecoach along the Oregon Trail. Some 1,000 people joined missionary Marcus Whitman in the "great migration" in 1843. Then, in the late 1840s, gold seekers headed to California, hoping to make their fortune.

Above: San Francisco became a thriving city after the discovery of gold in 1849. This view overlooks the city from Telegraph Hill in 1850.

James Marshall's discovery of gold nuggets brought tens of thousands of "forty-niners" to California.

San Francisco

In the early 1840s, fewer than 50 people lived in the little hamlet of Yerba Buena, renamed San Francisco in 1847. With the discovery of gold, the town became the major supply center for miners. Its population rose from around 800 in 1848 to 25,000 in 1849, and in 1850 the town officially became a city. As people scrambled to get rich, business boomed, but so did violent crime. San Francisco continued to grow, and by 1870 had a population of nearly 150,000.

Panning involved swirling the gravel sediment from the riverbank around in a pan with some water. The gold flakes (or occasionally nuggets) would sink to the bottom of the pan.

The Discovery of Gold

John Sutter was an early trader living in the Sacramento Valley in California. He hired James W. Marshall, a carpenter, to help him build a mill. There, at the site of the mill, Marshall found some gold nuggets in 1848. Sutter and Marshall became business partners and tried to keep their discovery a secret, but word soon got out, and the following year thousands of people from all over the world traveled to California in search of gold. They were called "Forty-Niners," because they were part of the gold rush of 1849.

Panning for Gold

Miners spent long, gruelling days panning for gold. Food and supplies were expensive and hard to get. After the earliest gold finds, prospectors turned to placer mining to gather less easily accessible gold.

A poster advertising passage to the gold region of California aboard the clipper ship Josephine.

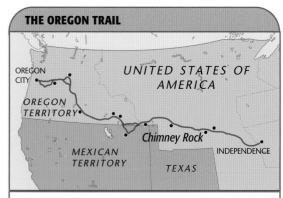

THE OREGON TRAIL

OREGON CITY
OREGON TERRITORY
UNITED STATES OF AMERICA
Chimney Rock
MEXICAN TERRITORY
INDEPENDENCE
TEXAS

Along the Route

One of the main starting points for the Oregon Trail was Independence, Missouri, where travelers would load up their wagons with supplies. The route passed through many towns that had grown up around forts, such as Fort Laramie. Some people, exhausted by the journey, settled in these towns. Short-cuts and alternate routes, called "cutoffs," were made to bypass difficult terrain.

Wells Fargo stagecoaches carried passengers, freight, and mail, as well as gold and silver from the mines.

Stagecoaches and the Pony Express

Before the railways were built, stagecoaches carried mail, supplies, and passengers across often dangerous country to the next town. The largest stagecoach company was Wells Fargo, founded in 1852 to carry gold and provide banking services. In 1857, the Butterfield Overland Mail Company began a twice-weekly postal service between St. Louis, Missouri, and San Francisco. The journey took about 25 days. Faster than stagecoaches was the Pony Express. Men on horseback would carry the mail a certain distance, and then pass it to the next rider along the way, like a relay race.

PONY EXPRESS !
CHANGE OF TIME!
REDUCED RATES!
10 Days to San Francisco!
LETTERS
WILL BE RECEIVED AT THE
OFFICE, 84 BROADWAY,
NEW YORK,
Up to 4 P. M. every TUESDAY,
AND
Up to 2½ P. M. every SATURDAY,
Which will be forwarded to connect with the PONY EXPRESS leaving
ST. JOSEPH, Missouri,
Every WEDNESDAY and SATURDAY at 11 P. M.
TELEGRAMS
Sent to Fort Kearny, on the mornings of MONDAY and FRIDAY, a line
next with PONY leaving St. Joseph, WEDNESDAYS and SATURDAYS.

From 1860 to 1861, horseback riders carried letters from Missouri to San Francisco in only 10 days by Pony Express.

The Oregon Trail

From the early 1840s, explorers, pioneers, and gold seekers used the Oregon Trail to travel west by covered wagon across America. The trail stretched from Independence, Missouri, for 2,000 miles (3,200 km) to the Columbia River in Oregon. Travelers undertook the six-month journey because they wanted land, wealth, adventure, or religious freedom. They often had to endure hunger, exhaustion, Native American attacks, extreme weather, floods, and diseases such as cholera. Travel on the Oregon Trail only declined in the late 1800s after trains replaced wagons for long journeys.

One of the landmarks for the early immigrants on the Oregon Trail was Chimney Rock, in what is now Nebraska.

A master and slave at Legree Plantation, Capers Island, South Carolina. Plantation houses often had wide verandas and shuttered windows for shade.

White Southerners

The period of Southern history before the Civil War is often referred to as "antebellum" (from the Latin for "before the war"). Some people have a romantic view of this time; Margaret Mitchell's 1936 novel *Gone with the Wind* depicted the grand plantations and genteel living, and reached a wide audience. It was indeed a time of great prosperity for the large plantation owners, who grew rich from cotton, tobacco, and sugar cane. But their society was underpinned by slavery—a cause of growing tension with the North.

Southern Whites dressed up to go out. Women carried parasols, as a suntan was considered unattractive.

Plantation House Architecture

During the first half of the 1800s, a type of neo-classical architecture called the Greek Revival style was very popular in the South. All types of buildings, including many plantation houses, were designed with white columns and grand porches like those of Greek temples. Some, such as Madewood Plantation House, built in 1848 in Napoleonville, Louisiana, were modelled on the Parthenon in Athens. Many buildings in Washington, D.C., such as the US Capitol, were also built in this style.

The Importance of Cotton

Following Eli Whitney's invention in 1793 of the cotton gin—a machine that separated cotton fiber from the seed pods—cotton became the main cash crop in the South. The plantations were worked by slaves (see pages 26–27), who did all the hard labor of picking, ginning, and baling the cotton. Plantation owners sometimes had several properties, and left the daily running of the plantation to an overseer. By 1850, the cotton industry had become vital to the economy of the South. Its importance was summed up in 1858 by senator James H. Hammond, who declared: "Cotton is king."

A large cotton plantation on the Mississippi. At harvest time, slaves (both men and women, including pregnant women) worked in the fields for 18 hours a day.

Steamboats

Steamboats were an important means of transportation for people in the South. The first steamboat on the Mississippi was the *New Orleans*, built in 1811. The following year, a regular steamboat service operated between New Orleans and Natchez, a distance of 268 miles (431 km). In 1816, improved designs meant that the boats could travel in shallower water. By 1830 there were 200 steamboats on the Mississippi carrying passengers and cargo.

Steamboats were driven by large paddlewheels. The fanciest boats had ornately decorated cabins, restaurants, and live music.

Defending Slavery

Some influential southern politicians passionately defended slavery. Senior politician John C. Calhoun (vice president 1825–32) argued that slavery was a "positive good" rather than a necessary evil. In a speech he made in 1837, he said that whites were naturally the dominant race and deserved to have slaves, and also that American slaves were treated better than slaves in other countries. Calhoun's views angered the many Northerners who opposed slavery. Such divisive sentiments became one of the main causes of the Civil War (see pages 30–33).

John C. Calhoun (1782–1850), from South Carolina, argued that slavery was good for both blacks and whites.

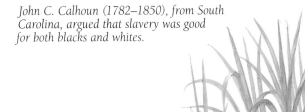

Sugar cane was crushed and refined in mills to make molasses, rum and fuel.

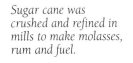

Sugar Plantations

In the early 1800s, some Southern planters began growing sugar cane, initially brought to America by Spanish explorers. It was a profitable crop, but required large amounts of land and heavy investment in machinery and slaves. Sugar plantations were especially common in Louisiana, where New Orleans plantation owner Etienne de Bore (1741–1820) developed the process of turning sugar into grains.

THE SOUTH

From 1800
Raised banks called levees are built along both banks of the Mississippi north of New Orleans to safeguard the land from flooding.

1816
Henry Miller Shreve launches his steamboat Washington, *which travels from New Orleans, Louisiana, to Louisville, Kentucky.*

1828
Congress passes the so-called Tariff of Abominations, which puts a high tax on imported goods. Britain, in response, imports less cotton from the Southern states, damaging their economy.

1832
South Carolina declares the 1828 tariffs to be unconstitutional, because they favor Northern manufacturing over Southern agriculture. Military conflict between the North and South is narrowly averted by the introduction of a compromise tariff in 1833.

1843
Norbert Rillieux (1806–1894) invents an evaporator pan system to separate sugar from sugar cane.

1854
The Kansas–Nebraska Act opens up the Midwest to settlement. Settlers there can choose whether or not to allow slavery.

Slavery and the Underground Railroad

Slaves were owned by many early Americans, particularly plantation owners in the South, who needed lots of workers to provide labor. Although abolitionists—people who opposed slavery—helped pass laws during the 1800s to restrict slavery, by 1860 there were about four million slaves in the South. Slaves were considered property and were often separated from their families and forced to work under very harsh conditions. Many tried to run away, and some succeeded, using a secret network of routes called the Underground Railroad.

SLAVERY

1793
Eli Whitney's invention of the cotton gin makes separating cotton from its seeds quicker and easier. More slaves are needed on plantations. Cotton becomes an important crop for the Southern economy.

1821
The US government passes The Missouri Compromise, admitting Missouri as a slave state and Maine as a free state, and prohibiting slavery in most of the western territory.

c.1830
Runaway slaves first use the Underground Railroad to reach freedom.

1849
Harriet Tubman makes her first rescue on the Underground Railroad.

1850
The Fugitive Slave Law is made much harsher. Slave owners are allowed to hunt for runaways anywhere in the country. People who help them, even in free states, may be punished. Slaves are not allowed to have a trial in court.

1854
The Kansas-Nebraska Act reverses the Missouri Compromise, allowing slavery in those territories.

Hitching posts like this black lawn jockey signalled a safe house to slaves using the Underground Railroad.

Slave Markets
Most slave families in the United States came originally from Africa. They were brought by ships, in which they were forced to live below deck in crowded, filthy conditions. Many died on the journey. When they arrived, they were sold at markets or at auctions to the highest bidders. The children of slaves were considered slaves too, and were sold in the same way. Potential owners would choose slaves just as they would choose new animals, looking at their muscles, teeth, and other physical attributes to make sure they were strong and would make good workers.

Slave auctions, watched by white citizens, were humiliating and terrifying for the slaves. Once sold, they had to go wherever their new owner took them.

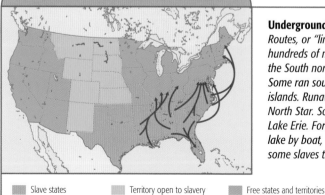

PRE-CIVIL WAR SLAVE AND FREE STATES

Underground Railroad Lines
Routes, or "lines," on the Underground Railroad covered hundreds of miles. They mostly ran from the slave states in the South northward to free states, such as Pennsylvania. Some ran southward through Florida to the Caribbean islands. Runaways traveling north were advised to follow the North Star. Some of the routes to Canada involved crossing Lake Erie. For part of the year it was possible to cross the lake by boat, but in winter ice floes barred the way, and some slaves tried to cross the ice on foot.

Slave states   Territory open to slavery   Free states and territories

Helped by "Moses"

Harriet "Moses" Tubman was born a slave in Maryland. In 1849 she escaped to the city of Philadelphia in Pennsylvania, which was a free state. There, she vowed to return to Maryland to help other slaves escape to freedom. Although the Fugitive Slave Law of 1850 made it a crime to help a runaway slave, "Moses" made 19 rescue trips and helped more than 300 slaves find freedom using the Underground Railroad.

Harriet Tubman (c.1820–1913) was called "Moses" after the Biblical prophet who led the Jewish people to freedom from Egypt.

Slaves on Cotton Plantations

Cotton became a very important crop in the South, and plantation owners used slaves for the hard work of planting and picking it. Field hands usually lived in very basic huts and supplemented their rations with food they grew in their gardens. The combination of relentless, backbreaking work and poor living conditions left them vulnerable to many diseases. They were constantly threatened with violent punishments or sale to another plantation, which would separate them from family and friends.

A slave family on a cotton plantation in Georgia, in about 1860. Even young children were put to work in the fields.

Below: Runaway slaves often traveled at night along rivers and creeks, because there was less traffic on the rivers, and so less chance of being seen. Bounty hunters, who were paid for capturing runaway slaves, pursued the fugitives with bloodhounds.

The Underground Railroad

The Underground Railroad was a network of escape routes taken by runaway slaves seeking freedom. Along each route, the slaves were helped by sympathetic people who opposed slavery. Often at great personal risk, they would break the law by providing the slaves with food, clothing, shelter, and directions to free (non-slave) states or Canada. Escaping slaves used a secret code that drew on railway terminology (hence the name "Underground Railroad"). For example, the people who helped the slaves were called "conductors," the safe houses were "stations," and the routes taken were "lines." Even after gaining freedom, slaves still faced poverty and discrimination, as well as the constant threat of being captured and returned to slavery in the South.

This engraving from about 1819 shows women working in a textile mill. Some factories, such as those of Francis Cabot Lowell, were initially known for their good working conditions.

Growth of Textile Mills

In New England in the northeast, textile mills were built for turning raw cotton, bought from the Southern plantations, into cloth. Knowledge of the machinery needed to spin and weave was brought from England by American merchant Francis Cabot Lowell (1775–1817). He improved the machinery and brought all the tasks under one roof. Mill towns for the workers grew up around the booming industry.

The Seneca Falls Convention

The summer of 1848 was an exciting time for women's rights supporters. The first women's rights convention was held in July in Seneca Falls, New York. It was organized by abolitionists Elizabeth Cady Stanton (1815–1902) and Lucretia Coffin Mott (1793–1880). About 300 people attended. Stanton later worked with civil rights leader Susan B. Anthony (1820–1906) to gain the vote for women.

Lucretia Coffin Mott, shown here in 1878, was considered one of the first American feminists.

Northern Cities Expand Upwards

New businesses brought more people to the cities in the mid 1800s. In cities like New York, there was little space to build but upwards. Taller buildings were built, using new innovations and cheaper materials. Innovations included the first "safe lift," designed by Elisha Otis (1811–61); the lift incorporated a safety device that prevented it from falling if the cable broke.

"Safe lifts" were first used by the public in 1857, in a tall New York department store.

The Erie Canal

New York City is built at the mouth of the Hudson River. When the Erie Canal was completed in 1825, it linked the Hudson River (and thus New York) to Lake Erie to the west. Settlers were able to travel from the city all the way to the Great Lakes first by river and then by canal, and trade opened up in both directions. Before long New York became the center of commerce in the United States.

The North: Factories and Cities

L ife in the North and South became increasingly different as the century wore on. In the early 1800s, most people in both regions were farmers, but before long manufacturing and industry became more important in the North. Cities expanded, and many immigrants arrived looking for work. Religious and social reform groups flourished, supporting causes such as better education, women's rights, temperance (not drinking alcohol), and the abolition of slavery. Divided opinion in the North and South on slavery was a main cause of the Civil War.

The original Erie Canal was 360 miles (580 km) long, and had 18 aqueducts and 83 locks. The Croton Water aqueduct, shown here being built, provided New York with clean water.

A poster advertising the anti-slavery novel Uncle Tom's Cabin, a best-seller in the 1800s.

135,000 SETS, 270,000 VOLUMES SOLD.

UNCLE TOM'S CABIN

FOR SALE HERE.

AN EDITION FOR THE MILLION, COMPLETE IN 1 Vol. PRICE 37 1-2 CENTS.
" " IN GERMAN, IN 1 Vol. PRICE 50 CENTS.
" " IN 2 Vol. CLOTH, 6 PLATES, PRICE $1.50.
SUPERB ILLUSTRATED EDITION, IN 1 Vol. WITH 153 ENGRAVINGS,
PRICES FROM $2.50 TO $5.00.

The Greatest Book of the Age.

Abolitionists

Northerners began to take a strong stand against slavery, and abolitionists came from many walks of life. William Lloyd Garrison's American Anti-Slavery Society demanded the immediate emancipation of slaves. The harsh Fugitive Slave Law of 1850 inspired Harriet Beecher Stowe (1811–96) to write her popular novel *Uncle Tom's Cabin* (1852), which exposed the inhumanity of slavery and further fuelled abolitionist passions.

Although thriving by the 1850s, New York City also suffered a series of economic crises. As this painting shows, in 1857 bankers on Wall Street panicked as grain prices dropped and businesses faced collapse.

New York City

By the mid 1800s, New York City had the advantage of good access to shipping, railroads, and canals, as well as a large number of people looking for work. American poet Walt Whitman described the bustle in New York as a "…ceaseless, devilish, provoking, delicious, glorious jam!"

Clothing Industry Revolutionized

Before the sewing machine was invented, people sewed clothing by hand at home, and clothes were expensive. The mass production of sewing machines in the 1850s meant that clothing, such as uniforms during the Civil War, could be manufactured cheaply in large quantities in factories. Isaac Singer (1811–75) achieved enduring success by designing a practical sewing machine that he marketed to housewives. Increasingly, however, Americans bought ready-made clothing.

A Singer sewing machine from the 1850s.

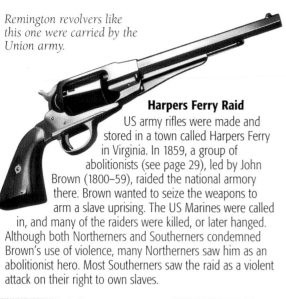

Remington revolvers like this one were carried by the Union army.

Harpers Ferry Raid

US army rifles were made and stored in a town called Harpers Ferry in Virginia. In 1859, a group of abolitionists (see page 29), led by John Brown (1800–59), raided the national armory there. Brown wanted to seize the weapons to arm a slave uprising. The US Marines were called in, and many of the raiders were killed, or later hanged. Although both Northerners and Southerners condemned Brown's use of violence, many Northerners saw him as an abolitionist hero. Most Southerners saw the raid as a violent attack on their right to own slaves.

John Brown (second from right) is captured by Marines at Harpers Ferry. His violent raid fuelled tension between the North and South prior to the Civil War.

Abraham Lincoln

When Abraham Lincoln, a Northerner who opposed slavery, became president of the United States in 1861, many of the Southern states had already withdrawn from the Union. In his inaugural speech he spoke about unity. Addressing the Southerners, he said: "In your hands, my dissatisfied fellow-countrymen, and not in mine, is the momentous issue of civil war." It was too late, however, to mend the rift between the North and South, and civil war broke out a month later.

Lincoln, who came from a poor family in Kentucky, believed above all else that the states should stay united.

Civil War Breaks Out

By the mid 1850s, slavery was a major issue for politicians (though not for most ordinary people) in the North and South. Some political leaders in the North wanted to see slavery banned throughout the country on moral grounds. Politicians in the South, many of whom owned slaves, felt their cotton-based economy and whole Southern culture were threatened by this. From 1860, eleven Southern states withdrew, or seceded, from the Union and formed the Confederate States of America (the Confederacy), led by President Jefferson Davis. The North, led by President Abraham Lincoln, denied them the right to secede, and went to war to preserve the Union.

The Civil War broke out on April 12, 1861, at the Union stronghold of Fort Sumter, shown here, in South Carolina. The Confederates fired on the fort after hearing it was to be sent more weapons, and the Union commander surrendered to them.

Union general Ulysses S. Grant (seated) was unprepared when the Confederates attacked at Shiloh. His narrow victory enabled the Union army to push on down the Mississippi River to Vicksburg.

The Confederacy has the Upper Hand

The Confederacy won some major victories in Virginia, including the Battle of Bull Run (the name of a stream near Manassas) and Fredericksburg. In two battles at Bull Run in 1861 and 1862, Lee's hugely outnumbered Confederate troops pushed Union forces back to Washington, D.C. Later in 1862, Union forces attacked the town of Fredericksburg, where Lee's Confederate soldiers were waiting for them, entrenched in the hills. More than twice as many Union soldiers were killed as Confederates, and the Union was again forced to retreat.

The Battle of Shiloh

The Battle of Shiloh took place on the western front of the Civil War, in southwestern Tennessee, on 6–7 April, 1862. Confederate troops made a surprise attack on Union forces led by General Ulysses S. Grant (1822–85) and nearly defeated them. Although Union troops eventually won the battle, they were too exhausted to chase the Confederates as they retreated. With more than 23,000 casualties, it was the bloodiest battle of the Civil War to date.

Robert E. Lee

Confederate general Robert E. Lee won many battles by outsmarting his northern opponents. Although he was strongly loyal to his state of Virginia, he was actually a great believer in keeping the Union together. His strength, courage, and generosity made him a hero among his men and an enduring symbol of the South.

President Lincoln asked Lee to be the commander of the Union army in 1861, but Lee, loyal to his home state of Virginia, chose to fight for the Confederacy instead.

The Battle of Bull Run, on 21 July, 1861, was the first major land clash in the Civil War.

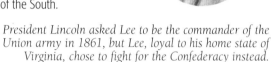

CIVIL WAR: EARLY BATTLES

1861
January
South Carolina, Mississippi, Florida, Alabama, Georgia, Louisiana, and Texas secede from the Union.

February
The Southern states create their own government and write a constitution.

April
Virginia, Arkansas, North Carolina, and Tennessee secede from the Union.

1862
March
The first battle between two ironclad ships ends in a stalemate.

May–August
General George McClellan leads Union troops in the Peninsular Campaign in Virginia. After initial victories his troops are defeated by Confederates.

September
In the Battle of Antietam, a Union victory, more than 16,000 men are killed in the bloodiest single day of the Civil War.

Civil War: The Conclusion

I n 1863, President Lincoln's Emancipation Proclamation came into effect, freeing all slaves in the Confederate states. Some 180,000 black men joined the Union army as a result. Outraged, the Confederacy became more determined than ever to win the Civil War. Superb strategy, focus, and drive had enabled the Confederate army to win some major battles during the first three years of the war. But in the end, the sheer size of the Union army gave them the upper hand. At the Battle of Gettysburg, the tide of war turned in the Union's favor.

Slaves celebrate Lincoln's Emancipation Proclamation.

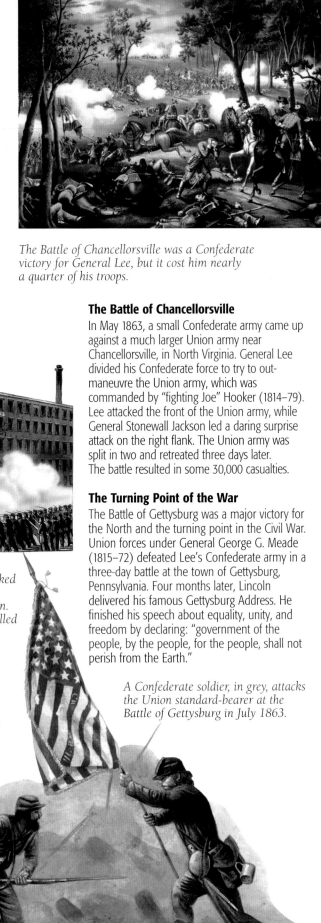

The Battle of Chancellorsville was a Confederate victory for General Lee, but it cost him nearly a quarter of his troops.

Draft Riots in New York

In March 1863, the US Congress tightened the laws requiring most white men up to the age of 45 to join the army. Only those who could either hire a substitute or pay the government a fee of $300 were able to avoid the draft. Many New Yorkers were angered that the rich could buy their way out of going to war. Rioting broke out on 13 July, particularly among the Irish immigrants, who felt their jobs were threatened by the newly freed slaves. For five days angry mobs ran riot in the city.

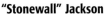

New York rioters attacked newspaper offices and killed several black men. US troops had to be called in to stop the riots.

"Stonewall" Jackson

Robert E. Lee's best general, Thomas Jonathan "Stonewall" Jackson (1824–63), was known for his resourcefulness, self-control, and bravery. He won several battles in the Peninsular Campaign, as well as the Battles of Bull Run, Harpers Ferry, and Fredericksburg. In May 1863, during the Battle of Chancellorsville, another victory, he was accidentally shot by one of his own men and died a week later. Lee said of Jackson's death that it was like "losing my right arm."

Jackson earned the nickname "Stonewall" during the first Battle of Bull Run, at which he held off a much larger Union army.

The Battle of Chancellorsville

In May 1863, a small Confederate army came up against a much larger Union army near Chancellorsville, in North Virginia. General Lee divided his Confederate force to try to out-maneuvre the Union army, which was commanded by "fighting Joe" Hooker (1814–79). Lee attacked the front of the Union army, while General Stonewall Jackson led a daring surprise attack on the right flank. The Union army was split in two and retreated three days later. The battle resulted in some 30,000 casualties.

The Turning Point of the War

The Battle of Gettysburg was a major victory for the North and the turning point in the Civil War. Union forces under General George G. Meade (1815–72) defeated Lee's Confederate army in a three-day battle at the town of Gettysburg, Pennsylvania. Four months later, Lincoln delivered his famous Gettysburg Address. He finished his speech about equality, unity, and freedom by declaring: "government of the people, by the people, for the people, shall not perish from the Earth."

A Confederate soldier, in grey, attacks the Union standard-bearer at the Battle of Gettysburg in July 1863.

General Lee surrenders

Toward the end of the Civil War, Confederate forces, vastly outnumbered by Union men, began to falter. Their supply lines were cut, and they were hungry and exhausted. At the Appomattox Courthouse in North Virginia, Lee finally surrendered to General Ulysses S. Grant, marking the end of the Civil War. The war had lasted for four years and killed more than 630,000 men.

General Lee (seated left) surrenders at Appomattox Courthouse. By the terms of the agreement, Confederate soldiers were allowed to return to their homes in the South.

Lincoln's Assassination

The Civil War left the United States in a mess. President Lincoln knew he had a lot of mending to do, but he was denied the chance. On 14 April, 1865, just days after the Civil War ended, he was shot in the back of the head while watching a play at Ford's Theater in Washington, D.C. His assassin was a Southern patriot and actor named John Wilkes Booth.

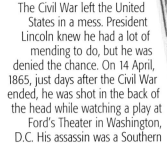

The Washington war department offered a reward for Booth's capture. He was found hiding in a tobacco barn and was killed on 26 April, 1865.

Below: After crossing the Mississippi River in May 1863, Union general Ulysses S. Grant and his Army of the Tennessee drove the Confederates into defensive lines around the city of Vicksburg, which Grant then besieged for over a month. On Vicksburg's surrender, the Union gained control of the Mississippi River.

CIVIL WAR: THE CONCLUSION

1863

January
President Lincoln's Emancipation Proclamation bans slavery in the Confederate states. This was the first step toward abolishing slavery altogether.

March
The Union government passes a new draft law, sparking riots in New York and other cities.

July
General George E. Pickett leads a successful attack against the Confederate Army, clinching the Battle of Gettysburg for the Union.

Reconstruction Era

After the Civil War, the South was in ruins. The government of President Andrew Johnson faced some major challenges, including rebuilding the South and bringing the Southern states back into the Union. This period, which lasted from 1865 to 1877, is known as the Reconstruction era. Although all the Southern states rejoined the Union and began to repair the damage, life changed little for many of the four million freed slaves, who faced poverty and discrimination.

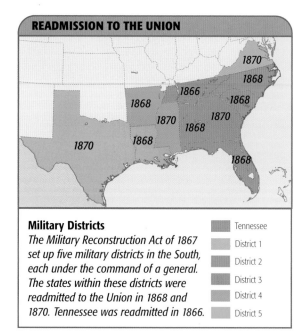

READMISSION TO THE UNION

Military Districts
The Military Reconstruction Act of 1867 set up five military districts in the South, each under the command of a general. The states within these districts were readmitted to the Union in 1868 and 1870. Tennessee was readmitted in 1866.

- Tennessee
- District 1
- District 2
- District 3
- District 4
- District 5

The North Prospers

In contrast to the South, the North thrived during the 1860s and 1870s. The Civil War had actually stimulated manufacturing and business, and technological advances in machinery made farming easier. Many Northerners were growing rich and finding time for leisure pursuits. In New York, Leonard Jerome, "The King of Wall Street," helped found the American Jockey Club and built the Jerome Park Racetrack in the Bronx.

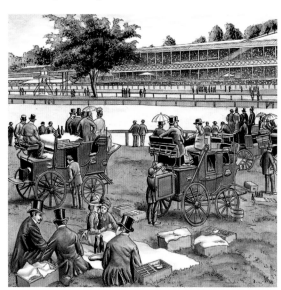

Jerome Park Racetrack in the late 1860s. Jerome was the maternal grandfather of the British Prime Minister, Winston Churchill (1874–1965).

A portrait of President Andrew Johnson (1808–75), who oversaw the reconstruction of the United States after the Civil War.

Carpetbaggers and Scalawags

After the Civil War, many Northerners moved to the South seeking opportunities to make money. They became known as "carpetbaggers," because they traveled with all their possessions in inexpensive bags made of carpet. Many joined the Republican Party, along with Southern white Republicans (known as "scalawags") and freed slaves, or Freedmen. The three groups formed a coalition in the state and local governments to push for civil rights and voting rights for the freed slaves.

Some corrupt carpetbaggers gained a bad name for taking advantage of freed slaves.

Three Phases

During the first phase of Reconstruction, known as Presidential Reconstruction (1865–66), President Johnson persuaded the Southern states to rejoin the Union, despite opposition from radical Republicans. During the second phase, known as Radical Reconstruction (1866–73), Congress passed the 14th amendment to the Constitution, which gave freed slaves civil rights, and the 15th amendment, which allowed them to vote in political elections. In the third phase, called "Redemption" (1873–77), white "supremacist" Southerners defeated the Republicans and took control of the South.

Black Codes

For many of the four million slaves who suddenly gained their freedom by the Emancipation Act, life in fact became harder than it had been before. Most freed slaves had no money or formal education, and they were treated worse than ever by hostile white people. Then, in 1865 and 1866, the Southern states passed laws called "Black Codes," which severely limited their rights. The government responded by passing Reconstruction Acts in 1867 that put the Southern states back under military control and forced them to grant rights to blacks.

A night train on the Hudson River Railroad in New York state.

CROSSING THE CONTINENT

PROMONTORY, UTAH

OMAHA, NEBRASKA

SACRAMENTO, CALIFORNIA

Central Pacific
Union Pacific
Added later

The Railroads

The world's first transcontinental railroad was completed in 1869. Two companies built the western portion. The Union Pacific company lay tracks going westward from Nebraska, while the Central Pacific Company lay tracks heading east from California. The tracks met at Promontory, Utah. The final spike to be hammered into the line was made of gold.

After the Reconstruction Act of 1867, black people were able to vote in Southern state elections for the first time.

Native Americans Forced Out

After the Civil War was over, American settlers once again began to head west, lured by the prospects of land, money, and adventure on the frontier. The land they wanted to settle, however, was the homeland of many western Native American tribes. For 25 years the United States battled against the Sioux, the Nez Percé, and the Apaches, finally succeeding in confining them to reservations. By taking their lands and killing the buffalo on which they depended, the white settlers won the West.

Chief Joseph (1840–1904) said in his famous surrender speech: "Hear me, my chiefs! My heart is sick and sad. From where the Sun now stands, I will fight no more forever."

A photograph of trader Jesse Chisholm, who drove a wagon across Oklahoma to set up a trading post in Kansas. His route became known as the Chisholm Trail.

The Chisholm Trail

In the late 1860s, settlers in the West were keeping vast numbers of cattle on the prairie grasslands. To get them to markets in the east, cowboys would drive the cattle for about 1,000 miles (1,600 km) across the open prairies from near San Antonio, Texas, north to Abilene in Kansas. At Abilene, trains stopped to pick up the cattle and take them east. Between 1867 and 1871, about 1.5 million head of cattle were driven along the Chisholm Trail, as it was known. Abilene grew into a boisterous town typical of the Wild West.

A "wanted" poster for Jesse James (1847–82).

The Nez Percé

Gold seekers invaded the first Nez Percé (French for "pierced nose") reservation in the 1860s. The government tried to move the Nez Percé people to a smaller reservation, but they resisted, and in 1877 a group led by Chief Joseph clashed with US army forces. Joseph and his people headed for Canada, marching some 1,400 miles (2,250 km), but were forced to surrender near the border.

Jesse James

Outlaws were one of the many dangers faced by the pioneers. Jesse James is probably the most famous of them. He and his gang held up trains, stagecoaches, banks, and shops at gunpoint and took people's money. When a reward was offered for the capture of Jesse or his brother Frank, dead or alive, one of their own gang shot Jesse in the head.

Apaches Moved to Reservations

For 25 years the United States army fought against Native American tribes to try to force them onto reservations. The Apaches of New Mexico and Texas, who were nomadic and not used to having to stay in one place, fought long and hard to keep their way of life. Apache resistance ended when the ferocious Chief Geronimo (1829–1909) surrendered in 1886. He later appeared at the 1904 World's Fair, selling souvenirs of himself.

The Apaches wore clothing made from animal skins and lived in simple shelters called tepees.

Sioux warriors wore deerskin shirts, often decorated with beads and feathers.

Custer's Last Stand

At the Battle of Little Bighorn (below), also known as "Custer's Last Stand," Civil War hero George Armstrong Custer (1839–76) led an attack against Sioux and Cheyenne warriors, including chiefs Crazy Horse and Sitting Bull. The Native Americans swiftly killed Custer and his whole unit. The death of their hero angered many whites and fuelled the campaign to force the Native Americans onto reservations.

NATIVE AMERICANS FORCED OUT

1862
The Homestead Act grants free land to settlers in the West. After five years, a settler can claim 160 acres (65 hectares) if he or she has built a house on it, dug a well, plowed 10 acres (4 hectares) and lived there.

1865
The Navajo surrender and are settled on a New Mexico reservation.

1877
The Nez Percé are forced to move to a smaller reservation. In response, Nez Percé warriors kill four white men, sparking the Nez Percé war.

1877
Sioux chief Crazy Horse surrenders to United States troops.

1881
The Missouri governor offers a reward for the capture of the notorious outlaw Jesse James.

1886
The Apache Wars end with the surrender of Chief Geronimo.

A Native American artist paints a scene of a ritual dance on to buffalo hide.

Left: A poster for Buffalo Bill's show, which romanticized the culture of the "Wild West."

"Buffalo Bill" Cody

William Frederick Cody (1846–1917) was the most famous buffalo hunter in the West. His amazing skill earned him the nickname "Buffalo Bill." From 1867 to 1868 he killed more than 4,000 buffalo for food for the workers on the Union Pacific Railroad. He worked as an army scout, hunting guide and actor in a traveling show called "Buffalo Bill's Wild West."

Hunting the Buffalo

Vast herds of buffalo roamed the prairies before whites settled there. The tens of millions of buffalo provided the Native Americans with meat for food and hides for clothing. In the late 1800s, however, white hunters killed them in their millions, and by 1889 the buffalo population was nearly extinct. One main aim of the hunters was to deprive the Native Americans of their main source of food so that they would have to agree to live on reservations.

Immigration

America in the mid 1800s was regarded by people all over the world as a land of opportunity and freedom. Millions decided to leave their own countries and move there to escape persecution, or the hunger and poverty caused by crop failures and unemployment. Between 1870 and 1900, nearly 12 million immigrants arrived. German, Irish, British, and Scandinavian immigrants initially dominated, supplanted after 1900 by Italians, Austro-Hungarians, and Russians. Public services such as state schools soon developed to cope with the rise in population.

The Beach Pneumatic Transit used a giant fan to propel its single underground rail carriage.

Some 40,000 Italians arrived in the USA between 1850 and 1880, largely from northern Italy. Many southern Italians came later.

New Transport for Cities

Immigrants poured into the cities looking for work, and soon new transportation systems were developed to ease congestion in the streets. In New York City, Alfred Ely Beach demonstrated his underground pneumatic train, the city's first underground railway, in 1870, and in the same year overland steam trains first ran a regular service.

The Immigrant Experience

Asian immigrants generally arrived on the West Coast and European immigrants on the East. Many had made long, difficult journeys by steamship and arrived with few possessions and little money. On arrival, they often encountered hostility from Americans who were suspicious of them because they looked different and worked hard for little money. Groups of immigrants often ended up in the worst neighborhoods, for example the Five Points slum in New York.

The Chinese Exclusion Act

The Chinese Exclusion Act, passed in 1882, marked the end of the US policy of welcoming immigrants from all over the world. Chinese immigrants escaping poverty and political persecution in China had been particularly drawn to California, where they made money working in the gold fields or building the transcontinental railroads. Many Californians resented them for taking their jobs and driving down wages. The Chinese Exclusion Act prohibited the immigration of Chinese laborers. It was renewed in 1892 and again in 1902.

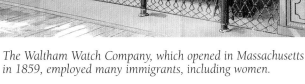

The Waltham Watch Company, which opened in Massachusetts in 1859, employed many immigrants, including women.

A Chinese immigrant working in a Californian gold field in 1849.

Work in Factories and Mines

Manufacturing was thriving in the northeastern USA at this time. Factories often employed immigrants because they were prepared to do dangerous jobs for low pay. On the East Coast, people from Ireland, Italy, Poland, and Russia often worked in grim conditions, but earned more than they were able to in their own countries. Women made up a large part of the workforce. In the West, Chinese immigrants worked as miners, which was often perilous.

Oklahoma Land Rush

After the Homestead Act of 1862 (see page 37), which offered free land to settlers, many landless immigrants headed west to claim a piece of land. In 1889 some particularly good land, serviced by a railroad and water towers, was offered in Oklahoma. At 12 noon on 22 April, people were admitted across the borders with Arkansas and Texas to claim a part of this land. The resulting town of Guthrie grew from a population of zero to more than 10,000 in a single afternoon.

Settlers lay claim to a plot of land at Guthrie, which became the first capital of Oklahoma.

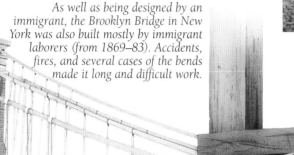

As well as being designed by an immigrant, the Brooklyn Bridge in New York was also built mostly by immigrant laborers (from 1869–83). Accidents, fires, and several cases of the bends made it long and difficult work.

Specialized Kinds of Work

Different ethnic groups tended to specialize in particular areas of work. The Slavs, for example, became steel workers, the Greeks opened small shops, the Jews in New York often worked in tailoring or ran delicatessens. In Boston, New York, and Chicago, many city jobs were done by German immigrants, like John Roebling (1806–69), who designed the Brooklyn Bridge.

Ellis Island

On the East Coast, the first immigration center was opened at Castle Garden, New York, in 1855, and it operated until 1890. It was replaced by Ellis Island, where nearly 12 million immigrants were processed between 1892 and 1954. Immigrants were interviewed and had to pass medical exams before being admitted to the United States, but only two percent were turned away. Today, more than 40 percent of Americans have ancestors who came through Ellis Island.

Immigrants at Ellis Island were checked to make sure they weren't suffering from any contagious disease.

Art, Music, and Literature

During the early 19th century, the arts in America tended to favor classical and European styles. The art movement known as the Hudson River School and the literary movement known as Transcendentalism celebrated America's natural beauty. By the late 1860s, slavery and the Civil War were having an influence, and increasingly artists and writers were expressing the hardships people faced. Slave narratives by Frederick Douglass and Harriet Jacobs exposed the cruelties of slavery, while in music, ragtime and the blues reflected the experience of many black Americans.

ART, MUSIC, AND LITERATURE

1826
America's first major novelist, James Fenimore Cooper (1789–1851), publishes his classic pioneer novel The Last of the Mohicans.

1828
Noah Webster publishes the American Dictionary of the English Language, *which promotes American (as opposed to British English) spellings and usage.*

1845
Abolitionist Frederick Douglass (1818–95) publishes his memoirs of life spent as a slave.

1872
The Metropolitan Museum of Art first opens in New York City.

1895
Stephen Crane (1871–1900) publishes his Civil War novel The Red Badge of Courage.

1899
Scott Joplin's "Maple Leaf Rag" becomes a hit.

Above: Thomas Cole of the Hudson River School used light to dramatic effect in his oil painting "Landscape (Moonlight)" c. 1833–34.

The Hudson River School

A number of artists in the early 19th century who painted the beauty and grandeur of nature in a realistic and detailed way became known as the Hudson River School. Their style is considered to be the first truly American style of painting. The founder of the movement was Thomas Cole (1801–48), who painted scenes of the Catskill Mountains above the Hudson River in New York state. Other Hudson River artists included Thomas Doughty and Asher Durand.

George Catlin's "Buffalo Dance", painted in 1844, records Native American culture.

Mark Twain grew up in the small town of Hannibal, Missouri.

Daniel Chester French (1850–1931) designed this 65-foot (20-m) tall statue, "The Republic," for the Columbian Exhibition of 1893, held in Chicago, Illinois.

Realism

One of the first American realists was the great American writer Mark Twain (1835–1910, born Samuel Langhorne Clemens), who portrayed life on the Mississippi River in novels such as *The Adventures of Tom Sawyer*. Realists wrote about the good and bad in people and everyday events in an objective way; they were neither romantic nor sentimental, and generally made no moral judgements.

George Catlin

George Catlin (1796–1872) painted scenes of Native American life that have become an important historical record of their heritage. After traveling with famous explorer William Clark into Native American territory in 1830, Catlin spent the next few years on the Great Plains, painting more than 500 scenes of Native American life.

Two Popular Styles

Neo-classical art and architecture, modelled on examples from ancient Greece and Rome, were popular in 19th-century America. Examples include many plantation houses in the South, and also the Lincoln Memorial in Washington, D.C. Naturalistic sculptures, such as those by Augustus Saint-Gaudens (1848–1907), celebrated patriotic subjects and Civil War heroes.

The Transcendentalists

A famous group of philosophers, writers, and social reformers lived in the town of Concord, near Boston, Massachusetts. Known as the Transcendentalists, they included Ralph Waldo Emerson (1803–82) and Henry David Thoreau (1817–62). Emerson wrote about self-reliance and finding truth in nature. Thoreau, who spent more than two years living in a one-room cabin in the woods near Concord, wrote about the value of living simply and protesting against injustice by breaking the rules. His writings on civil disobedience inspired future leaders, including Martin Luther King, Jr. (1929–68).

Portrait of Ralph Waldo Emerson.

Ragtime and Blues

Two important kinds of music were developed by black Southerners in the late 19th century, and they continue to influence popular music today. Ragtime featured melodies with uneven beats, usually on the piano. Scott Joplin (1868–1917), the "King of Ragtime," became famous for his "Maple Leaf Rag" in 1899. Blues (singing or playing to a particular rhythm) may have developed from "field hollers"—the calls that black plantation workers made to each other. Blues had a major influence on the development of jazz.

Louisa May Alcott

Jo March, the heroine of Louisa May Alcott's *Little Women* (1869), is one of the great characters of American children's fiction. Alcott's autobiographical novel tells the story of four sisters living in New England during the Civil War. Alcott grew up in Concord among the Transcendentalists, who included her father, Bronson Alcott. She became a social reformer and worked to gain the vote for women.

A poster for Scott Joplin's rag "The Entertainer," published in 1902. It remains a popular piano tune today.

A scene from the 1994 film Little Women, *based on the hugely popular novel by Louisa May Alcott (1832–88). Jo March was the first really individual young heroine in American fiction.*

CANADA: PEOPLES AND REBELLIONS

1812
The British in Canada support the Native Americans and First Nations peoples whose land is being taken by American settlers. America invades Canada and fights the British in the War of 1812 (see pages 14–15).

1816
A Hudson's Bay Company governor is killed by Métis allies of the North West Company. This marks the birth of the Métis nation.

1821
Montreal businessman James McGill (1744–1813) endows McGill University.

1829
The first Welland Canal is completed, linking Lake Erie to Lake Ontario.

1831
Quebec City and Montreal are officially incorporated as cities.

1834
Toronto is officially incorporated as a city.

1836
The Champlain and St Lawrence Railroad, Canada's first railway, is officially opened.

Native Peoples

Canada was already inhabited by many different native peoples before the Europeans arrived. There were native Indians, or First Nations, living throughout the region and speaking a number of different languages. And in the cold, far northwest were the Inuit, who survived by hunting and fishing. Many Europeans married native peoples, and their descendants were known as Métis. The Métis developed their own language, and mixed native and European traditions.

The thunderbird is a powerful mythical creature in many First Nations cultures.

Hudson's Bay Company
INCORPORATED 2ND MAY 1670.

Red River Settlement

In the early 1800s, Scottish philanthropist Thomas Douglas, 5th Earl of Selkirk, obtained a grant of land from the Hudson's Bay Company in Canada to found a new settlement for some of the poor farmers of Scotland and Northern Ireland. The first settlers arrived in 1812, and more came in 1815. Rival fur traders from the North West Company and many native peoples were hostile to the settlers, and killed 22 of them at the massacre of Seven Oaks (1816). The settlement recovered, however, and prospered.

1818 TREATY WITH BRITAIN

British
American
Spanish
Russian

Lake of the Woods

The 49th Parallel

In 1818, the Anglo-American Convention established the border between the British Canadian colonies and the United States. The boundary was latitude 49 degrees north, called the 49th parallel. It stretched from the Lake of the Woods (where Ontario, Manitoba, and Minnesota meet) west to the Rocky Mountains.

Canada: Peoples and Rebellions

After the American War of Independence, thousands of colonists who were loyal to the British fled north to Canada. The region already had a large French population—French settlers had arrived in the 17th century—as well as its own native First Nations and Inuit peoples. Conflicts inevitably arose, particularly over land ownership, and battles were fought between the First Nations, supported by the British, and the Americans. The borders changed many times, and increasingly Canada's peoples began to share a common goal: the desire for self-rule.

Hudson's Bay Company fur trappers traveled on foot through forests and across mountains, as well as by canoe along Canada's extensive rivers. Among the animals they caught were beavers. The beaver fur was made into felt and used to make hats for the European market.

Trading Companies Unite

Two fur trading firms, the Hudson's Bay Company and the North West Company, were keen rivals during the late 1700s and early 1800s. They used any means, including vandalism, bribery, and violence, to compete to sell more furs. Most of their resources were going into fighting each other, so in 1821 the British government took measures to merge them into one company under the Hudson's Bay name. Today, Hudson's Bay is still one of Canada's most powerful companies.

Rebellions of 1837

In the early 1800s, Upper Canada (now Ontario) and Lower Canada (now Quebec) were both governed by cliques of rich people. Many people became angry by the self-serving policies of these powerful people, and in 1837 groups in both provinces revolted. William Lyon Mackenzie (1795–1861) led the revolt in Upper Canada and Louis Joseph Papineau (1786–1871) in Lower Canada. Although the revolts were quashed by the governments, they led to many reforms, including the Act of Union, which united Upper and Lower Canada in 1840.

Rebels seized weapons from a Toronto armory and marched down Yonge Street, sparking Upper Canada's rebellion of 1837.

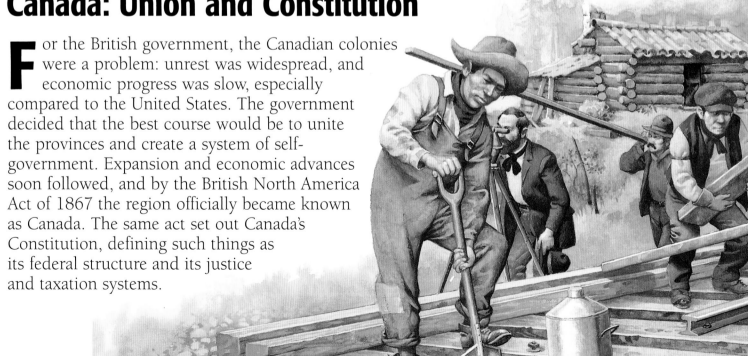

CANADA: UNION AND CONSTITUTION

1846
The Oregon Boundary Treaty establishes a border between British North America and the United States at 49 degrees north latitude.

1853
The Grand Trunk Railroad between Montreal and Portland, Maine, is completed, creating North America's first international railroad.

1854
The Reciprocity Treaty abolishes customs tariffs and helps increase trade between Canada and the United States.

1879
Sir John A. Macdonald (1815–91), the first prime minister of Canada, encourages westward expansion and growth in manufacturing.

1897–98
Miners seeking gold pour into the Klondike (Yukon Territory).

A Shortage of Labor

During the 1840s, Canada had a shortage of labor. Thousands of French-Canadians were emigrating from Canada to the USA, and there simply weren't enough people to farm the vast open prairies efficiently. The invention of a new horse-drawn reaping machine by American inventor Cyrus H. McCormick dramatically changed farming in the region from the 1850s onward. This once labor-intensive task was now able to be done much more quickly.

The Act of Union

Following the rebellions of 1837 (see page 43), the British government sent John Lambton, 1st Earl of Durham (1792–1840) to investigate the colonial governments. In his famous report, Lord Durham gave details of economic problems and conflicts between the English and the French people. He recommended a union between Upper Canada and Lower Canada. The Act of Union, passed in 1840 and enacted in 1841, joined Upper and Lower Canada as the Province of Canada.

Confederation and a New Railway

In 1867, the 1840 Act of Union was replaced by the British North America Act, which united the Province of Canada (Ontario and Quebec) with the colonies of New Brunswick and Nova Scotia. In 1871, the province of British Columbia on the west coast agreed to join this Confederation. The government, in return, took on the colony's debt and agreed to extend the Canadian Pacific Railway to British Columbia. Workers on the railway had to contend with treacherous mountain conditions and a shortage of money, but in 1885 Canada's first transcontinental railroad was completed. The main line ran between Montreal in the east and Port Moody, just outside Vancouver, in the west.

Cyrus H. McCormick (1809–84) and his reaping machine in 1837. The machine was distributed widely on the new railways that were being built, and was demonstrated to farmers by a vast network of trained salesmen.

Thousands of Chinese laborers worked long hours for little pay building the Canadian Pacific Railroad.

Canada: Union and Constitution

For the British government, the Canadian colonies were a problem: unrest was widespread, and economic progress was slow, especially compared to the United States. The government decided that the best course would be to unite the provinces and create a system of self-government. Expansion and economic advances soon followed, and by the British North America Act of 1867 the region officially became known as Canada. The same act set out Canada's Constitution, defining such things as its federal structure and its justice and taxation systems.

The "Mounties"

In 1873, Canada's first prime minister, Sir John A. Macdonald, created the North West Mounted Police (known as the "Mounties"). The force was organized like a British cavalry regiment, and its aim was to bring law and order to the Northwest Territories, where American whisky traders were causing trouble. The Mounties also kept order during the building of the Canadian Pacific Railway and the Klondike Gold Rush, and they enforced the law on the First Nations peoples, with whom they developed good relations.

The North West Mounted Police wore striking red jackets and stetson-style hats.

THE DOMINION OF CANADA

GREENLAND

BAFFIN BAY

BAFFIN ISLAND

ALASKA

YUKON TERRITORY

NORTHWEST TERRITORIES

PACIFIC OCEAN

BRITISH COLUMBIA

HUDSON BAY

MANITOBA

ONTARIO

QUEBEC

PRINCE EDWARD ISLAND

NEW-FOUND-LAND

NEW BRUNSWICK

QUEBEC •

MONTREAL •

NOVA SCOTIA

ATLANTIC OCEAN

• VANCOUVER

RED RIVER COLONY

OREGON COUNTRY

UNITED STATES

Canada, 1867
Territory added 1870
Provinces added by 1873
Territory added 1880
British crown colony
Canadian territorial claim surrendered to USA

Provinces and Territories

In 1867, the Confederation of Canada's four provinces (Ontario, Quebec, New Brunswick, and Nova Scotia) created "one Dominion under the name of Canada." This area was hugely enlarged in 1870, when the Hudson's Bay Company transferred to the government of Canada an area around Hudson's Bay known as Rupert's Land and the vast North-Western Territory (the two regions now formed the Northwest Territories). The province of Manitoba was also created and joined the Confederation in 1870. It was followed by British Columbia in 1871 and Prince Edward Island in 1873. Yukon Territory joined in 1898.

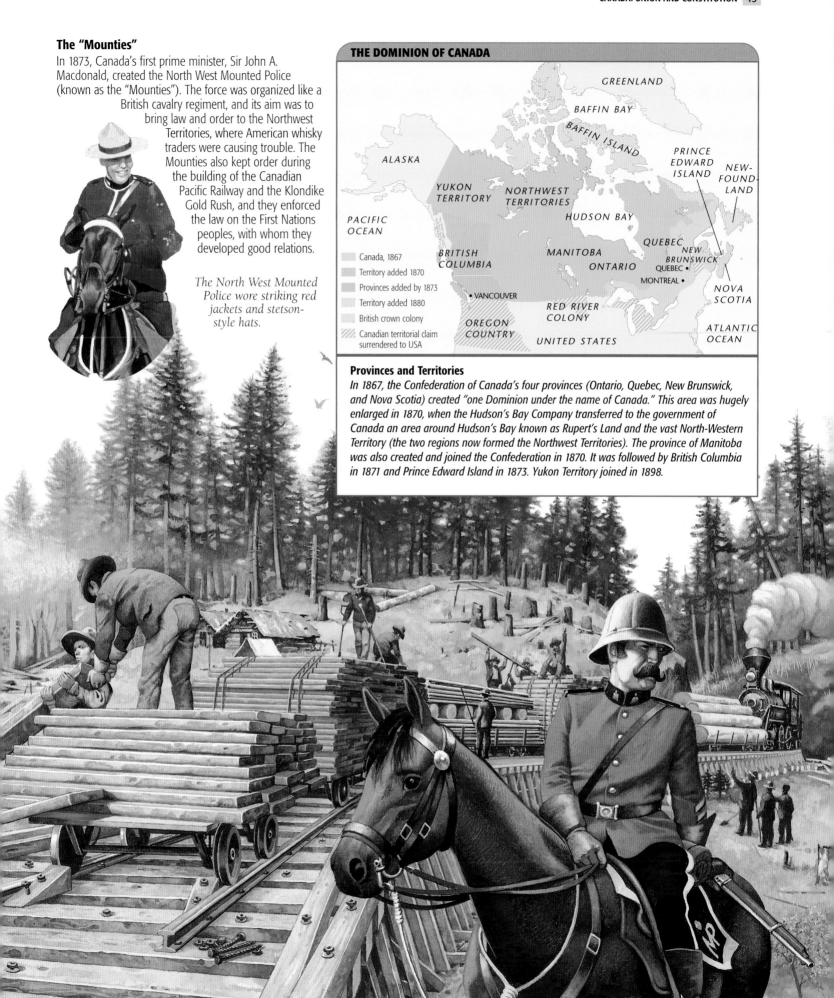

There were great technological achievements at the beginning of the 20th century. They included the first powered flight, by the Wright brothers, in 1903. Five years later another American, Henry Ford, launched his popular Model-T motor car. In other parts of the world, the early 20th century was a time of great social change. There were revolutions in Russia and China. Old empires that had been successful for centuries—such as that of the Ottomans—were in decline. In Europe, there was a build-up of military power among many nations. Alliances were cemented and political tension mounted, until war finally broke out in 1914.

This chapter tells the story of the pre-war period and describes the causes and horrors of the First World War (1914–18). It also covers developments in science and the arts, discovery and exploration, as well as the struggles and achievements of the growing women's movement.

Women in the United Kingdom campaigned together for the right to vote, and also for peace. New Zealand was the first country to grant women the vote, in 1893. Women in the United States won the right to vote in 1920.

TIMELINE

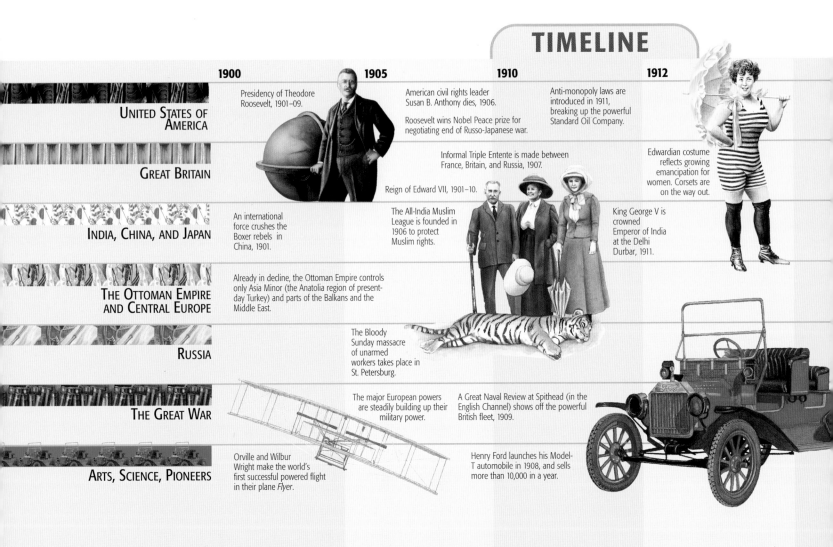

	1900	1905	1910	1912
UNITED STATES OF AMERICA	Presidency of Theodore Roosevelt, 1901–09.	American civil rights leader Susan B. Anthony dies, 1906. Roosevelt wins Nobel Peace prize for negotiating end of Russo-Japanese war.	Anti-monopoly laws are introduced in 1911, breaking up the powerful Standard Oil Company.	
GREAT BRITAIN		Reign of Edward VII, 1901–10.	Informal Triple Entente is made between France, Britain, and Russia, 1907.	Edwardian costume reflects growing emancipation for women. Corsets are on the way out.
INDIA, CHINA, AND JAPAN	An international force crushes the Boxer rebels in China, 1901.	The All-India Muslim League is founded in 1906 to protect Muslim rights.		King George V is crowned Emperor of India at the Delhi Durbar, 1911.
THE OTTOMAN EMPIRE AND CENTRAL EUROPE	Already in decline, the Ottoman Empire controls only Asia Minor (the Anatolia region of present-day Turkey) and parts of the Balkans and the Middle East.			
RUSSIA		The Bloody Sunday massacre of unarmed workers takes place in St. Petersburg.		
THE GREAT WAR			The major European powers are steadily building up their military power.	A Great Naval Review at Spithead (in the English Channel) shows off the powerful British fleet, 1909.
ARTS, SCIENCE, PIONEERS	Orville and Wilbur Wright make the world's first successful powered flight in their plane *Flyer*.		Henry Ford launches his Model-T automobile in 1908, and sells more than 10,000 in a year.	

Turn of the Century and the Great War

Sigmund Freud, an Austrian neurologist, became the founding father of psychoanalysis.

A German Fokker Dr-1 triplane (with three sets of wings), as flown by the famous Red Baron during the Great War.

1914

Film studios are established in the Hollywood district of Los Angeles.

Suffragettes march on Washington, D.C.

Irish Home Rule Act provides for a separate Parliament in Ireland.

War is triggered by the assassination of Franz Ferdinand, heir to the Austro-Hungarian throne.

Russia joins the Allies in the First World War as part of the Triple Entente with Britain and France.

Germany declares war on Russia and then France.

German troops invade Belgium. Britain declares war on Germany.

1915

A direct wireless service is established between the US and Japan.

The British government appeals for women to join a Register of Women for War Service.

The first Zeppelin raids are made on London.

Japan presents China with an ultimatum: Twenty-One Demands. These include the demand that China agrees to Japanese control over Manchuria.

The British steamship Lusitania is sunk without warning off the coast of Ireland by a German submarine. 1,198 people drown.

1916

Woodrow Wilson is re-elected President by a narrow margin.

The Ottoman Turks fight a guerrilla war with the Arabs, who are helped by British army officer T. E. Lawrence (1888–1935).

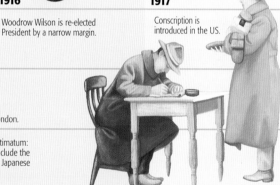

1917

Conscription is introduced in the US.

General Sir Edmund Allenby (British commander of the Palestine Front) captures Jerusalem from the Ottomans.

The Russian Revolution.

The United States declares war on Germany.

The Third Battle of Ypres (also known as Passchendaele) is fought in Belgium..

1918

President Wilson's proposals for future peace, the "Fourteen Points," are delivered to Congress.

The 'flu epidemic spreads.

November 11, the Great War officially ends.

Grain riots in southern India, and 'flu kills hundreds of thousands of people.

The Early 20th Century

The nations of Europe faced major upheavals during the period 1900 to 1918. Before the war, there were social changes in some countries, but reforms were held up by the events of 1914. In Ireland, for example, the introduction of home rule was suspended, leading to rebellion. For four years, the First World War, also called the Great War, dominated people's lives, as millions of men were sent off to fight.

The ball was a fashionable event among the members of high society in the 1900s. This painting shows a gala evening in Vienna, the capital of Austria-Hungary.

In 1904, King Edward VII visited the Austro-Hungarian spa town of Marienbad (Marianske Lazne in the present-day Czech Republic).

La Belle Époque

In France, the years before the First World War became known as the Belle Époque ("beautiful period"). For middle- and upper-class people, it was a time of social elegance and cultural refinement. For the wealthy, life was settled and comfortable, and there was a growing freedom for artists and intellectuals. However, there was hardship among working-class families, many of whom turned to labor movements to better their situation. As war approached, many socialists believed that working men would never fight each other, but for most people national interests overcame class differences.

The Shadow of War

Early in the century, many European nations were politically stable. An exception was Portugal, where revolutionaries overthrew the king and formed a republic. But France and Britain felt threatened by Germany's growing power, Austria-Hungary was in disagreement with Serbia, and Russia was worried about its borders around the Black Sea. Conflicts and tensions led to the increased importance of political alliances.

End of Empires

Two major empires—the Russian and Ottoman—declined during the first decade of the century. The first revolution struck Russia in 1905 (see page 80), and in the final year of the Great War the last Romanov tsar was murdered. Ottoman decline (see pages 64–65) led to military defeats and the end of the empire after the Great War. The defeated Dual Monarchy of Austria-Hungary was also replaced by separate republics.

The Russian royal family, photographed in 1914. They were all killed four years later.

The Cost of the War

Out of more than 65 million men sent to war, some 10 million were killed and 21 million were wounded. Millions more were severely damaged by the horrors they witnessed. Women and children at home suffered great hardship (see pages 74–75). Some men wrote about their experiences, including the so-called war poets. One of the most famous was Wilfred Owen, who was given a military award but was killed in action just a week before the end of the war.

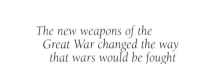

The Military Cross was awarded to British army officers for "gallantry during active operations against the enemy."

Women's rights campaigner Christabel Pankhurst (see page 59) incites the crowds in Trafalgar Square, London.

A New Kind of War

When war came, the political leaders of the nations involved assured their people that it would be over quickly. But the battle plans of both sides proved to be optimistic and sometimes unworkable, leading to stalemate. The situation was not helped by the use of new weapons, such as machine guns, tanks, airplanes, and poison gas. On the Western Front, deadlocked trench warfare dragged on, with huge numbers of lives being sacrificed to gain a few miles of churned-up land.

The new weapons of the Great War changed the way that wars would be fought in the future.

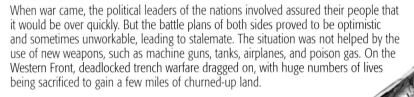

Ireland

From the late 19th century, there were strong moves to free Ireland from British rule and allow an Irish parliament to decide its own affairs ("home rule"). In 1905, the organization Sinn Fein ("We Ourselves") wanted to achieve independence from Britain by political means, while the secret Irish Republican Army (IRA) wanted to fight for independence. A Home Rule Bill was passed by the British in 1914, but was bitterly opposed by the Protestant majority in Ulster. Two years later, an Easter Rising in Dublin was brutally put down, leading to further support for the republicans.

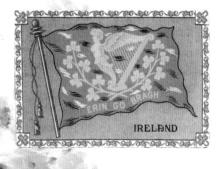

The question of Irish home rule was put on hold when war broke out just after the 1914 Home Rule Bill was passed.

The Wright brothers' Flyer had a small petrol engine. Its first flight, on 17 December 1903, lasted just 12 seconds. The final flight of the day lasted 59 seconds and covered 853 feet (260 m).

First Flights

In 1903, bicycle-makers Orville and Wilbur Wright made the world's first successful powered flights, at Kitty Hawk, North Carolina. They used a method of twisting the wings to control their early aircraft. In the following years, aviation developed quickly. By 1911, the American inventor Glenn Curtiss (1878–1930) was building the first planes for the US Navy, having shown that they could take off and land on ships.

Child Labor

The development of the US textile industry had depended heavily on child labor, as it had done in Britain and other European countries. There was little regulation, and such laws as existed varied throughout the states. This meant that unscrupulous factory-owners could exploit young workers, whose parents needed their income. The first federal law restricting child labor was not brought in until 1916.

Children working at a Carolina cotton mill in 1908.

The USA at the Turn of the Century

In the United States there was a continuing rise in industry and big business during the early years of the 20th century. Motor cars were mass-produced, and the age of aviation began. These developments had a great influence on American society in general, as more people moved from the countryside to the growing cities. By 1916, almost half of the population of 100 million people lived in urban areas.

An early Curtiss biplane. Some useful developments were a wheeled undercarriage and an upright sitting position for the pilot.

Chinese Exclusion Act

A temporary Chinese Exclusion Act had become law in 1882. It was renewed ten years later and, in 1902, the Act was made indefinite. This was the first US immigration law aimed at a particular ethnic group. It was caused by concern in the western states at the large number of Chinese workers on the expanding railroads. Like many others, Chinese immigrants had also been tempted by the California gold rush.

Many immigrant families kept up their own traditions. These Chinese parents are celebrating their son's birthday.

Above: the killing of the president of USA, William McKinley.

About 28,000 buildings were destroyed by the San Francisco earthquake and fire. Burst water pipes hampered attempts to put the fires out.

The San Francisco Earthquake

Early on the morning of 18 April 1906, the city of San Francisco shook for up to a minute. The terrible damage caused by the earthquake was made worse by raging fires, many of which came about because of overturned stoves. The fires burned for three days, and the disaster killed at least 3,000 people and left 225,000 homeless. Survivors did their best to find safe areas outside the city.

The Square Deal

President Theodore Roosevelt introduced a program of social reform that was known as the Square Deal. Roosevelt himself used the term after settling a miners' strike in 1902. He believed that industry and trade unions could get along together, so long as workers were treated fairly (given a "square deal"). This led to Congress establishing a Department of Commerce and Labor in 1903.

President Roosevelt stands next to a globe. His policy in foreign affairs was to "speak softly and carry a big stick," combining diplomacy with military strength.

THE USA AT THE TURN OF THE CENTURY

1901
On 6 September, President William McKinley (1843–1901) is shot by anarchist Leon F. Czolgosz at the Pan American Exposition in Buffalo, New York; McKinley dies 8 days later.

1901–09
Presidency of Theodore Roosevelt (1858–1919).

1903
The US acquires construction rights to the Panama Canal after supporting a revolution in Panama that helped it gain independence from Colombia.

1907
Oklahoma becomes a state.

1908
A "gentlemen's agreement" is made between the US and Japan, reducing immigration but stopping discriminatory laws.

1912
Arizona and New Mexico become states.

1911
Anti-monopoly laws break up John D. Rockefeller's powerful Standard Oil Company.

1913
The US government gains the power to levy an income tax.

1914
The world's first airline operates flying-boat flights in Florida, USA, between St. Petersburg and Tampa.

1916
The first federal child labor law is passed by the US Congress, including a minimum working age of 14.

The Birth of Film

After the first public screening of moving pictures in Paris in 1895, filmmaking made great progress during the first twenty years of the 20th century. Movies became popular both in Europe and the United States. Talkies had not yet been invented, but the silent films were often accompanied by live music. Later, titles were inserted in scenes to show some dialogue. By 1915, film companies were all looking for star performers.

Helen Holmes prepares to leap onto a moving train in a trademark piece of athletic action.

American actress Lillian Gish (1893–1993) was one of the greatest stars of the silent screen.

Stunt Action

In the early days of film, actors performed their own stunts. This was a dangerous business. One of the best stunt-actresses was Helen Holmes (1893–1950), who began her film career in 1912. Two years later she starred in *The Hazards of Helen*, a series of 26 "thrill-a-minute" episodes. The heroine usually chased bad guys and had to jump on and off moving vehicles to catch them.

Special Effects

Filmmakers realized that they could make things more exciting by using special effects. In the early days, many effects were produced within the camera, or by using miniatures or back projection. French director Georges Méliès (1861–1938) experimented with movies, using a glass-enclosed studio for stop motion, superimposing images and other tricks. He also used color by hand-painting the film. Between 1899 and 1912 Méliès made more than 400 films.

Left: A still from Georges Méliès' science-fiction film A Trip to the Moon (1902).

Silent Superstar

British-born American comedian Charlie Chaplin (1889–1977) took the world of silent comedy films by storm. He was enormously popular playing a likeable tramp dressed in baggy trousers, wearing a bowler hat and shuffling along in outsized shoes. Chaplin made *The Tramp* in 1915, and he was soon writing and directing as well as starring in his own films. Filmgoers called him "the funniest man in the world."

Right: Charlie Chaplin in front of the camera as the tramp character he called "the little fellow."

THE BIRTH OF FILM

1902
The first permanent cinema (Tally's Electric Theater) opens in Los Angeles, California.

1905
The first nickelodeon, a small movie theatre costing a nickel (5 cents) admission, opens in Pittsburgh, Pennsylvania.

1907
The first multiple-reel films appear in the US.

1908
Ten film companies form the Motion Picture Patents Company (MPPC). By now there are 10,000 nickelodeons in the US.

1912
Lillian Gish makes her debut with her sister Dorothy in D. W. Griffith's An Unseen Enemy.

1913
The Keystone Studio signs up Charlie Chaplin when he tours the US with a pantomime company.

1914
Studios are established in the Hollywood district of Los Angeles.

1915
D.W. Griffith's Intolerance, an epic historical film, opens in New York.

A poster advertising
The Great Train Robbery.

Artistic Techniques

American director D. W. Griffith (1875–1948) used new techniques to improve silent films. He moved the camera much more than others, introducing shots from various angles and distances, including close-ups. His most famous film was *The Birth of a Nation* (1915), an epic about the American Civil War. The film was praised for its technique, but it was also criticized as being racist.

Poster for Cabiria *by Giovanni Pastrone (1914). It was the second blockbuster in the history of world cinema, after* Quo Vadis? *by Enrico Guazzoni (1876-1949).*

Below: Still from The Birth of a Nation, *with Lillian Gish on the right. The film was more than two hours long and became a huge hit.*

Storytelling

In 1903, the American director Edwin S. Porter made one of the first films to tell a continuous story—all in 12 minutes. The action of *The Great Train Robbery* was "sensational and startling" (see poster, above). It showed the robbery itself, the robbers being chased, and their eventual capture. It set the scene for many Western films to come.

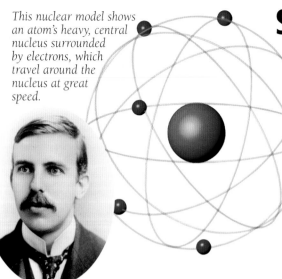

This nuclear model shows an atom's heavy, central nucleus surrounded by electrons, which travel around the nucleus at great speed.

Science and Technology

Great scientific advances were made in the early years of the 20th century. Those scientists who made the most revolutionary contributions were rewarded with a new honor—the Nobel Prize. Developments in physics and chemistry also led to medical advances, helping to treat disease and creating healthier living conditions for many people. In the field of engineering, motor cars became more widely available as new methods made them cheaper to produce.

A gramophone-record cover showing the importance of rail transport in 1900.

Nuclear Science

New Zealand-born physicist Ernest Rutherford (above) (1871–1937) is often called the father of nuclear science. He discovered that atoms—the basic particles of all matter—have a nucleus at the center. In 1911 he put forward his own nuclear model of the atom, for which he is most famous. During the First World War, Rutherford worked on ways of detecting submarines.

Wireless Communication

Telegraph signals had been sent along wires since the 1830s, but at the beginning of the 20th century a new wireless form of communication was discovered. The Italian inventor and electrical engineer Guglielmo Marconi sent his first radio signals in 1895. Six years later, he transmitted a signal across the Atlantic Ocean (see map, right). The earliest practical use of the "wireless" (or radio) was communication with ships, and developing knowledge soon led to the first radio broadcasts for news and entertainment.

TRANSATLANTIC SIGNAL

From England to Newfoundland
Many scientists thought that because radio waves travel in a straight line, they could not be sent a long way because of the curvature of the earth. On 12 December 1901, Marconi proved them wrong. He repeatedly transmitted the three dots of the Morse code letter "S" from Poldhu, in Cornwall, to St. John's, in Newfoundland (Canada)—a distance of more than 2,100 miles (3,400 km).

Guglielmo Marconi (1874–1937) sits at a desk full of electrical equipment. The wired devices were used to send and receive wireless signals.

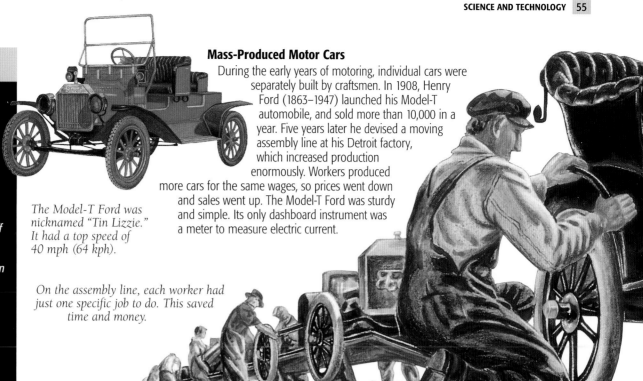

SCIENCE AND TECHNOLOGY

1900
German physicist Max Planck (1858–1947) discovers that the radiation of light occurs in units of energy, called quanta.

1901
First Nobel Prizes: Chemistry–Jacobus Hoff (Netherlands) for discovering chemical laws; Medicine–Emil von Behring (Germany) for diphtheria antitoxin; Physics–Wilhelm Roentgen (Germany) for X rays.

1902
US steel manufacturer Andrew Carnegie founds the Carnegie Institution of Washington as an organization for scientific discovery.

1906
British biochemist Frederick Hopkins (1861–1947) discovers that foods contain "accessory food factors," later called vitamins.

1907
A regular transatlantic wireless telegraph service is introduced.

1908
Ernest Rutherford wins the Nobel Prize for Chemistry (for research into chemical elements).

1909
Belgian-born US chemist Leo Baekeland (1863–1944) patents a synthetic resin (or early plastic) called Bakelite.

1910
German chemist Paul Ehrlich introduces chemotherapy (the treatment of disease with chemical drugs).

Mass-Produced Motor Cars

During the early years of motoring, individual cars were separately built by craftsmen. In 1908, Henry Ford (1863–1947) launched his Model-T automobile, and sold more than 10,000 in a year. Five years later he devised a moving assembly line at his Detroit factory, which increased production enormously. Workers produced more cars for the same wages, so prices went down and sales went up. The Model-T Ford was sturdy and simple. Its only dashboard instrument was a meter to measure electric current.

The Model-T Ford was nicknamed "Tin Lizzie." It had a top speed of 40 mph (64 kph).

On the assembly line, each worker had just one specific job to do. This saved time and money.

Nobel Prizes

Swedish businessman Alfred Nobel (1833–96) left a large sum of money to found annual awards for people who achieved great things "for the benefit of mankind." The first Nobel Prizes–for Chemistry, Physics, and Medicine or Physiology, as well as for Literature and Peace–were awarded in 1901. Polish-born French scientist Marie Curie won the 1903 physics prize (with her husband Pierre and Antoine Becquerel) for research on radiation. Eight years later she won the prize for chemistry on her own.

Marie Curie (1867–1934) made remarkable discoveries about radioactivity. She named the metallic element polonium after her native Poland.

Albert Einstein

Einstein was a German-born physicist, who became a Swiss citizen in 1905. In the same year he published a series of papers, with theories that showed new ways of thinking about time and space. Einstein's revolutionary theory of relativity said that while the speed of light is constant, time and motion are relative (or changeable) to an observer. Earlier scientists had insisted that time itself was always constant. Einstein widened the theory in 1916, and five years later received a Nobel Prize for Physics.

Albert Einstein (1879–1955), photographed in 1905. He worked in the Swiss patent office before he published his great theories.

Two British Kings

At the beginning of the 20th century, Britain was one of the world's most powerful nations. It had a vast empire and dominated areas of industry and commerce, including shipping and banking. The nation's foreign policy had been one of "splendid isolation," but now efforts were made to form alliances with Japan, France, and Russia. Edward VII, who succeeded Queen Victoria in 1901, made a significant contribution to British diplomacy in the years leading up to the First World War; his son, George V, had a less decisive role.

A three-handled Spode cup commemorating victories in the Boer War and declaring "Equal rights for all."

Edward VII, portrayed in royal regalia in 1902, the year of his coronation.

The Edwardian Age

Edward VII, whose reign became known as the Edwardian era, was a very popular king and a leader of British society. He enjoyed sports, and horses from the royal stables won the Derby three times. But he was also interested in foreign affairs, making an important official visit to France and later becoming the first reigning monarch to visit Russia.

Entente Cordiale

In 1904, France and Britain agreed to settle long-standing colonial disputes. The two countries reached an Entente Cordiale, or "friendly understanding." Among other things, they recognized each other's African interests, especially France's in Morocco and Britain's in Egypt. The agreement was not popular with Germany, which tried to put pressure on it, but only succeeded in strengthening the Anglo-French alliance.

Second Boer War

The British had fought the Boers (Dutch for "farmers") in 1881 for control of certain parts of southern Africa. Having lost territory then, the British fought the Dutch immigrants again from 1899 to 1902 in an attempt to take over the Boer republics of the Transvaal and Orange Free State. The British victors brutally herded many thousands of Boers into camps.

Below: This postcard makes fun of the Entente Cordiale. It shows President Émile Loubet, followed by Edward VII and French foreign minister Théophile Delcassé.

Prime Minister Asquith

Herbert Henry Asquith became prime minister in 1908. His Liberal government had an informal agreement of cooperation with the newly formed Labour Party and brought in important social reforms aimed at helping the working class. These included the Old Age Pension Act and increased taxes for the wealthy. Some reforms were resisted by the upper house of parliament (the House of Lords), and Asquith succeeded in reducing the Lords' power and opposition.

Portrait of Herbert Henry Asquith (1852–1928), who was prime minister until 1916. Later, he became the Earl of Oxford and Asquith.

THE BRITISH EMPIRE

Colonies Across the World

The map shows the extent of British colonial interests in 1912. Inherited from the Victorian era, these stretched from Canada to Australia and New Zealand. India and large parts of Africa were also still under British control. Other European powers were trying to expand their empires in Africa and Asia, leading to great rivalry.

George V comes to the throne

George V (1865–1936) was the second son of Edward VII, but became heir to the throne when his elder brother died in 1892. George became king on his father's death in 1910, and the following year he and his wife, Queen Mary, visited India and attended the Delhi Durbar, a splendid parade of imperial might. During the first few years of his reign, Germany began to build up its armaments.

Below: A magnificent luncheon was held at the Guildhall in London to celebrate King George V's coronation.

BRITAIN BEFORE THE FIRST WORLD WAR

1901–10
Reign of Edward VII.

1902
The Peace of Vereeniging ends the second Boer War. An Anglo-Japanese Alliance is signed in London.

1902–05
Arthur Balfour (1848–1930) is Conservative prime minister of Britain.

1905–08
Henry Campbell-Bannerman (1836–1908) is Liberal prime minister, with Asquith in his cabinet.

1906
The Liberals win an important general election; the Labour Representation Committee (formed in 1900) is renamed the Labour Party.

1907
An Anglo-Russian agreement leads to the informal Triple Entente between France, Britain, and Russia.

1909
A Great Naval Review at Spithead (in the English Channel) shows off the powerful British fleet.

1911
The government's Parliamentary Act limits the power of the House of Lords.

Gibson girls were outdoor, athletic types. They showed a spirit of adventure with a touch of mischief.

Gibson Girls

American illustrator Charles D. Gibson (1867–1944) was a specialist in pen-and-ink drawing. His illustrations of attractive, fun-loving young women appeared in weekly journals around the turn of the century and were extremely popular. The "Gibson girls", as they were known, were seen as the American ideal of fashionable femininity. They captured the spirit of the age.

WOMEN BEFORE THE WAR

1902
Australia gives women the right to vote in national elections.

1903
Emmeline Pankhurst and daughter Christabel found the National Women's Social and Political Union.

1906
Finland becomes the first European country to give women the vote.

1907
Finland has the world's first female members of parliament. The American Equality League of Self-Supporting Women is founded.

1913
Women gain the vote in Norway. The British "Cat and Mouse Act" allows the temporary release from prison of suffragettes whose health is in danger from hunger striking. Suffragette Emily Davison deliberately runs in front of a horse owned by King George V at the Derby race and is killed.

1914
Beatrice Webb and her husband Sidney join the Labour Party.

Suffragettes

The suffragettes were women who sought the right to vote in political elections (this right is called suffrage). From 1903 they organized demonstrations, chained themselves to railings and used other forms of protest to try and get women the vote. In Britain, they were led by Emmeline Pankhurst (1858–1928). She and her daughters Christabel and Sylvia were treated harshly by the authorities and imprisoned. Many suffragette prisoners who went on hunger strike were force-fed.

Women Before the War

Roles and opportunities for women began to change during the early years of the 20th century. Some women started to find work as typists and telephonists, while others found careers as writers. Votes for women had been secured in New Zealand in 1893, and women's movements gradually made greater political demands in other countries around the world. In Britain, a growing number of suffragettes overcame harsh treatment to make progress possible for women of all social classes.

Members of the suffragette movement celebrate their release from prison in 1908. It was another 20 years before British women got full voting rights.

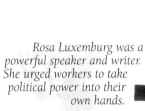

Above: German score of a 1913 operetta, The Ideal Wife, *featuring the tango, which was clearly a big selling point.*

Dance Crazes

Dance music was very popular throughout the period. The favorite form of piano music was ragtime, which influenced the development of jazz. Wind-up gramophones were becoming popular, so young people could play music to dance to, as well as going to dance halls. From 1910 a new dance came from Argentina to the United States and Europe—the tango. This dance involved a close embrace that shocked many older people at the time.

Rosa Luxemburg

Many women took part in revolutionary politics. Polish-born German communist Rosa Luxemburg (1871–1919) followed the teachings of Karl Marx. She helped found the Polish Social Democratic Party and, later, the German Communist Party. From 1907 to 1914 she taught at the Social Democratic Party School in Berlin. "Bloody Rosa," as she was sometimes called, was a great believer in the power of mass strikes.

Rosa Luxemburg was a powerful speaker and writer. She urged workers to take political power into their own hands.

This stained-glass window commemorating the Fabian Society was commissioned by dramatist George Bernard Shaw in 1910.

Beatrice Webb

The English socialist Beatrice Webb (1858–1943) came from a wealthy background. A great believer in equality and democracy, she became a social worker in London, where her experiences among poor people underlined her beliefs. She joined the socialist Fabian Society and married one of its executive members, Sidney Webb. Beatrice served on a royal commission investigating poverty in Britain. Together, Beatrice and Sidney established the political journal *New Statesman*.

Captain Scott in his winter base, during his second and last expedition to Antarctica.

Scott of the Antarctic

British naval officer Captain Robert Falcon Scott (1868–1912) led two expeditions to Antarctica. He sailed south first in *Discovery* (1900–04) and then in *Terra Nova* (1910–12). The second expedition turned into a so-called "Race to the South Pole" with Amundsen (see below). Scott reached the Pole in January 1912, only to find that he had been beaten to it. He and his four companions died on the return journey.

Roald Amundsen

Norwegian explorer Roald Amundsen (1872–1928) had great success in both polar regions. In 1903–06 he was first to sail through the Northwest Passage, the Arctic sea route leading from the Atlantic to the Pacific Ocean. Five years later Amundsen became the first man to reach the South Pole—on December 14, 1911—beating Scott by 5 weeks.

Amundsen (on the left, with one of his team of four) carries out a survey at the southernmost point on Earth.

Exploration and Discovery

During the previous century many of the great European explorers had concentrated on Africa and the tropical regions of the world. At the beginning of the 1900s the polar regions were left as some of the world's least explored areas. This caused races to the North and South Poles that led to well-documented stories of hardship and heroism. In Asia and South America, archeologists were making further astonishing discoveries about the world's earlier civilizations.

To the North Pole

American explorer Robert Peary led an expedition to Greenland in 1891, with his wife Josephine, colleague Matthew Henson, and future rival Frederick Cook. Eighteen years later—on April 6, 1909—Peary and Henson, along with four Inuit helpers, arrived at the North Pole. Then Peary learned that Cook claimed to have reached the Pole a year earlier. This was disputed, and experts credit Peary with having been first.

Robert Peary (1856–1920) learned his Arctic skills, including clothing, diet, and dog-handling, from the Inuit people.

Lost City of the Incas

American archeologist Hiram Bingham (1875–1956) taught Latin American history at Yale University. But he liked to be thought of as an explorer rather than an academic. In July 1911, Native American guides led him to an overgrown site in the Andes mountains of Peru. Bingham had been searching for remains of the Inca people, whose empire had been destroyed by invading Europeans in the 16th century. He soon realized from the wonderful stonework he saw that he had rediscovered an Inca city with a sacred plaza and a circular temple.

Right: When Bingham discovered the Inca city, called Machu Picchu, it was overgrown. Today, the cleared and excavated site is a great tourist attraction.

Harriet Quimby's trademark flight suit was made of purple satin.

Trans-Antarctic Expedition

Sir Ernest Shackleton (1874–1922) was on Captain Scott's first polar expedition, and Shackleton almost reached the South Pole himself in 1909. On his British Imperial Trans-Antarctic Expedition of 1914–16, Shackleton's ship *Endurance* got stuck in the ice and was eventually crushed. He and his crew drifted for five months on ice floes before reaching Elephant Island by sledge and boat. Shackleton then sailed for 800 miles (1,300 km) to find help. He died in the Antarctic at the start of his next expedition.

This photograph shows some of Shackleton's dogs beside his ice-wrecked ship.

Aviation Pioneer

In 1911, aviatrix Harriet Quimby became the first American woman to receive a pilot's licence. She soon became the first woman to make a night-time flight and, in 1912, the first female pilot to fly across the English Channel. She made the flight in a plane designed by Louis Blériot, who had achieved the feat two years earlier. Quimby's flight lasted 59 minutes. Later in the year, she was killed at the Boston Aviation Meeting when her plane crashed.

Asia in the Early 20th Century

There were major developments in the largest and most powerful Asian countries during this period. The Qing Dynasty lost power in China, and revolution led to the setting up of a republic. In India, British colonial control was coming under pressure from Hindu and Muslim nationalists. Meanwhile, imperial Japan became the first Asian nation to defeat a European power (Russia) in war and was able to expand its colonies.

In 1901 the Boxer rebels were rounded up. Many were shot.

The Boxer Rebellion

In 1900, a group of Chinese rebels rose against Westerners, including Christian missionaries and their Chinese converts. Called Boxers from the name of their secret society, the Righteous and Harmonious Fists, the rebels marched on Beijing. They burned houses and schools, attacking anyone who supported foreigners. A year later, the rebellion was crushed by an international force of troops from eight different nations.

Japanese flags were flown to celebrate a great victory over Russia.

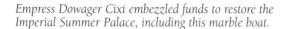

Empress Dowager Cixi embezzled funds to restore the Imperial Summer Palace, including this marble boat.

Empress Dowager Cixi

During the reign of the Manchu emperor Guangxu, from 1875 to 1908, Guangxu's adoptive mother Cixi acted as regent. She dominated the Chinese government and prevented the young emperor from modernizing the fading imperial system. Previously consort of one emperor and then mother of another, the empress dowager resisted reform, holding back China's opportunity for peaceful change. In 1908, on her deathbed, Cixi ordered that the emperor be poisoned.

Russo-Japanese War

The Russo-Japanese War of 1904–05 arose from the countries' conflicting interests in Manchuria. The Japanese used modern equipment and superior leadership to defeat the Russian land forces and Baltic fleet. Their victory inspired other colonized peoples as the first example of an Asian nation defeating a European power. At the resulting peace conference in New Hampshire, USA, Japan gained control of southern Manchuria and Korea.

Revolution in China

In 1905, Chinese revolutionary organizations formed a United League, choosing Sun Yat-sen as their leader. Over the next six years, the rebels attacked the Manchu imperial government, but without success. Finally, in 1911, a revolutionary group managed to overthrow the provincial government in Wuhan. This signalled the end of the Qing dynasty of the Manchus, as other Chinese provinces declared their republican independence.

Former army leader Yuan Shikai was the first president of the Republic of China from 1912 to 1916.

ASIA IN THE EARLY 20TH CENTURY

1900–01
Ito Hirobumi is premier of Japan for the fourth time.

1901
The United States establishes a colonial government in the Philippines.

1905
The Japanese defeat the Russian navy in the Battle of Tsushima Straits.

1906
The All-India Muslim League is founded to protect Muslim rights.

1910
Japan annexes Korea.

1912
Japanese Emperor Meiji dies, ending the era of "enlightened rule." In China, republicans establish a Nationalist Party (Kuomintang). In the Dutch East Indies (modern Indonesia), the Islamic Association gains power.

1913
Indian poet Rabindranath Tagore (1861–1941) is the first non-Westerner to win a Nobel Prize for Literature.

1914
Japan joins the Allied Powers by declaring war on Germany. Mohandas (Mahatma) Gandhi (1869–1948) returns to India from South Africa.

1917
Chinese emperor Pu Yi is restored to the throne for just 12 days (from July 1 to July 12).

Tiger hunting was popular among British colonials in India.

British India

In 1905, the division of the province of Bengal into separate Hindu and Muslim sections led to violent protests. This persuaded the British to appoint an Indian national to the viceroy's executive council, and in 1911 Bengal was reunited. Three years later, Indian troops were fighting for Britain against Germany. Nevertheless, Indian politicians kept up their demands for reform.

Last Chinese Emperor

Cixi had ordered that the former Qing emperor's nephew, Pu Yi, take the throne. He did so, two months short of his third birthday. The boy was taken from his mother and installed in the Forbidden City in Beijing. His father acted as regent, but Pu Yi was worshiped in the same way as all previous Chinese emperors. Revolutionaries forced him to give up the throne at the age of six.

Pu Yi, as he was portrayed in the film The Last Emperor *(1987).*

Ito Hirobumi

Elder statesman Ito had been Japanese premier four times before he was made resident general in Korea in 1905. He helped modernize Japan, stressing cooperation between politicians and bureaucrats. However, he never gained the trust of the Koreans. In October 1909 Ito was assassinated in Harbin, China, by three bullets from the gun of a young Korean nationalist. The following year, Japan took full control of Korea.

Portrait of Ito Hirobumi (1841–1909), who was made a Japanese prince in 1907.

Ottoman Decline, Balkan Wars

The Ottoman Empire had become smaller and weaker during the previous century. In 1878 it lost Bulgaria to the Russians, and in 1897 the Greeks declared war following an uprising in Crete. Montenegro, Romania and Serbia also gained their independence. As their power declined, the Ottoman Turks saw it in their interest to side with Germany in the First World War. Except for Bulgaria, their former Balkan provinces continued to fight the Ottomans on behalf of the Allies.

DECLINE OF THE OTTOMAN EMPIRE

- Ottoman Empire 1800
- Ottoman territory lost 1805–1914
- Ottoman Empire 1914

Losing European Territory
In 1908 King Ferdinand of Bulgaria declared his country's full independence from the Ottoman Empire. Adding to the earlier loss of former provinces, by 1914 this left the Ottomans with eastern Thrace (modern European Turkey) as their only European possession. The map shows how the Ottoman Empire shrank in size.

Young Turks

Turkish revolutionary groups opposed the tyrannical Ottoman sultan, Abdul Hamid II. In 1908 a group called the Committee of Union and Progress, with members known as the Young Turks, led a revolt. They first forced the sultan to restore parliament, and then deposed him. Their aim was to return the Ottoman Empire to its former greatness, and their success led to some modern reforms. They introduced a spirit of Turkish nationalism, but their foreign policies were misguided.

Abdul Hamid II (1842–1918) was Ottoman sultan from 1876 to 1909. He opposed, although not very effectively, all Western interference in Ottoman affairs.

New Alliances

In order to try and achieve the aims of the Young Turks, the Ottoman Empire allied itself with Germany in August 1914. Fearing that the Armenians in the northeast of the empire would support Russia instead, the Ottoman government in 1915 (and later) deported about 1,750,000 Armenians to Syria and Mesopotamia. Hundreds of thousands died on the way. Bulgaria also joined Germany in the Great War, hoping to regain territory lost in the Second Balkan War (see page 65).

The Greek battleship Georgios Averof steams into Constantinople in 1918. The Greeks joined the Great War on the side of the Allies in 1917.

Peoples of the Region

Most of the Balkan nations had been part of the Ottoman Empire for hundreds of years. But there were many different ethnic groups, cultures and languages within the nations, which caused tensions. Kurdish efforts towards self-government were crushed by the Turks early in the 20th century.

Croat

Bulgarian

Albanian

Kurdish

Habsburg emperor Franz Josef (reigned 1848–1916) discusses Austro-Hungarian foreign policy.

Bosnia-Herzegovina

Since 1878 Bosnia-Herzegovina had been controlled by Austria-Hungary. In 1908 the empire formally annexed the region, causing unrest among Serb and Slav nationalists. The military governor of Bosnia dissolved parliament and declared a state of emergency. The heir to the imperial throne visited the Bosnian capital of Sarajevo and was killed (see page 68). His death started a train of events that soon resulted in the outbreak of the Great War.

Lawrence of Arabia

In 1916, British army officer T. E. Lawrence (1888–1935) joined the Arab revolt against the Ottoman Turks. Lawrence helped the Arabs wage a successful guerrilla war against the Ottomans, by wrecking trains and other tactics. In this way the Arabs prevented thousands of Turkish troops from taking part in the Palestine campaign, helping the Allies. Lawrence led a triumphant Arab force into Damascus in October, 1918.

Thomas Edward Lawrence wrote of his exploits in The Seven Pillars of Wisdom.

Balkan Wars

In the First Balkan War (1912–13), Serbia, Bulgaria, Greece and Montenegro formed an alliance against the Ottoman Empire. This Balkan League had a force of 750,000 men that overpowered the Ottomans, who lost almost all their European possessions. When the victors disagreed over territory, Bulgaria began the Second Balkan War (1913) by attacking Serbia and Greece. The Bulgarians were defeated and again lost much of the land they had just gained.

Ferdinand, king of Bulgaria, walks over captured flags during the First Balkan War.

see page 68

OTTOMAN DECLINE, BALKAN WARS

1903
The Ottomans allow German banks to fund the planned building of a railway between Berlin and Baghdad.

1909
The Ottoman Army acquires its first aircraft.

1912
Montenegro starts the First Balkan War by declaring war on Turkey.

1913
The Ottoman Empire loses Crete, part of Macedonia, southern Epirus and many Aegean islands to Greece. Bulgaria starts the Second Balkan War.

1914
German prince Wilhelm zu Wied is briefly ruler of newly independent Albania.

1917
General Sir Edmund Allenby (British commander of the Palestine Front) captures Jerusalem from the Ottomans.

1918
The newly created Kingdom of Serbs, Croats and Slovenes regains control of Kosovo (also claimed by Albania).

War Plans and Weapons

From the beginning of the century the major European powers steadily built up military power, strengthening alliances and making plans for war. Germany had a large, well-trained army and was gaining a powerful naval force. Russia made plans to mobilize its forces against both Germany and Austria-Hungary. The destructive power of all the armies was increased by new weapons, including machine guns and giant howitzers.

Heavy machine guns generally fired about 450 rounds of ammunition per minute.

Admiral Sir John Jellicoe, commander of the British Grand Fleet from 1914.

Essen in the Ruhr Valley was the center of German industrial might. Its factories produced steel and many of Germany's weapons.

Sea Power

When Britain launched its large, fast, heavily armed battleship Dreadnought in 1906, it gave the Royal Navy a huge advantage over Germany and Austria-Hungary. This revolutionary vessel was built in a record 14 months. Germany responded quickly. By 1914 the German navy had 14 large battleships to Britain's 20. Battleships were protected at sea by smaller destroyers and cruisers, and the Royal Navy had more of these vessels too.

Dreadnought was 526 feet (160 m) long and had a speed of 22 knots (41 kph).

GERMANY'S SCHLIEFFEN PLAN

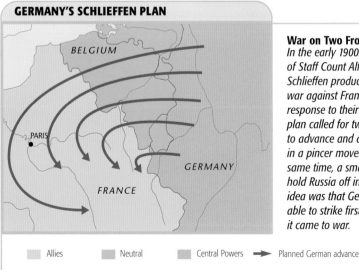

BELGIUM

PARIS

GERMANY

FRANCE

Allies   Neutral   Central Powers   → Planned German advance

War on Two Fronts

In the early 1900s, German Chief of Staff Count Alfred von Schlieffen produced a plan for war against France and Russia in response to their alliance. The plan called for two military wings to advance and defeat the French in a pincer movement. (At the same time, a smaller army would hold Russia off in the east.) The idea was that Germany would be able to strike first and decisively if it came to war.

France's Plan XVII

Plan XVII was adopted in 1913 by commander-in-chief Marshal Joffre, who pushed hard for increased military spending in France so that the French armies would be ready to mobilize and prepared for the defence of France. Once the war broke out, France took the opportunity to advance into Alsace and Lorraine, which it had lost to Germany in 1871.

COLONIAL EMPIRES IN 1914

British	Italian	Portuguese	Belgian
French	Russian	Japanese	American (USA)
German	Dutch	Spanish	Danish

An Imperial Age

In 1914 the British Empire still covered almost a quarter of the globe, and Britain knew that it could count on its colonies in time of war. The Russian Empire was vast, but much of its Asian territory in Siberia was unpopulated. The Europeans had divided up Africa between them. As war approached, there was little to suggest that the age of empires was almost over.

Germans are mobilized in Berlin and head off to the Western Front by train.

Vital Railways

Throughout Europe, railways formed a vital supply route. Troops were deployed and then supplied by train, so railway networks and timetables helped shape the military build-up. Military authorities took over rail use for mass mobilization. The British army, for example, formed a Railway Operating Division. Tracks were essential for troop movements, therefore their destruction would cause great problems for advancing troops. So once war began, attackers could be quickly cut off from reinforcements and supplies, giving an advantage to well-supplied defenders.

The M11 howitzer was developed at the Skoda works in Pilsen in 1906. It was built secretly and was ready for action by the Austro-Hungarian and German armies in 1914. Nicknamed "Schlanke Emma" ("Slender Emma"), this giant weapon could fire shells to a range of 7 miles (11 km).

War Breaks Out

By 1914 the political alliances among European nations, along with increased nationalism and military build-up, made for an extremely tense situation. War was finally triggered by the assassination of the heir to the Austro-Hungarian throne, which led to the alliances being called to action. Five weeks after the assassination, German troops were invading neutral Belgium. Politicians and the public on both sides hoped the war would be short, but military experts feared the reverse.

Franz Ferdinand (1863–1914) and his wife, Countess Sophie, were both killed by the assassin's bullets.

Field Marshal Paul von Hindenburg (middle, foreground) and General Erich Ludendorff (to his left) were hailed as heroes in Germany after victories on the Eastern Front.

Assassination in Sarajevo

Archduke Franz Ferdinand, heir to the Austro-Hungarian throne, visited Bosnia (then a region of his empire). There he was shot dead by Gavrilo Princip, a member of a group called Young Bosnia (which was being exploited by a Serbian nationalist group, the Black Hand). The nationalists were protesting against the oppression of Bosnian Serbs. The assassination led to demands within Austria-Hungary for an attack on Serbia, which gained backing from the German Kaiser. The Serb capital Belgrade was bombarded a month later.

On Other Fronts

When the German navy attacked Russian bases in the Black Sea in October 1914, the Allies came to Russia's support and declared war on the Ottoman Empire. The Ottomans blocked the sea route to southern Russia, and British and French warships attacked the Dardanelles strait. The following year, Australian, New Zealand, British, and French troops landed on the Gallipoli Peninsula in Turkey, but the campaign ended in failure with great loss of life.

Germany Battles on Two Fronts

In the west, the German army swept into neutral Belgium in August 1914 and headed towards France, causing Britain to declare war on Germany. The powerful German offensive led to great battles along the Western Front (see Marne, opposite). In the east, Russian troops invaded German territory faster than expected. But their armies became separated, and the Germans won a great victory at the Battle of Tannenberg (in East Prussia).

Major Offensives
On the Eastern Front, the Russians had many more troops than the Germans, but their equipment was inferior. Russian communications were also less effective, and the Germans followed up Tannenberg with another victory at the Masurian Lakes (in present-day northern Poland). By the end of 1914, trench warfare had been established on this front.

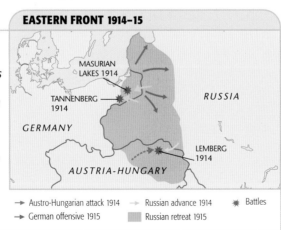

EASTERN FRONT 1914–15

MASURIAN LAKES 1914

TANNENBERG 1914

RUSSIA

GERMANY

LEMBERG 1914

AUSTRIA-HUNGARY

→ Austro-Hungarian attack 1914   → Russian advance 1914   ✳ Battles
→ German offensive 1915   ▨ Russian retreat 1915

An ANZAC (Australian and New Zealand Army Corps) soldier. More than 11,000 ANZAC troops were killed at Gallipoli.

First Battle of the Marne

By early September 1914, German troops had reached the River Marne, just 30 miles (50 km) east of Paris. Then General Joffre launched a French counterattack, supported by the British Expeditionary Force. Fierce fighting stopped the breakthrough, and the German troops started to withdraw. Eventually they retreated about 40 miles (65 km). It was a victory for the Allies, but the German army was not beaten. The Marne battle showed that this was not going to be a short war.

German biplanes fly over the River Marne. During the famous battle of 1914, the French army suffered 250,000 casualties.

THE WAR IN 1914

1914
June 28
Archduke Franz Ferdinand is assassinated in Sarajevo.

July 23
Austria-Hungary issues an ultimatum to Serbia.

July 28
Austria-Hungary declares war on Serbia.

August 1–3
Germany declares war on Russia and then France.

August 4
German troops invade Belgium. Britain declares war on Germany.

August 10
Austria-Hungary invades Russia, starting war on the Eastern Front.

September 6–10
First Battle of the Marne.

September 11
The Austro-Hungarians are forced by Russia to begin withdrawal from Galicia.

November 1–5
Russia and Allies declare war on Ottoman Empire.

December 15
Austro-Hungarians withdraw from Belgrade.

Peace Protests

Not everyone agreed with the war. In 1914 many women who had been campaigning for equal rights (see page 58) turned their attention to the struggle for peace. The following year about 1,300 women from Europe and North America formed the Women's International League for Peace and Freedom in the neutral Netherlands.

Women campaigned in their own peace movement.

PEACE

Opposing Sides

The two opposing sides in the Great War, as it was known at the time, were made up of alliances between different empires and nations. They formed the Central and Allied Powers. Though it came to be known later as a "world war," most of the fighting was carried out by land armies in Europe. Other countries outside Europe (including the Ottoman Empire on one side and the Asian part of the Russian Empire on the other) were drawn in by imperial or political alliance.

This poster shows the uniforms and flags of the four members of the Central Powers: Austria-Hungary, Germany, Ottoman Empire (Turkey) and Bulgaria.

ALLIED POWERS

In 1914
Belgium
The British Empire (including UK, Australia, Canada, Ceylon, India, Newfoundland, New Zealand, Rhodesia, South Africa and the West Indies)
France
Japan
Montenegro
Russia
Serbia

Joined 1915
Italy
San Marino

Joined 1916
Portugal
Romania

Joined 1917
Brazil
China
Cuba
Greece
Liberia
Panama
Siam
USA

Joined 1918
Costa Rica
Guatemala
Haiti
Honduras
Nicaragua

Central Powers

The Dual Monarchy of Austria-Hungary was led by the Habsburg ruler, Franz Josef (1830–1916), who was Emperor of Austria and King of Hungary. Austria-Hungary had formed an alliance with the newly formed German Empire in 1882. The Ottoman Empire, led by the Sultan of Turkey, made a defensive alliance with Germany in July, 1914. Bulgaria (a former province of the Ottoman Empire) joined the Central Powers in the following year.

The Allies

The first countries to join Serbia as Allies included the Triple Entente powers (see page 56) of Britain, France and Russia. Colonies in the British Empire joined the UK in war. Japan also joined in 1914 because of its alliance with Britain, and many countries from around the world joined the Allies over the next four years (see box, left). The United States was at first neutral, but crucially became an "associated power" in April 1917.

Wilhelm II (1859–1941) was the eldest son of Frederick III and Princess Victoria, daughter of Queen Victoria of England.

An American army recruit signs up and collects his uniform. Conscription was introduced in the United States in May, 1917.

The Kaiser

Kaiser Wilhelm II was German emperor from 1888 to 1918. The last ruler of the Hohenzollern dynasty, he was a cousin of both George V of England and Nicholas II of Russia. His education had included military training, and he built up Germany's army and navy. As head of state, he was also commander-in-chief of the German armed forces.

Kitchener's Call to Arms

Horatio Herbert Kitchener (1850–1916) was appointed British Secretary of State for war in 1914. A distinguished soldier and field marshal himself, Lord Kitchener showed such determination that it made him a symbol of the British will to win. Though he believed in conscription, he accepted Prime Minister Asquith's belief that this was impossible before 1916. Kitchener therefore set about recruiting and organizing a mass volunteer army.

Printed by the Victoria House Printing Co., Ltd.

A German infantryman with the old-style spiked helmet, which was replaced with a rounded steel version in 1916.

A French infantryman with a standard-issue Lebel rifle and bayonet.

Infantry

Infantrymen (foot soldiers) formed the armies' basic assault weapon. They carried a rifle, which could be fitted with a bayonet for use in close combat. Infantry commanders in 1914 tended to believe they could be successful without the need for artillery support. However, the experience of war taught them that a more cautious advance, designed to break down well-protected, established defenses, was more likely to be successful, particularly if it was well prepared and supported by heavy artillery.

This famous recruitment poster, showing the face of Lord Kitchener, first appeared in the London Opinion *magazine in 1914.*

DIVIDED EUROPE

Neutral countries
Battlefront

Central Powers	Allies	Allies
Germany	Great Britain	Belgium
Austria-Hungary	France	Italy
Bulgaria	Russia	Romania
Ottoman Empire	Serbia	Portugal

Allies, Central Powers and Neutrals

This map of allegiances shows how the Central Powers were surrounded by the Allies, apart from in the southeast (the Ottoman Empire) and the north (neutral countries). The Scandinavian nations remained neutral, though the Norwegian merchant fleet carried Allied cargo and was badly damaged. Neutral Spain sold goods to the warring nations. The yellow lines show the main fronts (or battle lines).

Trench Systems

Frontline trenches—nearest the enemy—were usually zigzagged and had barbed wire in front. They were reached by small passages from support trenches, where men could rest when they were not on duty. Further back were reserve trenches. The two sides' frontline trenches were separated by a "no-man's-land," which varied in width from tens to hundreds of meters. When one side launched an attack, soldiers had to go "over the top" and rush towards the enemy.

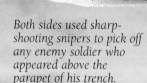

Both sides used sharp-shooting snipers to pick off any enemy soldier who appeared above the parapet of his trench.

Some deep trenches were lined with timber. Soldiers on duty had to watch out for snipers.

Defense in Depth

The German army built deep systems of trenches along the Western Front. From 1915, the Germans used concrete to strengthen fortified areas and dug deep bombardment shelters. Their systems included second-line trenches, and in 1916 large defensive trenches formed a system known as the Hindenburg Line. German defense in depth meant that the Allies suffered great casualties when they advanced and tried to capture line after line of trenches.

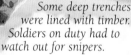

Field telephones like this one were used for communication, and there were a small number of wireless sets.

War in the Air

At the beginning of the war, aviation was still in its infancy. Britain, France, Germany and Russia were all adding air units to their armies, using planes to observe enemy movements on the ground and then dropping bombs by hand. By 1916, fighter planes were taking part in close-combat dogfights, trying to shoot each other down with machine guns. As aircraft improved, flying faster and higher, whole squadrons took part in these air battles.

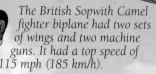

The British Sopwith Camel fighter biplane had two sets of wings and two machine guns. It had a top speed of 115 mph (185 km/h).

Trench Warfare and Dogfights

Trench warfare was a major feature of the Great War. On both sides, a battalion of men would serve a spell at the front, then a period in support, followed by time in reserve. After a short rest, the cycle of trench duty would start all over again. There were huge casualties on both sides along the Western Front. The increased use of aircraft made trenches even more dangerous places to be.

Christmas Truce

On the first Christmas Eve of the war, British troops on the Western Front heard their enemies singing German carols. The British joined in with their own songs, as guns on both sides gradually fell silent. Some opposing soldiers met up in "no-man's-land" and there was even an informal international game of soccer. This friendly ceasefire was totally unofficial, and top commanders frowned on it.

During the unofficial truce, German and British soldiers shook hands.

Poison Gas

The use of lethal chlorine gas by the Germans in April 1915 caused total panic, as Allied troops suffocated in seconds. The gas was released from canisters, but a changing wind could damage the attackers too, as happened to the British when they first used it. Later, mustard gas was also employed and was even added to high-explosive shells. The German army used most gas, followed by the French and the British.

Gas masks were introduced by both sides to protect their troops.

Baron Manfred von Richthofen (1892–1918) got his colorful nickname, the Red Baron, because of his squadron's red planes.

The Red Baron

German flying ace Manfred von Richthofen, known as the Red Baron, was the war's top-scoring pilot. He shot down 80 enemy aircraft, five more than René Fonck of France. Von Richthofen served first as a cavalry officer, before joining the German Army Air Service. He became commander of Fighter Group 1, and was killed when his plane was shot down by ground fire during a dogfight in the last year of the war.

A German Fokker Dr-1 triplane (with three sets of wings), as flown by the Red Baron. This single-seat fighter had the same top speed as the Sopwith Camel.

New Mobile Weapons

In 1915 the British developed a new weapon, which they called a "landship," but code-named "tank" because it looked like a water tank. The code-name stuck, and the first tanks went into production. These new armored combat vehicles traveled on caterpillar tracks and were ideal for trench warfare. The French army also developed and used them successfully, but the Germans did not introduce theirs until 1918 and made very few.

Some early tanks had a machine gun in a revolving turret. Small tanks could smash through barbed wire, but had trouble crossing wide trenches. Larger versions were soon developed.

TRENCH WARFARE AND DOGFIGHTS

1915
On April 22, the Germans use poison gas against Allied lines (French and Algerian troops) in the Second Battle of Ypres; the British retaliate on September 25 at the Artois-Loos offensive. Dutch designer Anthony Fokker, working for Germany, develops a machine gun that times shots between an aircraft's spinning propeller blades.

1916
By February, the Aéronautique Militaire (French air force) has 1,149 aircraft. In August, Manfred von Richthofen becomes a fighter pilot on the Western Front; the German Army Air Service forms specialist fighter units. On September 15, Britain brings the first tanks into action during the Battle of the Somme.

1917
On April 26, a great dogfight takes place between a total of 94 British and German aircraft. In July, the Sopwith Camel goes into full service with the British Royal Flying Corps. On November 20, 474 British tanks break through German lines in the Battle of Cambrai.

1918
On April 1, the British air services unite as the Royal Air Force. In August, Canadian fighter ace Billy Bishop (who shot down 72 German aircraft) joins the British Air Ministry. In September, US officer Billy Mitchell commands the largest air assault (1,500 Allied aircraft) in a mission over German lines in France.

Women and the Home Front

This British poster advised people to learn to identify aircraft, so that they could shelter from the enemy.

During the war a large number of women in Europe exchanged their full-time jobs —for example in domestic service or in textile industries—for other kinds of work. Some undertook munitions production, others did farm work. Women were also needed as nurses and in back-up jobs to the armed forces. Many had to adapt quickly to being head of the household, although their status and rights were still not equal to those of men.

Land Girls

In Britain, the Women's Land Army was organized by the Board of Trade, rather than the War Office. WLA members, known as "land girls," did agricultural work. By the end of 1917, more than 250,000 women were working on British farms. They did the work of men who were away fighting and helped greatly with food supply.

A young Land Army woman cuts hay.

The Zeppelin's crew of 20 were carried in a gondola beneath the airship.

L 32

Air Raids

Gas-filled Zeppelin airships (named after German designer Count Ferdinand von Zeppelin) made their first bombing raids in 1914, on the Belgian city of Liège. The rigid airships could fly high and for long distances. The following year they started attacking Paris and London, striking fear into the hearts of many civilians. During 31 raids on London, 670 people were killed. Altogether the Germans used 115 Zeppelins during the war.

PATRIOTIC SERVICE for BRITISH WOMEN

WOMEN WANTED URGENTLY

to enrol for the duration of the war in the

W·A·A·C

WOMEN'S · ARMY · AUXILIARY · CORPS
and the

W·R·N·S

WOMEN'S · ROYAL · NAVAL · SERVICE

ENROL TO-DAY

Apply at the nearest EMPLOYMENT EXCHANGE for full particulars. Ask at Post Office for the address.

British women were encouraged to enrol for "patriotic service." The WAAC was founded in 1917 and numbered 57,000 by 1918.

Nursing the Wounded

Professional nurses were joined by volunteers in military hospitals at home and in the field. The male-dominated authorities that were against women's involvement in the war were happy for them to help the wounded. In field hospitals, women were exposed to horror and danger. Many served far from home; Australian nurses, for example, worked as far afield as France, Egypt, and India.

English nurse Edith Cavell, who was nursing in Belgium, was executed by the Germans in 1915 for helping Allied soldiers escape.

Female Recruits

In some countries women were enrolled into supporting military organizations. Members of the British Women's Army Auxiliary Corps wore khaki uniforms and worked as clerks, telephonists, and gas-mask instructors. Their female leaders were not commissioned as officers, but were called controllers and administrators. Private soldiers were "workers." Similar auxiliary groups formed in other countries, and in Russia they had a more military role.

Entertaining the Troops

Since it was very difficult for theatrical groups to travel anywhere near the battlefield, troops of all nationalities mostly had to put on their own amateur shows if they ever had the time or energy. One exception was the French "army theater." French troops built their own stages, and were rewarded with visits by professional entertainers, including the famous French actresses Jeanne Bartet and Sarah Bernhardt.

French soldiers on leave were entertained by dancing shows in Paris and other cities. Light-hearted amusements lifted morale.

WOMEN AND THE HOME FRONT

1914
In Britain, the Women's Volunteer Reserve is founded. The Women's Hospital Corps sets up a military hospital in Paris, and later in London. In the Ottoman Empire, women begin working in offices, hospitals and schools for the first time.

1915
The British government appeals for women to join a Register of Women for War Service.

1916
American author Edith Wharton is made a French Chevalier of the Legion of Honor for her work with war refugees. In Britain, the Women's Royal Naval Service recruits cooks, clerks and wireless telegraphers (numbering 5,450 by 1918).

1917
Women play a leading role in the February Revolution (it took place in March according to the revised calendar of 1918) in Russia; a Russian women's battalion is founded.

1918
In the Ottoman Empire a female labor battalion is established. In Britain, both meat and sugar are rationed.

Women wartime workers in a German munitions factory.

Making Munitions

Women in all countries were needed as factory workers. In munitions factories, the work was hard and dangerous, since the materials for making weapons were poisonous and flammable. Though female workers were essential, they were still paid less than men. Most of the work was voluntary, but in Germany some women were forced into employment to help the war effort. Around 700,000 women worked in German munitions factories, and there were even more in Britain.

A German U-boat (from Unterseeboot, or submarine). Its main weapons were torpedoes with explosive warheads.

Major Offensives

On the Western Front, attacks by both sides generally ended in stalemate. This deadlocked trench warfare involved a huge loss of life. There were also enormous casualties on the Eastern Front, where the Germans and Austro-Hungarians attacked in 1915 and pushed the Russians back. At sea, German attacks on merchant ships helped persuade the United States to join the Allies, making a crucial difference to the balance of power.

Second Battle of Ypres
In late April 1915, the German Fourth Army began attacking Allied positions around the town of Ypres, on the Western Front in Flanders. The attack included the first large-scale use of poison gas, which led to the Germans making ground against British, French and Canadian troops. They were unable to take Ypres itself, however, and so used heavy artillery to demolish it. The Allies lost almost 70,000 men—twice as many as the Germans.

This painting of the Second Battle of Ypres shows the chaos and horror of war.

War at Sea
In 1915 Germany began a submarine blockade of the British Isles, attacking merchant ships bringing supplies across the Atlantic. The sinking of the *Lusitania*, a passenger ship on the way from New York to Liverpool, caused outrage in Britain and anti-German feeling in the United States. British and German warships had their one direct encounter in the following year, at the Battle of Jutland.

During the First World War, America produced thousands of recruitment posters encouraging people to sign up.

Verdun
The 10-month-long Battle of Verdun, in 1916, was the longest of the war. It was launched by the Germans in order to try and knock the French army out of the war. The German army was led by Crown Prince Wilhelm, eldest son of the Kaiser, and the French by Philippe Pétain, who famously promised, "They shall not pass." At the end of the offensive, Germany had gained a few miles along the Western Front. Figures for those killed and wounded are uncertain, but are in the region of several hundred thousand for both sides.

French soldiers in damaged Verdun, 1916.

Battle of the Somme

In July 1916 in France, British troops attacked north of the River Somme and French troops attacked south of the river. On the very first day, the British suffered 58,000 casualties, a third of them killed. General Douglas Haig led more attacks, supported by the French, but the Germans brought in reinforcements and little success was achieved. Terrible losses drained the manpower resources of both sides. The battle cost about 620,000 British and French and 500,000 German lives, and the Allies ended up gaining about 7.5 miles (12 km) of battle-scarred ground.

Soldiers on the Somme battlefields often had to fight, eat, sleep, and die in the thick mud, which penetrated everything. This horse-drawn unit is struggling to transport ammunition in the appalling conditions.

War diary entries, like this British Intelligence report made on the first day of the Somme offensive, provide information on troop movements.

Nivelle Offensive

France's General Nivelle planned a 1917 spring offensive near the River Aisne, aiming to smash through the German lines quickly. Some other military leaders opposed the operation, and when it failed, the French army was crippled and Nivelle was dismissed. There was mutiny among French soldiers, who had lost faith in their commanders and could see little point in more bloodshed. Pétain restored order, but the British had to take over the offensive role in France.

General Robert Nivelle (1856–1924) became commander-in-chief of French forces in December 1916. He was replaced by Marshal Pétain four months later.

WESTERN FRONT 1916–17

PASSCHENDAELE 1917
VIMY RIDGE 1917
ARRAS 1917
BELGIUM
THE SOMME 1916
LUX
GERMANY
FRANCE   PARIS
CHEMIN DES DAMES 1917
VERDUN 1916

Attacks Made Minor Gains

In 1916, the main attack from the Germans was at Verdun. The Allies' major offensive was along the Somme, which was partly a counterattack to try and draw German troops away from Verdun. Long, hard-fought battles with enormous casualties led to very small changes in the location of the Front. In early 1917, the Germans withdrew behind the Hindenburg Line.

- - - - Front line in 1917   Hindenberg line   Major battles

Armistice and Afterward

The poppy became a symbol to commemorate those who died in the war.

After failed German offensives early in 1918 and a defeat in northern France in the summer, the Kaiser installed a new government in Berlin. Many German politicians wanted to seek a peace agreement, but before they could do so, mutiny broke out in the navy and revolution among workers. In November, Wilhelm II was forced to abdicate, Germany became a republic and its representatives signed an armistice. The war was over.

Spring Offensives

In spring 1918, the Germans used reinforcements from the east to make five major attacks on the Western Front. Their aim was to win the war in France before any build-up of US forces. The attacks made early gains, but both sides suffered heavy losses. The final advance was turned back near the River Marne, just 50 miles (80 km) from Paris.

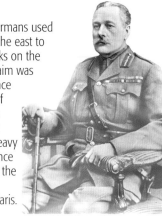

Field Marshal Sir Douglas Haig (1861–1928) commanded the British Expeditionary Force. Some of his tactics were criticized by Prime Minister David Lloyd George.

German Problems

Towards the end of the war there were severe food shortages in Germany. Bread had been rationed since 1915, and other foods were scarce. The situation was made worse by raging inflation. In 1918 a loaf of bread cost a quarter of a Mark; by 1922 it cost 3.50 Marks, and the following year rose to 100,000 Marks!

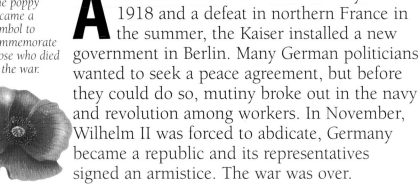

Inflation meant that after the war German banknotes became almost worthless.

The Kaiser Abdicates

By autumn 1918, Germany was near collapse. Its people lost faith in their leaders and there were riots. In early October power was transferred to parliament and the imperial chancellor announced the abdication of Wilhelm II on November 9. The Army helped its former emperor flee to the neutral Netherlands, where he officially gave up his throne. Wilhelm stayed there for the rest of his life.

The Royal Palace in Berlin was the Kaiser's main residence. After his abdication, it became a museum.

Fourteen Points

In January 1918, US President Woodrow Wilson named Fourteen Points as a proposal for a peace settlement. They included proposals for free trade and independence for Turkey and Poland. The final point called for an association of nations to help keep world peace. The proposals formed a basis for later discussions, but other Allied nations felt that they were not tough enough on Germany.

President Wilson's proposals for a peace settlement were widely publicized.

Armistice

Immediately after the Kaiser abdicated, German politicians met the Allied supreme commander in the forest of Compiègne, near Paris. They signed an armistice, and the ceasefire came into effect at 11 a.m. on 11 November, 1918 (at the 11th hour of the 11th day of the 11th month). Germany surrendered its arms and had to leave its occupied territories within 14 days. The following year, Allied countries declared 11th November to be Armistice Day, to commemorate those killed in the war.

Survivors

In addition to the 10 million soldiers killed, around nine million civilians died as a result of the war. Those who survived suffered severe hardship. Towns, villages and farmland were ruined, especially in northern France and Belgium. Many wounded soldiers came back to their families to discover that they had to find new homes.

Refugees left their homes to flee the fighting. Many returned to find destruction.

A London newspaper announces the armistice.

GERMAN TERRITORIAL LOSSES

Lost Territory
Defeat led to Germany giving up territory to Belgium, Denmark, France and Poland. Germany also lost its overseas colonies. France gained control of the Saar coalfields, and Saarland was controlled by the League of Nations. Allied troops occupied the Rhineland.

- Lost
- Occupied by Allied troops
- Saar

Map labels: DENMARK, EAST PRUSSIA, WEST PRUSSIA, HOLLAND, GERMANY, BELGIUM, POLAND, FRANCE, CZECH REPUBLIC, SWITZERLAND, AUSTRIA

ARMISTICE AND AFTERWARD

1918
Mar 3
The Central Powers and Russia sign a peace agreement (Treaty of Brest-Litovsk).

Mar 21
Germans open their Spring Offensive (also called Kaiserschlacht or Second Battle of the Somme).

Apr 9
Second Spring Offensive begins along the River Lys.

Apr 14
Marshal Ferdinand Foch of France becomes Allied Supreme Commander on the Western Front.

May 27
Third Spring Offensive begins near the River Aisne (Third Battle of the Aisne).

Sep 29
Bulgaria surrenders.

Oct 4
The German government asks for a ceasefire.

Oct 30
The Ottoman Empire makes peace.

Nov 3
Austria-Hungary makes peace.

Nov 4
English war poet Wilfred Owen is killed in action in France.

Nov 9
Germany is proclaimed a republic.

Nov 11
Germany signs an armistice; official date of the end of the Great War.

Canadians celebrate Armistice Day. More than 56,000 Canadian soldiers were killed in the Great War.

The Russian Revolution

People supported the revolution because they wanted to end poverty and injustice. The Bolsheviks promised "peace, land, and bread."

At the beginning of the 20th century, the vast Russian Empire was ruled by a tsar (or emperor) and a small group of wealthy aristocrats. Most Russians were poor peasants farming the land, though industrialization had taken many to work in the growing cities. Political revolutionaries wanted to change the system and bring better living conditions to the majority. As they gained support, there was a series of revolutions that led to Russia becoming a communist republic.

Bloody Sunday

On January 22, 1905, 200,000 unarmed workers marched to the tsar's Winter Palace in St. Petersburg. The workers wanted reforms, but the imperial troops opened fire on the marchers and many were killed. This became known as the Bloody Sunday massacre, and it sparked a revolutionary reaction. By October there was a general strike, which forced the tsar to introduce an elected parliament (the Duma) with the power to pass laws. However, the tsar and his officials continued to interfere with the Duma.

The terrible events of Bloody Sunday were portrayed by Russian artist Vladimir Makovsky in his painting Death in the Snow.

Poverty and Discontent

Under the tsar, peasants worked hard to farm land rented from rich landowners. They struggled to make ends meet and were often in debt because of high rents and taxes. Some of their money helped to pay for new factories and railways, as industry grew in Russia, but this was of little benefit to the poor. The gap between wealthy aristocrats and pitifully poor workers led to growing discontent.

Peasant children often had to go hungry. Their parents were desperate for a better life.

Conflict with Japan

The Russo-Japanese War of 1904–05 ended in a humiliating defeat for the Russians (see page 62). The final land battle in China left the Russian army with 89,000 casualties, and was followed by the Russian Baltic Fleet being destroyed at sea. Defeat left a desperate situation, with mutiny in the army, riots in the streets and food shortages everywhere.

Left: In this illustration from a 1904 journal, a correspondent films the Russian cavalry in Manchuria (northeast China).

Statue of the revolutionary leader Lenin (1870–1924), whose real name was Vladimir Ilyich Ulyanov.

Bolshevik Revolution

In October 1917, revolutionary Bolsheviks led workers and soldiers to the Winter Palace, the former royal residence in Petrograd (formerly St Petersburg) that had become government headquarters. The Bolsheviks formed a new government headed by Lenin. His new regime promised great changes, including an end to Russia's involvement in the Great War.

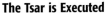

27 Февраля 1917 года
КРАСНАЯ ГВАРДІЯ
Васильевского Острова

Above: Armband of a Red Guard supporting the Bolsheviks.

The Tsar is Executed

After the Duma called on the tsar to abdicate, Nicholas II gave up the throne on March 15, 1917. The provisional government imprisoned Nicholas and his family, and they were moved several times. When it seemed possible that they might be rescued by anti-Bolshevik forces the following year, all the family were taken into a cellar and shot.

Right: Tsar Nicholas II (1868–1918) was the last Romanov ruler of Russia.

Picasso's Violin and Guitar *(1912) combines the shapes of the two instruments.*

THE ARTS

1900
Sigmund Freud's The Interpretation of Dreams *is published.*

1902
Just So Stories *by Rudyard Kipling (1865–1936) are published.*

1905
German Expressionist artists found a group called Die Brücke *(The Bridge) in Dresden.*

1911
Gustav Mahler (1860–1911) works on his final, unfinished symphony, No. 10. Expressionist artists found a group called Der Blaue Reiter *(The Blue Rider) in Munich.*

1912
An abstract form of Cubism, called Orphism, is developed in France. American poet Ezra Pound (1885–1972) founds a movement called Imagism.

1913
The first volume of Remembrance of Things Past *by Marcel Proust (1871–1922) is published.*

1915
The Dada movement, stressing the illogical and absurd, is founded in Zurich.

1916
The Judgment, *by Franz Kafka (1883–1924), is published.*

Pablo Picasso (1881–1973) moved to France in 1904.

Cubism

The art movement known as Cubism revolutionized European painting and sculpture. The movement began in France about 1907 and flourished until 1914. The leaders of Cubism were the Spanish-born artist Pablo Picasso and French artist Georges Braque. They used geometric (or "cubic") shapes to represent solid forms in two dimensions, often using many different views of an object in a single image.

Chagall's Birthday *(1915) is typical of his fanciful style. The man in the picture floats upside down and contorts his body.*

Musical Trends

French composer Claude Debussy (1862–1918) introduced a new musical approach known as impressionism. Some of his works include sounds that give the impression of wind or the sea. The works of Austrian composer Arnold Schoenberg (1874–1951) and Russian-born Igor Stravinsky (1882–1971) were more revolutionary and experimental. They used unusual rhythms and conflicting sounds that were not always popular at the time.

The young Stravinsky. He wrote famous ballet scores, such as The Firebird *(1910) and* The Rite of Spring *(1913).*

Picasso's Violin and Guitar *(1912) combines the shapes of the two instruments.*

Dreamlike Fantasy

Artists such as Russian-born Marc Chagall (1887–1985), who went to Paris in 1910, combined elements of fantasy and dreams. Chagall was greatly influenced by Cubism. Many of the figures and animals in his pictures float through the air, and art historians consider that his style influenced the 1920s movement of Surrealism.

The Arts

There were many new movements in the early 1900s. European and North American painters, writers, and musical composers were looking for new directions. They moved away from traditional 19th-century approaches and became more experimental. Painters, for example, turned from realistic representation to more abstract styles. Later in the period these movements were influenced by the First World War, which brought great social and political upheaval. The war also left many artists feeling bitter and pessimistic, which may be reflected in their work.

Questioning Art

Revolutionary artists such as French-born Marcel Duchamp (1887–1968) posed the question, "What is art?" In 1913, Duchamp produced his first "ready-made," which was simply an ordinary bicycle wheel. Two years later, he went to the United States, where he was already well known for his unconventional paintings. Many people said his works were meaningless, or even disgraceful, but they certainly invited gallery-goers to look at everyday objects in a new way.

Duchamp sent this urinal, entitled Fountain, *to the first exhibition of the Society of Independent Artists, in 1917.*

Art Nouveau

The decorative style of "new art," named after a Paris art gallery, flourished from about 1890 to 1910. It was used a great deal in graphic design, for books and posters, as well as for jewelry, glassware and ornamental objects. Many of its works incorporated the shapes of flowers and plants. The style became known by many different names, including Jugendstil in Germany, Sezessionstil in Austria, and Stile Floreale in Italy. In the United States, the designer Louis Comfort Tiffany (1848–1933) created colorful glassware in the art nouveau style.

This elaborate candlestick from 1900 is designed in the Art Nouveau style. It takes the form of a woman entwined with thistle-shaped flowers.

Viennese Culture

Turn-of-the-century Vienna, capital of Austria-Hungary, was a flourishing cultural centre. The pioneering psychiatrist Sigmund Freud (1856–1939) established an International Psychoanalytical Society there. Freud's new ideas influenced many Viennese writers and artists, including playwright and novelist Arthur Schnitzler (1862–1931) and painter Gustav Klimt (1862–1918). Gustav Mahler and his fellow composer Schoenberg were also working there at this time.

Sigmund Freud developed new theories about the symbolism of dreams.

Fulfilment (1905–09) by Gustav Klimt, who founded an avant-garde group called the Sezession in Vienna.

At the end of the Great War in 1918, many people felt there was going to be a new, peaceful world order. However, the fun times of the roaring twenties were quickly followed by a worldwide economic crisis. At the same time, Italy fell under the grip of fascism and Stalin's brand of communism gained control of the Soviet Union. In Germany, where many people felt they had been treated too harshly by the 1919 peace settlement, Hitler promised to build a powerful new empire. The Nazi dictator's imperialist plans led directly to the outbreak of another disastrous world war.

This chapter tells the story of the interwar period, from the Treaty of Versailles to the German invasion of Poland. It also covers the events of the Second World War itself, from its beginning to the dropping of atomic bombs on Japan that brought it to a close.

Two fascist leaders: Il Duce (Mussolini) and Der Führer (Hitler).

TIMELINE

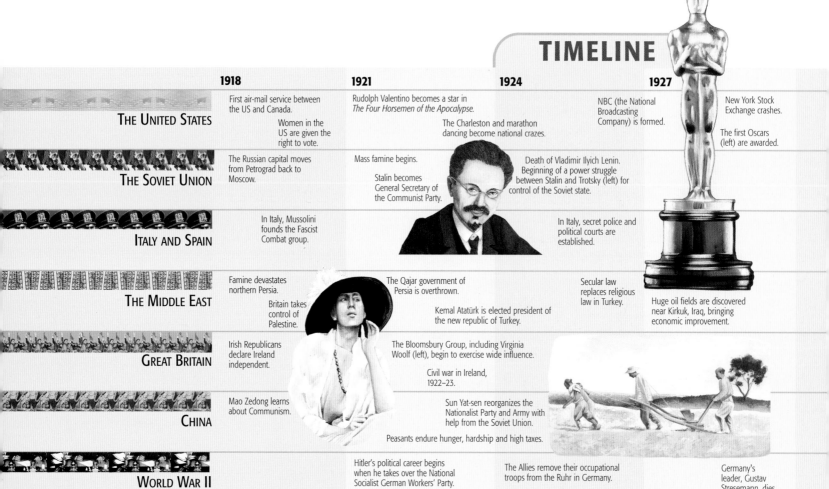

	1918	1921	1924	1927
THE UNITED STATES	First air-mail service between the US and Canada. Women in the US are given the right to vote.	Rudolph Valentino becomes a star in *The Four Horsemen of the Apocalypse.* The Charleston and marathon dancing become national crazes.	NBC (the National Broadcasting Company) is formed.	New York Stock Exchange crashes. The first Oscars (left) are awarded.
THE SOVIET UNION	The Russian capital moves from Petrograd back to Moscow.	Mass famine begins. Stalin becomes General Secretary of the Communist Party.	Death of Vladimir Ilyich Lenin. Beginning of a power struggle between Stalin and Trotsky (left) for control of the Soviet state.	
ITALY AND SPAIN		In Italy, Mussolini founds the Fascist Combat group.	In Italy, secret police and political courts are established.	
THE MIDDLE EAST	Famine devastates northern Persia. Britain takes control of Palestine.	The Qajar government of Persia is overthrown. Kemal Atatürk is elected president of the new republic of Turkey.	Secular law replaces religious law in Turkey.	Huge oil fields are discovered near Kirkuk, Iraq, bringing economic improvement.
GREAT BRITAIN	Irish Republicans declare Ireland independent.	The Bloomsbury Group, including Virginia Woolf (left), begin to exercise wide influence. Civil war in Ireland, 1922–23.		
CHINA	Mao Zedong learns about Communism.	Sun Yat-sen reorganizes the Nationalist Party and Army with help from the Soviet Union. Peasants endure hunger, hardship and high taxes.		
WORLD WAR II		Hitler's political career begins when he takes over the National Socialist German Workers' Party.	The Allies remove their occupational troops from the Ruhr in Germany. At the Locarno Conference, treaties are signed guaranteeing peace in Europe.	Germany's leader, Gustav Stresemann, dies.

From Versailles to World War II

Londoners celebrate the end of the Great War.

The atomic bombs dropped on Japan in 1945 spread lethal radiation over a wide area.

1930	1933	1936	1939	1942

A quarter of the US population is unemployed.

Roosevelt introduces his New Deal reforms to help lift the economic depression.

Roosevelt wins re-election.

Millionaire pilot Howard Hughes sets a transcontinental flight record.

Roosevelt becomes the first US president to appear on television, as he opens the World's Fair in New York.

The American fleet at Pearl Harbor is attacked by Japan.

Millions of Russians die of famine 1932–33.

Stalin's "purge" trials eliminate thousands of political opponents and army generals.

Trotsky founds the Fourth International (1938) in opposition to Stalin.

The Soviet Union joins the war against Germany, its former ally, when Hitler invades.

Fascist dictator of Italy, Benito Mussolini, invades Abyssinia.

Franco becomes chief of the Spanish army's general staff.

Mussolini forms an alliance –the Pact of Steel–with Hitler in May 1939.

Franco's dictatorship starts (lasts until 1975).

Iraq gains independence after the British mandate officially ends, 1932.

Saudi Arabia gains independence.

Arabs revolt against British rule in Palestine (first "intimated").

Oil is discovered in Saudi Arabia by an American company.

1941, Reza Shah Pahlevi ascends to the throne of Iran when his father is deposed by British and Soviet troops for collaborating with the Nazis.

The Statute of Westminster establishes the Commonwealth of Nations, 1931.

In January 1934, the British Union of Fascists (BUF) holds a rally attended by more than 10,000 supporters.

Sir Frank Whittle invents the Jet Engine in 1937.

In January, King George V dies. Edward succeeds him as king. In December, Edward VIII abdicates.

George VI is the first British monarch to visit the USA.

George VI institutes the George Cross and George Medal for acts of bravery by civilians.

The Chinese Communist Party confirms Mao Zedong in the new post of chairman.

Beginning of the Sino–Japanese War, causing a second United Front of Chinese forces; the Soviet Union and China sign a non-aggression pact.

Hitler becomes Chancellor of Germany.

Germany leaves the League of Nations.

Hitler introduces conscription.

Germany rearms and occupies the Rhineland.

Hitler outlines secret plans to conquer Austria and Czechoslovakia.

Britain and France pledge to declare war against Germany if Hitler invades Poland.

War is declared 3rd September 1939.

Tanks and other military equipment were systematically destroyed after the war.

Between the Wars

People thought the 1914–18 conflict was the "war to end all wars." Millions had died, and the victors saw an opportunity to create a new world order. Yet just 21 years later, the world was at war again. Many problems of the interwar years helped cause this. They included failings in the peace settlement, a global economic crisis, and great splits between fascists, communists, and capitalists.

Treaty of Versailles

The treaty set out the terms of peace between the Allied Powers and Germany. The German representatives were required to sign it without negotiation and with the threat that the war would resume if they did not. The main provisions disarmed Germany, revised European boundaries, and called for reparations (compensation payments) from Germany, which was declared solely responsible for the war. These terms were seen as too lenient by the French and others.

The last lines of the treaty, signed by the "Big Four"—Woodrow Wilson (USA), David Lloyd George (UK), Georges Clemenceau (France) and Vittorio Orlando (Italy).

Below: The German Military Cemetery at Vladslo, Belgium. Many German survivors felt that the war had swept away the finest of a whole generation.

The treaty was signed in the Palace of Versailles, the 17th-century former French royal residence just outside Paris. The US Senate never ratified (accepted) the treaty.

The Prince of Wales (later Edward VIII, see page 107) toured parts of the British Empire in 1930.

Colonial Changes

Post-war treaties altered the balance of power in European overseas colonies. Under the Treaty of Versailles, Germany lost its foreign territories. With the agreement of the League of Nations, but without consulting any local people, Britain was given control of German East Africa and France gained most of the Cameroons. Germany's Pacific colonies were divided between Japan, Australia and New Zealand. Britain and France also gained mandated territories in the Middle East from the defeated Ottoman Empire (see page 104).

League of Nations

The Paris Peace Conference established the League of Nations in January 1920, with headquarters in Geneva, Switzerland. The League acted as a peacekeeping agency, based on the principle of collective security—each member state agreed to help defend any other member attacked by another country. It also controlled specialist agencies, such as the Court of International Justice and the International Labor Organization. Sixteen years later, the League failed to stop the build-up to another world war (see page 114).

This caricature of the League of Nations, entitled 'The Promised Land: the United States of Europe', appeared in a Paris satirical journal in 1931.

EUROPE, 1919

LUX = LUXEMBOURG   NL = NETHERLANDS
SWZ = SWITZERLAND

Redrawing the Map

The collapse of Austria-Hungary led to the creation of new states, including Czechoslovakia and the Kingdom of Serbs, Croats and Slovenes (renamed Yugoslavia in 1929). Germany also lost territory from its homeland. Poland gained most of East Prussia, dividing Germany and creating a Polish Corridor to the Baltic Sea. France regained the provinces of Alsace and Lorraine, and coal mines in the Saar region.

The Rise of the Dictators

The first country to fall under the power of a fascist dictator was Italy. Mussolini began exercising total authority there in 1925 (see page 102). Four years later, Stalin—the "man of steel"—wielded absolute power in the Communist Soviet Union (see page 100). Hitler declared his Third Reich, with himself as Führer (Leader) in 1934 (see page 112). After a military coup two years later, Franco took over in Spain (see page 110).

Benito Mussolini and Adolf Hitler, together in Munich in 1937. They died within two days of each other in 1945.

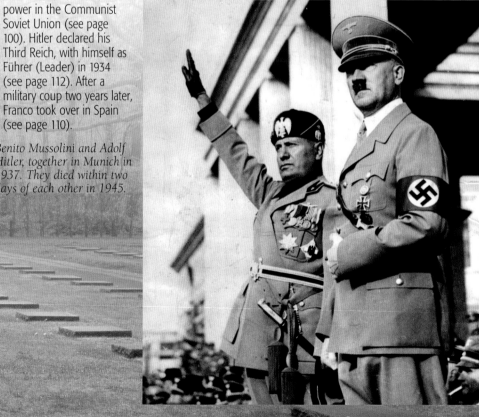

America: the Roaring Twenties

By 1920 many Americans wanted to forget the horrors of the Great War. US politicians wanted to keep out of European affairs, and the Senate refused to approve the Treaty of Versailles or join the League of Nations. The successful economy meant a rising standard of living. Those young people who could now afford it were keen to enjoy themselves, wearing new fashions and dancing to new kinds of music. The decade became known as the Roaring Twenties.

Racial Tension

Some white Americans were opposed to black people having the vote and other civil rights. They terrorized black people and tried to scare them into not voting. The most feared group of extremist white people was the Ku Klux Klan, which by the mid-1920s had about four million members. It was responsible for bombings and lynchings. Members also turned their vicious hatred on Jews and other minority groups.

Ku Klux Klan members wore white robes and hoods to frighten black people and hide their own identity.

Policemen pose beside an illegal still, used to produce alcohol such as whisky.

Prohibition

Members of the temperance movement and others believed that drinking alcohol led to increased poverty and crime in American society. They encouraged new laws prohibiting the making and selling of alcohol. But during the Prohibition period (1920–33), the laws were very difficult to enforce. People drank bootleg (illegal) liquor in bars called speakeasies, and some also made their own illegal spirits at home. Many came to think that Prohibition simply encouraged ordinary citizens to break the law.

Gangland Crime

Prohibition led to more crime instead of less, because it gave gangsters the opportunity to control illegal alcohol. Gang leaders such as Al Capone (nicknamed "Scarface") dominated the criminal underworld in cities such as Chicago. They ran other rackets, as well as dealing in bootleg liquor, frightening people into allowing the gangsters to "protect" them. There were frequent shootouts between the rival gangs as they fought for control of gangland districts.

A wanted poster for "Machine Gun" Kelly, who was finally arrested for armed robbery and kidnapping.

FEBRUARY 18, 1926 Teaching old

The Jazz Age

During the 1920s, jazz music spread to the big US cities. New dances became all the rage, including the Charleston and the Black Bottom. Young women had their hair styled into short bobs, wore shorter dresses, and rolled their silk stockings down to their knees. They added lipstick, eye shadow, and nail polish to their look, and became known as "flappers."

This 1926 magazine cover shows a flapper teaching an "old dog" how to Charleston.

An early radio.

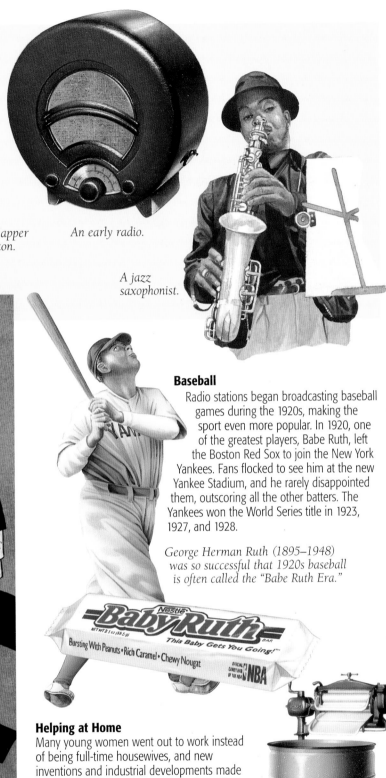

A jazz saxophonist.

Baseball

Radio stations began broadcasting baseball games during the 1920s, making the sport even more popular. In 1920, one of the greatest players, Babe Ruth, left the Boston Red Sox to join the New York Yankees. Fans flocked to see him at the new Yankee Stadium, and he rarely disappointed them, outscoring all the other batters. The Yankees won the World Series title in 1923, 1927, and 1928.

George Herman Ruth (1895–1948) was so successful that 1920s baseball is often called the "Babe Ruth Era."

Helping at Home

Many young women went out to work instead of being full-time housewives, and new inventions and industrial developments made life easier for them. Electric domestic appliances helped them spend less time on chores such as cleaning, washing, and cooking. Vacuum cleaners, washing machines, and electric irons saved hours of work, while refrigerators meant that women did not have to shop every day.

Wringer-mangles for drying clothes were attached to early washing machines.

1920
The US 18th Amendment forbids people to make or sell intoxicating liquor; the 19th Amendment is ratified, giving US women the right to vote.

1921
Baseball legend Babe Ruth scores 177 runs in a single season (still an all-time record).

1922
Anti-Prohibition rallies are held in Chicago and other cities.

1923
The Charleston and marathon dancing become national crazes.

1925
Clarence Birdseye starts the frozen-food industry.

1926
The Radio Corporation of America forms the National Broadcasting Company (NBC), the first permanent national wireless network.

1927
Al Jolson appears in the first successful talking movie, The Jazz Singer.

1928
Walt Disney introduces Mickey Mouse in Steamboat Willie, the first animated film with sound.

1929
Capone gunmen murder rival Bugs Moran's gangsters in the so-called St. Valentine's Day Massacre.

The Transportation Revolution

Radio (this one dates from 1925) and new forms of transport rapidly made the world seem smaller.

After the First World War, the rising standard of living in the United States meant that many people could travel more. Improved methods of transportation—especially rail and, increasingly, road—allowed people to move around the growing cities and live further from their place of work. Air travel was fastest for longer distances, and American and European entrepreneurs were working toward linking the two sides of the Atlantic by plane.

On the Move

In the 1920s, travel began to influence popular culture. Songs were written about the expanding cities, including, in 1922, "Chicago" and "Way Down Yonder in New Orleans." A couple of years later, more songs celebrated the new interest in travel, such as "Alabamy Bound" and "California Here I Come." By 1932, Chicago's Midway Airport was the busiest in the world.

An early aerial photograph: the city of Chicago in about 1930, with growing traffic on Michigan Boulevard.

TO WIN THE HEARTS and stir the pride of those you love the most—we suggest a Buick - Go to the Buick showroom today, and finish your Christmas shopping

THE GREATEST BUICK EVER BUILT

This Buick advertisement appeared in 1926, when the company produced more than 260,000 cars.

Air Mail

The idea of being able to deliver mail speedily over long distances had great appeal. Air-mail deliveries had begun in 1911 in both the US and Britain, and by 1924 there were regular mail flights right across the American continent. Their speed made aircraft a popular alternative to rail transport for postal services. This helped the development of aviation and provided jobs for enthusiastic young pilots such as Charles Lindbergh (see page 91).

The letter bottom right was carried on the first non-stop transatlantic flight in 1919. British aviators John Alcock and Arthur Whitten Brown flew from Newfoundland to Ireland in a converted Vickers Vimy bomber.

Motoring On

Mass production methods in large factories meant that more motor cars could be produced and sold at cheaper prices. In 1924, the Ford Motor Company produced two million Model-T cars, and a few years later the price of a "Tin Lizzie" dropped to less than $300 (a third of its original price). There was plenty of competition for Henry Ford. While his company concentrated on affordable motoring, others such as the Buick Motor Company aimed at the luxury market.

THE TRANSPORTATION REVOLUTION

1919
First international air-mail service starts between the US and Canada; a passenger air service opens between Florida and Cuba.

1926
Charles Lindbergh is hired as chief pilot by a company flying mail between St. Louis and Chicago.

1927
The Ford Motor Company ends production of its Model T automobile, as Henry Ford drives the 15 millionth "Tin Lizzie" off the production line.

1933
Boeing launches the world's first streamlined all-metal airliner, the Boeing 247, with room for 10 passengers.

1934
The first diesel-powered streamlined passenger train begins regular service between Chicago and Minneapolis–St. Paul.

1938
The British Mallard A4-class 4-6-2 locomotive sets a new world-record speed for a steam train of 126 mph (203 kph).

1930s INTERCONTINENTAL AIR ROUTES

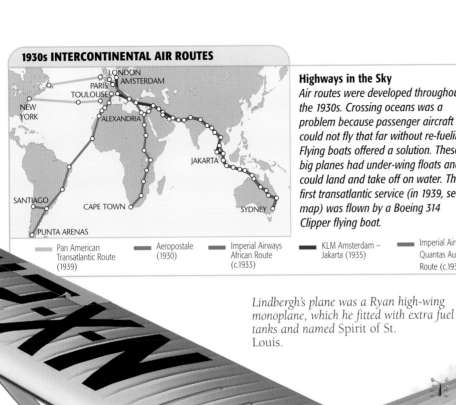

LONDON
AMSTERDAM
PARIS
TOULOUSE
NEW YORK
ALEXANDRIA
JAKARTA
SANTIAGO
CAPE TOWN
SYDNEY
PUNTA ARENAS

Pan American Transatlantic Route (1939)

Aeropostale (1930)

Imperial Airways African Route (c.1933)

KLM Amsterdam – Jakarta (1935)

Imperial Airways/ Quantas Australian Route (c.1934)

Highways in the Sky
Air routes were developed throughout the 1930s. Crossing oceans was a problem because passenger aircraft could not fly that far without re-fueling. Flying boats offered a solution. These big planes had under-wing floats and could land and take off on water. The first transatlantic service (in 1939, see map) was flown by a Boeing 314 Clipper flying boat.

Transatlantic Solo Flight
In 1927, American aviator Charles Lindbergh made the first solo flight across the Atlantic. His long journey from New York to Paris covered 3,610 miles (5,810 km), took 33 hours and won him a prize of $25,000. People all over the world read about the feat in their newspapers, and Lindbergh became an international star. His fame helped boost the aircraft industry and made air travel more popular.

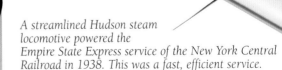

Lindbergh's plane was a Ryan high-wing monoplane, which he fitted with extra fuel tanks and named Spirit of St. Louis.

A popular celebrity, Charles Lindbergh (1902–74) was nicknamed "Lucky Lindy."

A streamlined Hudson steam locomotive powered the Empire State Express *service of the New York Central Railroad in 1938. This was a fast, efficient service.*

Railways
The US railway network covered the whole country. In the 1920s, most long-distance freight was moved by rail, and passengers also traveled by train. But the road system was improving, and cars and buses were becoming more popular. During the 1930s, the large railway companies lost money, and many went bankrupt. Those that survived did their best to attract passengers with the quality of their service, offering improved carriages, good food, and fast, powerful locomotives.

The Great Depression

Boom before bust. Christmas shopping in 1928.

During the American business boom of the 1920s, people were keen to invest and speculate on the Stock Exchange. Share prices went up and up. Some overestimated their value, and everything changed in 1929, when the New York Stock Exchange crashed. This started a huge international business slump, reaching its lowest point in 1932. As trade collapsed, millions of people lost their jobs and many struggled simply to survive.

Wealthy people who lost money tried to sell everything they could to raise cash.

World Trade

The US crash affected world trade, and bank and business failures led to a global economic crisis. At first Europe was worst affected, and bread lines and soup kitchens began to appear in Britain and elsewhere. Those countries that produced food and raw materials for the USA and Europe found that people could no longer afford their goods, and they too suffered.

In the United States and elsewhere, soup kitchens were set up to feed the poor and homeless.

Terrifying walls of dust created "black blizzard" dust storms in South Dakota in 1934.

Effects in the USA

For more than three years after the Stock Exchange crash of 1929, share prices kept on falling and businesses failed. Millions of Americans lost their savings, and many even lost their homes because they could not repay loans. By 1932, thousands of families were wandering the country, seeking shelter, and begging for food. Many starved or died of disease. For those who survived, life was very different from the Roaring Twenties, as their insecurity and financial worries grew.

The Curse of Unemployment

In the US the unemployment rate reached 9 percent in 1930. Three years later roughly a quarter of the working population—13 million people—was unemployed. The situation was no better in other parts of the world. In 1932, unemployment reached 30 percent in Germany, 24 percent in Belgium, and 21 percent in Britain. Overall, in that year world unemployment rose to nearly 30 percent. To make things worse, those in work suffered pay cuts as businesses struggled.

I KNOW 3 TRADES
I SPEAK 3 LANGUAGES
FOUGHT FOR 3 YEARS
HAVE 3 CHILDREN
AND NO WORK FOR
3 MONTHS
BUT I ONLY WANT
ONE JOB

Both skilled and unskilled workers found it hard to get a job.

Bonnie and Clyde

Criminal duo Bonnie Parker (1910–34) and Clyde Barrow (1909–34) became notorious in American newspapers for their daring armed robberies. Both originally from Texas, they teamed up in 1932 and began a series of raids on small-town banks, petrol stations, stores, and restaurants. They were finally tracked, ambushed, and gunned down by police in Louisiana in May, 1934.

The Dust Bowl

During the 1930s, severe droughts struck the southern Great Plains of the United States. As the soil dried out, crops began to fail. Prairie grasses died, and soon vast dust storms started blowing up. They damaged huge areas of Colorado, Kansas, New Mexico, Oklahoma, and Texas. The affected region came to be known as the Dust Bowl.

Bonnie and Clyde beside their getaway car, which is riddled with bullet holes.

THE GREAT DEPRESSION

1929
In March, US President Herbert Hoover says in his inaugural address, "In no nation are the fruits of accomplishment more secure." In October, the New York Stock Exchange crashes.

1930
The Smoot-Hawley Tariff Act raises duties, harming imports but not helping US trade.

1931
The 102-storey Empire State Building is completed in New York as the tallest building in the world. The popular song "Brother, Can You Spare a Dime?" expresses Depression feelings.

1932
Troops drive a group of protesting unemployed war veterans out of Washington. New York City Police estimate that 7,000 adults shine shoes for a living in the city.

1933
In July, share prices at last stop falling (at 15 percent of their 1929 value). End of the Prohibition period.

1934
Germany adopts a "New Plan" for trade regulated by the state.

Crowds of worried people gathered in New York streets as news of the Stock Exchange crash spread.

This British newspaper report appeared the day after the crash. It reported prices tumbling "like an avalanche."

The Wall Street Crash

Throughout the 1920s, the value of shares on the major Stock Exchange in Wall Street, New York, kept on rising. The US economy was doing extremely well. Then on 24 October, 1929, share prices suddenly fell rapidly, leading shareholders to sell their stock. This reduced prices further. The day of the Wall Street Crash came to be known as Black Thursday. Some banks lost so much money that they were forced to close, causing panic among customers. By 1932, nearly every US bank had closed.

A 1932 campaign badge for the Democratic presidential candidate, Roosevelt, who said: "I pledge you, I pledge myself, to a new deal for the American people."

The New Deal

When Roosevelt became president in 1933, he introduced a range of measures to get the United States out of its Great Depression. His New Deal of social and economic reforms aimed to restore confidence in the banks, reduce unemployment, and help the poor. The program did not solve all the problems, but it did help those facing most hardship.

FDR

Franklin Delano Roosevelt (1882–1945), known as FDR, is the only US president to be elected four times. He was in office for more than 12 years, leading his nation through World War II. He had been paralysed by poliomyelitis in 1921, but never allowed this to hold him back. Roosevelt famously said in 1933 that "the only thing we have to fear is fear itself," and he was fearless in seeing through his New Deal reforms.

The Hundred Days

Most of Roosevelt's New Deal laws were brought in between March and June 1933, a period called "the Hundred Days." First, the new president closed all the nation's banks; only financially sound ones were allowed to re-open. Then he created new agencies. The National Recovery Administration (NRA) helped businesses and workers; the Agricultural Adjustment Administration (AAA) helped farmers; and the Civilian Conservation Corps (CCC) launched a relief program for the poor.

A NEW DEAL FOR THE USA

1933
Roosevelt's first law as president is the Emergency Banking Act. The Tennessee Valley Authority (TVA) helps control floods and generate electricity.

1934
The Securities Exchange Commission regulates the stock market.

1935
The Works Progress Administration provides jobs for more than 8 million Americans. The National Labor Relations Board helps industry and trade unions.

1936
Roosevelt wins re-election.

1937
The Farm Security Administration helps farmers buy equipment.

1938
The Fair Labor Standards Act bans child labour and sets a minimum wage.

Poster for the 1940 film of Steinbeck's novel. Director John Ford won an Oscar for his work.

Helping the "Forgotten Man"

Roosevelt said he wanted his government to help the "forgotten man" at the bottom of the economic heap. He was thinking of the poor and the unemployed, including those who lost their homes. In 1939 American author John Steinbeck's novel *The Grapes of Wrath* told the story of a poor farming family that was forced to leave Oklahoma and head for California in search of a better life.

Migrant Families

Like the family in *The Grapes of Wrath*, many US farmers were badly hit by droughts and dust storms in the 1930s (see page 92). Many stuck it out as long as they could, but were eventually forced to leave their homes and try to find farming work and build new lives in other states. They packed up their possessions and set off to look for jobs pulling carrots or picking fruit or cotton.

This Oklahoma family packed up all their belongings in their car and headed for "the cotton fields of Arizona" on their way to California.

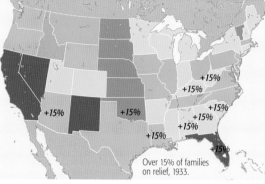

WORST AFFECTED AREAS

+15%
+15%
+15%
+15%
+15%
+15%
+15%
+15%
+15%

Over 15% of families on relief, 1933.

Families on Relief

The economic situation varied across the United States. As this map shows, in many of the southern states more than 15 per cent of families were on New Deal relief before the end of 1933. As people moved in search of work and to avoid drought and dust storms, the population in the central strip of states decreased. Many headed west.

POPULATION INCREASE AND DECREASE

20% + 　15–20% 　10–15% 　5–10% 　0–5% 　decrease

Roosevelt's "Tree Army"

The Civilian Conservation Corps (CCC) put people to work in useful projects, such as planting trees, building flood barriers and repairing forest roads. Workers were given free accommodation in camps, where they received food, medical care and a wage of a dollar a day. Altogether the CCC gave work to about 3 million men, and the "Tree Army" planted more than 3 billion new trees over 9 years.

Civilian Conservation Corps recruits planting trees in 1933. The trees replaced those destroyed by forest fires and were intended to stop erosion and dust storms caused by drought.

Rudolph Valentino played a desert chieftain opposite Agnes Ayres in The Sheik (1921). The film was followed in 1926 by Son of the Sheik.

Poster for the first successful talkie, which included songs such as "My Mammy."

The Silent Era

In the early 1920s, films grew in popularity as a form of mass entertainment. The growing movie studios made stars of actors such as Douglas Fairbanks Sr, Mary Pickford and Charlie Chaplin, who all worked for the United Artists studio. One of the most popular stars was the Italian-born actor Rudolph Valentino (1895–1926), who became famous for his romantic roles.

Coming of the Talkies

By 1925, several systems had been developed to add sound to films. Audiences were enthusiastic, but the studios were less convinced. Nevertheless, in 1926 Warner Bros brought out *Don Juan*, starring John Barrymore, which had a musical accompaniment recorded by the New York Philharmonic Orchestra. They followed this up the next year with *The Jazz Singer*, in which Al Jolson sang and spoke some dialogue. The new talking pictures were a huge success.

Walt Disney

Born in Chicago in 1901, Walt Disney moved to Los Angeles in 1923 to make movies. He set up a small studio and started producing cartoons with animal characters. Disney used sound and himself provided the voice for his most famous character, Mickey Mouse. In 1932 he made *Flowers and Trees* in Technicolor. Five years later, the Disney studio created the first full-length animated feature film with human characters and popular songs.

In 1932 Walt Disney won an Honorary Academy Award for Mickey Mouse and an Oscar for best short cartoon.

This famous sign was put up in Hollywood Hills in 1923.

The Hollywood Dream Factory

In the 1920s, Hollywood, a district of Los Angeles in California, became the center of the motion-picture industry. Companies that had studios there set up a system that gave them control over the entire production of their films, including the many different people involved. This led to a golden age of American films. From 1930 to 1945 Hollywood studios produced more than 7,500 movies.

Above: Orson Welles, seated far right, directs a scene in Citizen Kane. The film was not a financial success on release, but it received nine Oscar nominations and won Best Original Screenplay. Oscars (right) were first awarded by the Academy of Motion Picture Arts and Sciences in 1929.

Paramount Studios in the 1930s, when the company had such star actors as Gary Cooper, Marlene Dietrich, and W.C. Fields.

Big Studios

During the 1920s, films were dominated by the ever-growing big studios—Columbia, Fox, MGM, Paramount, RKO, United Artists, Universal and Warner Bros. These companies made and distributed films and owned cinemas. Their producers were tough businessmen. A studio signed up directors, writers, designers and technicians, as well as actors, so that they were on the payroll and worked only for that studio.

Greatest Film of All Time?

In 1941 one of the smallest of the major studios–RKO Radio Pictures–released a film called *Citizen Kane*. It is considered a masterpiece of cinematic technique, and in 2007 the American Film Institute made it number one in its list of all-time great US movies. The film, which is about a newspaper magnate, was directed by and starred Orson Welles (1915–85), who was given complete control over production of the film by RKO.

Genres

The studio system concentrated on genres, or specific types, of film. Westerns, gangster movies and comedies were all popular genres. Director John Ford increased the popularity of the Western with *Stagecoach* (1939). The film won two Oscars and made a star of John Wayne, who went on to make many more cowboy films. In the same year a new studio called Selznick Pictures had a sensational hit with *Gone With the Wind*, an American Civil War drama.

Golden Age

Popular Hollywood films provided entertainment for millions of people during the difficult period of the Depression (see pages 92–93). Actors became huge stars. As the political situation became more worrying towards the end of the 1930s, Hollywood studios made patriotic films with happy endings. This was a golden age for the studio system of movie production, and new, expensive films were heavily promoted.

A famous scene from King Kong (1933), *with the ape on top of the Empire State Building.*

Charlie Chaplin made fun of fascism in his 1940 film The Great Dictator.

Leon Trotsky

Trotsky helped lead the 1917 revolution and was the second most powerful man in Russia, after Lenin. In the Communist government Trotsky became Commissar for Foreign Affairs and then Commissar for War. He founded the Red Army (which was named after the color of the Communist flag), recruiting workers and peasants. He appointed former officers of the imperial army to lead them. Trotsky's use of the military to overhaul the Russian railway led to opposition from trade unionists.

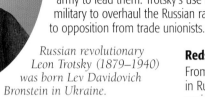

Russian revolutionary Leon Trotsky (1879–1940) was born Lev Davidovich Bronstein in Ukraine.

This Communist army recruitment poster of 1920 reads: "You! Are you a volunteer yet?"

Reds versus Whites

From 1918 to 1920, there was civil war in Russia. The Red Army fought against a group of anti-Communist armies (known as Whites), including Ukrainian nationalists. The Whites were politically supported by Russia's First World War allies, including Britain and France, who opposed Communism. The White armies were nowhere nearly as organized as the Reds, and by November 1920 their final group was defeated in the Crimea.

SOVIET UNION 1922–25

map showing:

SOVIET UNION

MONGOLIA

CHINA

Creation of the USSR

In December 1922, the Russian government united with Communist neighbors to found the Union of Soviet Socialist Republics (USSR, or Soviet Union). There were four founding republics—Belarus, Russia, Transcaucasia (modern Azerbaijan, Armenia, and Georgia), and Ukraine. The map shows the Union's territory in its early years.

- USSR in Oct. 1922
- Gained 19 Nov. 1922
- Frontier of USSR in 1923
- Gained by 1925
- Japanese until 1925
- Gained 30 Dec. 1922
- Other Communist states

Lenin and the Bolsheviks

When the revolutionary Bolsheviks formed a new government in 1917, they promised the Russian people great changes. The new regime was led by Lenin (1870–1924, real name Vladimir Ilyich Ulyanov), who was chairman of the Council of People's Commissars. Lenin redistributed their vast country's land to the peasants, but he also saw a need for a strong central government. The Bolsheviks hoped that their revolution would lead to a spread of Communism in other Western countries.

Birth of the Soviet Union

The Bolshevik Revolution of 1917 had led to a new government in Russia, headed by Lenin. In March the following year, the Russian Communists made peace with Germany, but were forced to give up territory, including the Baltic states, Finland, Poland, and the Ukraine. Lenin concentrated on the reforms promised by his party, and in 1922 Russia joined with the Ukraine and two other neighboring republics to form the Soviet Union.

Lenin speaks to a crowd of supporters on May 1, 1918.

The End of Lenin's Rule

From 1922 until his death two years later, Lenin suffered strokes and poor health. This meant a period of instability as others competed for power. The undisputed winner of the contest was Stalin. The new General Secretary gained the support of other committee members to oust Trotsky, who was later expelled from the party and exiled.

Lenin's body was displayed in a glass coffin inside a wooden mausoleum beside Red Square, in Moscow. Later, the mausoleum was rebuilt in red granite (left).

Izvestia

The daily national newspaper *Izvestia* (meaning "Delivered Messages" or "News") was founded in 1917 by the Petrograd Soviet of Workers' Deputies. After the formation of the USSR, it became the official newspaper of the Soviet government, outlining policy and expressing official views. *Izvestia* survived the collapse of Communism in 1991 and is still published today.

The Izvestia building in Moscow shows the full title of the newspaper: News of Soviets of Peoples' Deputies of the USSR.

BIRTH OF THE SOVIET UNION

1918
Russia signs the Treaty of Brest-Litovsk with Germany, withdrawing from the First World War. The Bolsheviks move the Russian capital back from Petrograd (formerly St. Petersburg) to Moscow.

1919
Lenin forms the Third International, an organization of world Communist parties. Russo-Polish War (1919–20).

1920
Polish leader Jozef Pilsudski defeats the Red Army and gains western Ukraine and Belarus.

1921
Rebellion by sailors at the Kronstadt naval base is crushed by the Red Army; this leads directly to Lenin's New Economic Policy.

1922
Lenin becomes seriously ill; in March, Joseph Stalin becomes General Secretary of the Communist Party.

1923
Lenin dictates a political Testament, warning against allowing Stalin too much power.

1924
Lenin dies on January 21; Petrograd is renamed Leningrad; Turkmenistan and Uzbekistan become new Soviet republics.

Stalin's Russia

After the death of Lenin and a victorious power struggle over Trotsky and others, Joseph Stalin gained total power. From 1929 he ruled unopposed as dictator of the Soviet Union. Stalin lived up to his adopted name of "man of steel," murdering opponents and sending millions to labor camps. His bold plans for industrialization were largely successful, but his hard-line policies for increasing agricultural output were disastrous, costing millions of lives.

This Soviet statue of 1935 represents successful industry and agriculture.

Young Stalin met with other revolutionaries and learned political skills, such as knowing which colleagues to trust.

Rise to Supreme Power

Stalin was born in Georgia, the son of a shoemaker and a washerwoman. He trained to be a priest before joining a secret Marxist group and, later, the Bolsheviks. He played an important part in the revolution of 1917, which was led by Lenin and Trotsky; after gaining power Stalin claimed to have been Lenin's co-leader. After becoming General Secretary of the Communist Party in 1922, Stalin set about gaining supreme power over the Soviet Union.

Peasants and Workers

Stalin planned to get farmers to produce enough grain to feed workers in the cities, so that industry could expand. Peasants were forced to give up ownership of their plots of land and work with others on large collective farms, which belonged to the state. Fewer unskilled farm laborers were needed, so many were sent to work in the growing factories. Those peasants who resisted were sent to labor camps or killed.

Women worked on collective farms, as well as in factories.

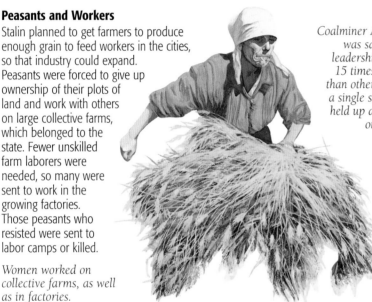

Coalminer Alexei Stakhanov was said by the Soviet leadership to have cut 15 times more coal than other workers in a single shift, and was held up as a model for others to follow.

Many new factories were built following the first Five Year Plan. Millions of workers moved to the growing cities to push through increased production.

End of the Kulaks

The kulaks were a class of wealthy landowning peasants who could afford to hire labour and lease portions of their land. They had been important people before the revolution, and they opposed Stalin's policy of collectivization (creating collective farms). The kulaks' land and property were taken by force, and they joined many of their former laborers in the Soviet gulags (labor camps).

Prisoners were forced to work hard in freezing conditions in the gulags of Siberia. Conditions were harsh, food was poor, and many died in the camps.

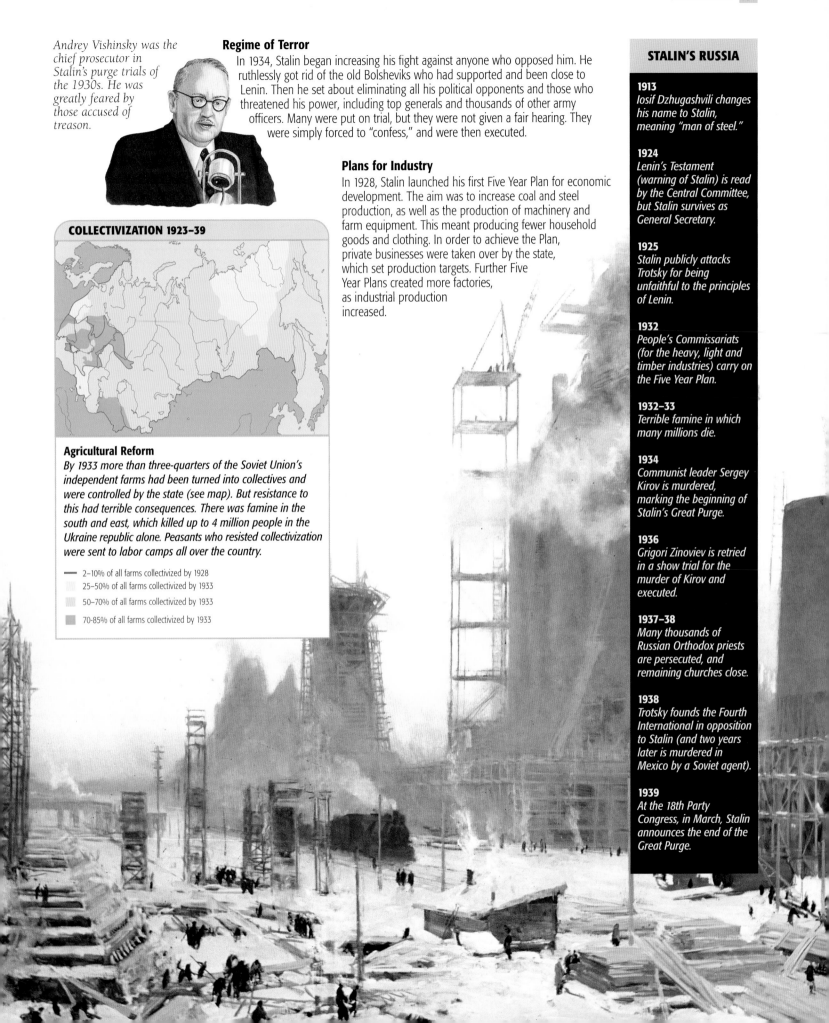

Andrey Vishinsky was the chief prosecutor in Stalin's purge trials of the 1930s. He was greatly feared by those accused of treason.

Regime of Terror

In 1934, Stalin began increasing his fight against anyone who opposed him. He ruthlessly got rid of the old Bolsheviks who had supported and been close to Lenin. Then he set about eliminating all his political opponents and those who threatened his power, including top generals and thousands of other army officers. Many were put on trial, but they were not given a fair hearing. They were simply forced to "confess," and were then executed.

Plans for Industry

In 1928, Stalin launched his first Five Year Plan for economic development. The aim was to increase coal and steel production, as well as the production of machinery and farm equipment. This meant producing fewer household goods and clothing. In order to achieve the Plan, private businesses were taken over by the state, which set production targets. Further Five Year Plans created more factories, as industrial production increased.

COLLECTIVIZATION 1923–39

Agricultural Reform

By 1933 more than three-quarters of the Soviet Union's independent farms had been turned into collectives and were controlled by the state (see map). But resistance to this had terrible consequences. There was famine in the south and east, which killed up to 4 million people in the Ukraine republic alone. Peasants who resisted collectivization were sent to labor camps all over the country.

- 2–10% of all farms collectivized by 1928
- 25–50% of all farms collectivized by 1933
- 50–70% of all farms collectivized by 1933
- 70-85% of all farms collectivized by 1933

STALIN'S RUSSIA

1913
Iosif Dzhugashvili changes his name to Stalin, meaning "man of steel."

1924
Lenin's Testament (warning of Stalin) is read by the Central Committee, but Stalin survives as General Secretary.

1925
Stalin publicly attacks Trotsky for being unfaithful to the principles of Lenin.

1932
People's Commissariats (for the heavy, light and timber industries) carry on the Five Year Plan.

1932–33
Terrible famine in which many millions die.

1934
Communist leader Sergey Kirov is murdered, marking the beginning of Stalin's Great Purge.

1936
Grigori Zinoviev is retried in a show trial for the murder of Kirov and executed.

1937–38
Many thousands of Russian Orthodox priests are persecuted, and remaining churches close.

1938
Trotsky founds the Fourth International in opposition to Stalin (and two years later is murdered in Mexico by a Soviet agent).

1939
At the 18th Party Congress, in March, Stalin announces the end of the Great Purge.

Fascist Italian flag flying from a fasces.

Fascism in Italy

Fascism is an authoritarian, nationalistic political movement and system of government. It takes its name from the fasces, a bundle of rods that represented the authority of ancient Rome. The movement was first introduced in Italy by Mussolini, who used the chaos and depression of the 1920s to gain support from landowners and industrialists, as well as extremists who cared little for equality and individual liberty.

Mussolini and his Blackshirts, photographed in 1922. The armed squads became more violent as they gained power.

Painting showing the bombing of Ethiopia by the Italian air force.

Colonial Empire

Mussolini was determined to increase Italy's influence as a major power. In 1935–36 Italian forces invaded Emperor Haile Selassie's Abyssinia (modern Ethiopia), despite opposition from the League of Nations. Other European countries opposed Italy's colonial policies, but they received backing from Germany. In 1939, Italy conquered Albania, which remained part of the Italian Empire until the Germans took over four years later.

The Leader

In 1922, large numbers of Blackshirts marched on Rome. The Italian king, Victor Emmanuel III, feared a civil war and felt forced to appoint Mussolini prime minister. Three years later, Mussolini declared a dictatorship, with himself at the head. He was called "Il Duce" (the Leader). Other political parties were banned, and the Fascist government took control of the police, industry, and the press.

Mussolini's Rise to Power

Benito Mussolini (1883–1945) started off believing in socialism, and at the age of 29 edited the left-wing Italian Socialist Party's newspaper. He served in the Italian army in the First World War, before founding the Italian Fascist Party, which combined socialist and extreme right-wing ideas. The Fascists were supported by black-shirted armed squads, who at first terrorized Communists and went on to target all opponents of Mussolini and fascism.

Rome–Berlin Axis

The Italian dictator was supported in his ambitions by the dictator of Germany, Adolf Hitler. In 1936, they both sent troops to support the Spanish Fascist dictator, Francisco Franco. Hitler and Mussolini announced a Rome–Berlin Axis (or center of power), around which they believed other European states would gather. The Axis was further strengthened by the addition of Japan in the Tripartite Pact of 1940.

Two Fascist leaders: Il Duce (Mussolini) and Der Führer (Hitler).

Mussolini had an office in the prestigious Palazzo Venezia in central Rome.

Desperate Downfall

In 1943, after Allied troops landed in Sicily, the Fascist Grand Council dismissed Mussolini and restored the king to power. Mussolini was imprisoned and then rescued by German soldiers. The former dictator became a German puppet ruler of the so-called Italian Social Republic in the north of the country. As World War II neared its end, Mussolini was captured by Italian anti-Fascist partisans and executed.

Opponents of the Fascist regime were terrorized, tortured, and killed.

ITALIAN EMPIRE, 1939

ITALY
ALBANIA
LIBYA
ERITREA
ABYSSINIA
SOMALILAND

▢ Italian Empire, 1939

Mussolini's Colonies

Italy had controlled Libya since 1912 and the small Dodecanese islands off Turkey since 1923. Mussolini's Fascist regime took Albania and expanded the region known as Italian East Africa. Italian troops added Abyssinia (Ethiopia) by invading without warning from areas already controlled by Italy—Somaliland (Somalia) and Eritrea.

Economic Aims

Mussolini's Fascists introduced programs to improve the economy by helping agriculture and creating employment. The "Battle for grain" program used existing and new farmland for growing the wheat that was needed to make Italy self-sufficient. The "Battle for land" reclaimed large areas of marshland, which were then used for farming. As the government took control of the economy, many Italian people welcomed its strong leadership and reforms.

A Fascist demonstration in Milan's Galleria arcade in 1934. Mussolini was presented by the Fascist Party as a great leader who could bring enormous success to Italy.

...SM IN ITALY

1919
Mussolini founds the Fascist Combat Group.

1921
The Blackshirts join the Fascist Party as a national militia.

1926
Secret police and political courts are established.

1929
Lateran Treaties between Mussolini's government and Pope Pius XI.

1936
The Rome–Berlin Axis is proclaimed.

1937
Italy joins Germany and Japan in an alliance against the Soviet Union.

1939
Italy and Germany make a formal alliance known as the Pact of Steel.

1940
Italy declares war on Britain and France and enters World War II.

1941
British forces help the Ethiopians drive Italians out of their country.

1943
In September, Italy surrenders to the Allies.

1945
Mussolini is shot; his body is hung upside down for display in Milan.

Reshaping the Middle East

The collapse of the Ottoman Empire in the early 20th century led to the foundation of the new republic of Turkey. The League of Nations divided other parts of the former empire into so-called mandated territories, administered by Britain and France. This approach caused conflict with Arab nationalists, and Jewish immigration heightened the tension in Palestine. Unsolved problems in the Middle East left a lasting legacy of conflict.

The Balfour Declaration (see below) was made in a letter from the British foreign secretary, Arthur James Balfour, to Lord Rothschild.

In 1919, the Zionist politician Chaim Weizmann (left, wearing Arab clothing as a sign of friendship) signed an agreement of Jewish-Arab cooperation with Emir Faisal (later king of Iraq).

BRITISH MANDATES

SYRIA

Palestine

Transjordan

BRITISH MANDATE OF PALESTINE

ARABIA

Palestine and Transjordan

The Balfour Declaration of 1917 stated British support for the establishment in Palestine of a national home for the Jewish people. Three years later, the UK was given a mandate to govern the whole region of Palestine (see map). In 1922, Palestine was limited to the area west of the River Jordan, and the area to the east became Transjordan.

End of the Ottoman Empire

Defeat in the First World War meant that the Ottomans lost all their territory outside Asia Minor. By the end of the war Britain and France occupied much of the Middle East region of the former empire. This led to the League of Nations going on to create the states of Iraq, Palestine and Transjordan (later Jordan) as mandated territories administered by Britain, while Lebanon and Syria came under French administration.

New Dynasty in Persia

The kingdom of Persia, which had been ruled by shahs of the Qajar dynasty since 1794, remained neutral during the First World War. In 1921 the Qajar government was overthrown and a cavalry officer named Reza Khan came to power. From 1925 he reigned as the Shah of Persia, and 10 years later the country changed its name to Iran (or "land of the Aryans").

The Golestan Palace in the Persian capital of Tehran once belonged to a group of royal Qajar buildings.

Kemal Atatürk (1881–1938), founder of modern Turkey.

Birth of Modern Turkey

The people of the region that remained of the former Ottoman Empire resented harsh treatment by the Greeks and their allies. In 1922, nationalist forces drove the Greeks from the region and abolished the office of sultan formerly held by the Ottoman rulers. They announced the new republic of Turkey and elected the nationalist hero Mustafa Kemal as president, naming him Atatürk–"Father of the Turks."

Desert Kingdom

The deserts of the Arabian peninsula had been controlled by tribal leaders and the Ottomans. From 1902, the Saud family gained control over more and more territory, but the British administered the region as a protectorate from 1915. Ibn Saud gained the holy cities of Mecca and Medina in 1925, and set about bringing the desert provinces together. By 1932, he was able to proclaim the lands under his control as the Kingdom of Saudi Arabia.

Oil was discovered in Saudi Arabia in 1936, changing the new kingdom's fortunes. The picture shows the first Saudi well gushing oil.

Colonial and Arab Disputes

King Faisal I of Iraq (ruled 1921–33) was a leader of Arab nationalism. The British government supported him as an influential statesman who could govern an independent Iraq after the British mandate ended in 1932. Since Iraq shared a long border with Saudi Arabia, British leaders attempted to bring about a settlement of old disputes between the two kingdoms. Agreements were reached, but future troubles were to prove that these were often short-lived.

RISING TENSION

By 1939, many of the countries of the Middle East region had officially gained independence, but some of the region was still administered by colonial powers (see map). Many Arab people were pressing for independence. They included the Palestinian Arabs, who protested about the increasing numbers of Jewish immigrants from Nazi Germany during the 1930s.

MANDATORY POWERS AND INDEPENDENT COUNTRIES, 1939

| Italy | Britain | France | Independent country |

In 1930, Faisal I of Iraq met Ibn Saud of Saudi Arabia aboard a British warship in the Gulf. The meeting, hosted by the British High Commissioner to Iraq and an RAF air marshal, ended in both sides recognizing the other's territory.

Britain's Imperial Sunset

Though Britain emerged from the First World War victorious, its human casualties, financial costs, and devastation left the country facing huge problems at home. Abroad, many of the United Kingdom's colonies were calling for independence, threatening the authority of the formerly all-powerful British Empire. Ireland became independent, along with other founder members of the Commonwealth of Nations, and Britain lost authority in India.

Londoners celebrate the end of the Great War.

After transport workers joined the General Strike, the government ordered armed escorts for important food convoys.

The Irish nationalist Michael Collins (1890–1922) became prime minister of the Irish Free State. He was killed by Republicans who opposed the Anglo-Irish Treaty.

Poster for the "Abundance of Africa," part of the British Empire Exhibition of 1924–25.

PAGEANT OF EMPIRE. WEMBLEY
21ST JULY TO 30TH AUGUST. 1924

The Abundance of Africa
EVERY EVENING AT 8·0 p.m.
21ST JULY TO 9TH AUGUST
11TH AUGUST TO 30TH AUGUST AT 7·30 p.m.

Independence for Ireland

In 1921, after years of fighting, Ireland was split into the British dominion of the Irish Free State and the Ulster counties of Northern Ireland, which remained part of the United Kingdom. The Irish Free State gradually cut its ties with the UK, and by 1937 was ready to gain full independence as Eire.

British Empire Exhibition

The aim of this exhibition, held at Wembley in 1924–25, was to strengthen trade with the colonies. At the opening ceremony, King George V sent a telegram that traveled right round the world in just over a minute. The three main buildings, linked by a "never-stop" railway, were devoted to industry, engineering and the arts. The exhibition attracted 27 million visitors.

General Strike

Britain faced severe economic problems after the War. The coal industry was hard hit, and when mine-owners cut wages and called for longer hours in 1926, the Trades Union Congress backed a General Strike. This lasted only nine days before the trade unionists accepted defeat, but the miners stayed out for another six months. Conservative Chancellor of the Exchequer Winston Churchill vigorously opposed the strike, which ended in failure for the workers.

BRITISH EMPIRE, 1921

Rule Britannia

In 1921, the British Empire covered more than a quarter of the globe (see map). But there was a move toward independence in the self-governing colonies, recognized by an Imperial Conference declaration in 1926. Five years later, Australia, Canada, the Irish Free State, New Zealand, Newfoundland, and South Africa became independent within the new Commonwealth of Nations.

■ British Empire in 1921

India

During the 1920s, Mohandas Gandhi and the Indian National Congress party pushed forward a programme of non-violent opposition to British rule. They encouraged civil disobedience, non-cooperation and a boycott of British goods. By 1935, Indians had more representation in provincial lawmaking and government, but the British viceroy still held overall power. Nevertheless, the independence movement was gathering pace, as the British Empire faced the loss of its "jewel in the crown."

Mohandas Gandhi (1869–1948), known as Mahatma ("great soul"), believed in self-reliance and simplicity. A British-educated lawyer, Gandhi was imprisoned several times in India.

Constitutional Crisis

Crisis struck the British establishment after Edward VIII succeeded his father, King George V, who died in 1936. Before his coronation, Edward let it be known that he wanted to marry an American divorcee, Mrs Wallis Simpson. Prime Minister Stanley Baldwin, the Archbishop of Canterbury, and many other important people objected, and Edward gave up the throne. Following the abdication, his brother became George VI.

In the 1930s, British banks issued brass money boxes like this one to encourage saving. Only the bank could open the box.

The former Edward VIII married Wallis Simpson in France in 1937. They became the Duke and Duchess of Windsor.

BRITAIN'S IMPERIAL SUNSET

1919
Republicans declare Ireland independent, leading to fighting between Irish rebels (the Irish Republican Army or IRA) and British forces.

1921
Anglo-Irish Treaty gives British dominion status to a new Irish Free State.

1922–23
Civil war in Ireland.

1924
Britain has its first Labour administration, relying on Liberal support.

1927
The Trade Disputes Act (repealed in 1946) makes general strikes illegal.

1930
Gandhi leads the Salt March to the sea, protesting against British taxes on salt manufacture.

1931
The Statute of Westminster establishes the Commonwealth of Nations.

1937
The Muslim League grows in popularity and power in India.

China in Turmoil

I n the early 1920s, much of the republic of China was ruled by warlords (regional military leaders), but soon there were great changes. The Nationalists exercised their power over the warlords, and the Communists organized themselves into a strong force. Civil war broke out between the two political powers, and the Nationalists and Communists were only brought together by a common enemy—Japan.

The Communist revolutionary leader, Mao Zedong (1893–1976).

Chinese peasants were so poor that they could afford little farming equipment.

Mao Zedong

Mao was born into a farming family in southern China. From the age of 7, he worked in his father's fields. He was 18 when rebels overthrew the imperial government and made China a republic. In 1921, Mao was one of the 12 founding members of the Chinese Communist Party in Shanghai. The young Communists wanted to unite their country by joining up with the Kuomintang (Nationalist Party).

Civil War

In 1927 war broke out between Chiang Kai-shek's Nationalists, based at their capital in Nanjing, and Mao's Communists, based in Shanghai. Chiang led a number of campaigns that were designed to wipe out his Communist rivals, including a massacre of Shanghai workers. Mao led hundreds of peasants to the mountains of Jiangxi province, in southeastern China. They formed the beginnings of the People's Liberation (or Red) Army.

Just like the Communists, Nationalist soldiers had to survive tough conditions and had a poor diet.

Postage stamp showing a portrait of Chiang Kai-shek.

ROUTE OF THE LONG MARCH

Chiang Kai-shek

Chiang Kai-shek (1887–1975), also known as Jiang Jieshi, was the son of a village merchant. As a young man he attended the Chinese Imperial Military Academy, and in 1923 ran his own military academy. Three years later, he was commander-in-chief of the National Revolutionary Army. Chiang led the successful Northern Expedition, a military campaign against powerful warlords in northern China.

This painting shows some of the women who made the Long March. They return enemy fire as they start to cross one of the many rivers along the way.

From Jiangxi to Shaanxi

Mao's Long March (see page 109) began when about 100,000 Communists left their base, broke through Nationalist lines, and headed west. Their route then turned north (see map). Altogether the Communist troops crossed 18 mountain ranges and 24 rivers, covering about 6,000 miles (9,700 km) in a year and 5 days.

— Route of Mao's Long March

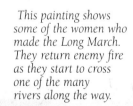

Japanese Invasion

In 1931, the Japanese invaded and occupied the huge northeastern province of Manchuria. Six years later Japanese forces moved further inland, causing Chinese Communists and Nationalists to unite against the invaders. Japan's army was better equipped than its opponents and soon captured Shanghai. As Nanjing fell, many thousands of men, women and children were massacred. The Sino-Japanese War was to carry on until 1945.

Cartoon illustrating the Japanese aggressive attitude toward its much bigger neighbor.

This calendar for year 23 of the Chinese Republic (1933), based on the lunar cycle, gives guidance on favorable days.

The Long March

By 1934, the Communists had suffered heavy losses in the civil war, and Mao Zedong's group was close to collapse. Mao's Communist army, together with 35 women, decided to move north. They were bombarded by the Nationalist air force and ground troops, and about half were killed in the first three months of the Long March. They were joined by other small Communist groups along the way, but only about 8,000 marchers completed the hazardous journey, which ended in Shaanxi province. The Long March strengthened Mao's leadership of the Communist Party and inspired many young Chinese to join him.

Civil War in Spain

After Spain became a republic in 1931, there was a widening gap between the political left and right wings. The Communists on the left sympathized with Republican aims, while the Fascists of the extreme right and the Catholic Church supported the Nationalists. Liberal ideals came up against authoritarian power, and the Civil War of 1936–39 tore the country apart. By the time the Nationalist commander General Franco was victorious, about 700,000 people had died in the struggle.

Many civilians took up arms in the war, using guerrilla tactics.

Poster of the Iberian Anarchist Federation (founded in 1927), which joined the fight against the Nationalists.

New Republic

King Alfonso XIII (1886–1941) ruled Spain during a period of dictatorship and social unrest. When Republican leaders won parliamentary elections in 1931, Alfonso was forced to leave the country. The government introduced a democratic constitution for the new republic, separating the state from the Church and giving more rights and freedom to the people, especially women. There was a new flag and a new anthem.

Republicans Versus Nationalists

In 1936 a military revolt against the Republican government was led by General Franco. The rebel Nationalists were supported by the Fascist party, Falange, which wanted to overthrow the democratic system. Republican loyalists resisted the takeover, leading to the violent conflict of civil war. In this battle of ideologies, Nazi Germany and Fascist Italy helped Franco's forces, while the Communist Soviet Union supported the Republicans. The US, UK, and France remained neutral.

General Francisco Franco (1892–1975), known as El Caudillo (the Leader).

General Franco

The son of a naval officer, Francisco Franco attended an infantry academy and became the youngest captain in the Spanish army in 1915. He commanded units in Morocco, where he put down rebellion against Spanish rule. Franco was promoted to brigadier general and became chief of general staff. In 1936 he led Spanish troops from Morocco to overthrow the Republican government.

SPAIN, 1936–39

LA CORUÑA
OVIEDO •X
X•GUERNICA
BASQUE TERRITORIES
FRANCE
• VALLADOLID
BARCELONA •
PORTUGAL
BRUNETE •X X• GUADALAJARA X•GANDESA
X• MADRID
X• TERUEL
VALENCIA •
• MÉRIDA
• SEVILLE
• GRANADA
• Ceuta
SPANISH-MOROCCO

July 21, 1936   Dec 31, 1937   February, 1939   Republican March 1939   X Important battles

Nationalist Gains

When war broke out, the Republicans controlled most of the east and north of the country. The map (left) shows how the Spanish Nationalists changed the situation and gained territory over the next 3 years. Important battles were fought in the heart of Spain, around the capital Madrid, as loyalists and rebels struggled for control.

NATIONALIST TERRITORIAL GAINS BY:

Above: Pablo Picasso's painting Guernica shows the horrors of the Civil War. In 1937 the historic Basque town of Guernica was virtually destroyed by German bombers supporting the Nationalists.

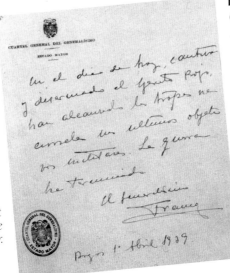

Franco's signed document declaring victory and the end of the war.

SPANISH CIVIL WAR

1931
Niceto Alcalá Zamora (1877–1949) is elected president of the Second Republic (the First Spanish Republic was 1873–74).

1932
An autonomous government is established in Catalonia.

1933
The extreme Nationalist political group Falange ("phalanx") is founded.

1934
Franco is promoted to major general (and a year later is appointed chief of the Spanish army's general staff).

1936
Salvador Dalí, one of the few artists to support the Nationalists, takes part in the London International Surrealist Exhibition.

1937
The Vatican recognizes Franco's Nationalist regime.

1938
International Brigades (about 20,000 non-Spanish volunteers, mainly Communists) fight for the Republicans, but the Soviet Union ends large-scale aid.

1939
Franco's dictatorship starts (lasts until 1975).

Nationalist Dictatorship

General Franco's forces took Barcelona in January 1939 and Madrid, one of the last Republican strongholds, two months later. The remaining Republican forces surrendered on April 1, leaving the Nationalists triumphant. Franco became head of state and the Falange was the only legal party in the new dictatorship. When the Second World War broke out later in the year, Spain remained neutral, although Franco's sympathies lay with Hitler's Germany.

Spanish poet and dramatist Federico Garcia Lorca (1898–1936) was shot and killed by Nationalists at the start of the Civil War.

Writers and Artists

Most Spanish writers and artists identified with the more liberal aims of the Republicans, and the government ran special missions to help young artists escape to the countryside. Sympathizers included the painters Pablo Picasso and Joan Miró (both living in France), filmmaker Luis Buñuel and writer Garcia Lorca. Foreign Republican supporters included the American novelist Ernest Hemingway and English writer George Orwell, who described his experiences in his personal account of the war, *Homage to Catalonia*.

The Nazis were proud of their murderous "Night of the Long Knives."

Hitler's Rise to Power

In the early 1920s, raging inflation ruined its currency. Then, when Germany failed to pay reparations for the Great War, France occupied the Ruhr region. The German economy collapsed and in 1933 the National Socialist German Workers' (or Nazi) Party used this desperate situation to gain power. The party's leader was Adolf Hitler, a former army corporal who rose to become the brutal dictator of Nazi Germany.

The Hakenkreuz ("hooked cross" or swastika) was an ancient symbol adopted by the Nazis.

From Corporal to Chancellor

Adolf Hitler, who was born in the Austrian town of Braunau, moved to Munich in 1913. When war broke out a year later, he joined the German Army and became a messenger. Hitler won an Iron Cross for bravery in crossing battlefields under fire and was promoted to corporal. After taking over the Nazi Party in 1921, he made it Germany's strongest political force. In 1933 President Hindenburg appointed Hitler Chancellor, head of the German government.

Adolf Hitler (1889–1945), giving the Nazi salute at the National Party Congress in Nuremberg in 1934.

Germany Under the Nazis

The Nazi Party's success was founded on the desperation of many Germans at the failure of their government to solve the country's terrible economic problems. The Nazis promised work for all by regulating wages and the production of goods. They gave many ordinary Germans a sense of unity and power, but at the same time smothered all opposition.

The Nazis manipulated public opinion by taking over the media and using extreme propaganda.

Night of the Long Knives

On 30 June 1934, the SS (Schutzstaffel, "protective unit") murdered many of Hitler's political opponents. Most of the victims belonged to the SA (Sturmabteilung, "assault division") Brownshirts, founded by Hitler himself 13 years earlier. Hitler announced that 77 individuals had been executed for conspiracy, including SA leader Ernst Röhm. The SS arrested and murdered many more, such as former chancellor, Kurt von Schleicher.

Poster for the 1936 Olympic Games.

Hitler Youth

German boys were supposed to join the Hitler Youth at age 13. They were trained in sport, camping and other activities, and strict discipline was enforced. Girls joined the League of German Maidens, where they learned gymnastics and were prepared for motherhood. By 1938, nearly 8 million young people had joined, but there were disagreements with schools that tried to keep up a more liberal tradition.

Racism and Persecution

Hitler and the Nazis used the Gestapo and SS to get rid of the groups they considered "non-Aryan," so that they could promote the idea of the German nation's "racial purity." The Gestapo had unlimited powers to hound and arrest Jews, trade unionists, homosexuals, gypsies, disabled people, and left-wing intellectuals. Discrimination against these groups quickly turned into persecution, and in 1935 rights were taken away from all German Jews. Many persecuted people left Germany.

Children joined the German Young People's organization at age 10, before moving on to the older boys' or girls' groups.

Jews were forced to wear a yellow star on their clothes.

Marlene Dietrich (1901–92) was one of the most famous people to leave Germany. She went to Hollywood to star in many films.

Berlin Olympics

For the Nazis, the 1936 Olympics made an opportunity to show the world that German athletes represented a superior race. "Non-Aryans" were kept out of the German team. Yet the Nazis tried to show their country to foreigners as a tolerant, peaceful place. Though Germany won most gold medals–33 to the USA's 24–the most successful athlete was a black American named Jesse Owens, who won four golds. Hitler avoided those medal presentation.

German Resistance

Opposition to Hitler and the Nazi Party was treason according to laws introduced in 1933. Nevertheless, some Communists, trade unionists and others distributed anti-Nazi leaflets. The Catholic Church opposed Hitler's program to kill physically and mentally disabled people, and clergymen and others helped and protected Jews.

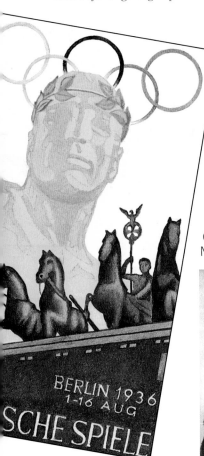

Brother and sister Hans and Sophie Scholl (shown in the center of the poster, left), joined with university students and professors in Munich to form a resistance group known as the White Rose. They were both captured and killed during the war.

In 1937, this anti-Nazi leaflet, headed "The final appeal," was sent secretly to France concealed inside a seed packet.

Germany Expands

Once he had total power, Hitler put his expansionist plans into action. In 1936 his forces occupied the Rhineland region, which had been demilitarized after the First World War. German troops met with no effective opposition from France or the League of Nations. Next on Hitler's list was Austria, which he invaded in March 1938 and proclaimed Anschluss (a forced "union" with Austria). A majority of Austrians welcomed becoming part of Großdeutschland ("Greater Germany").

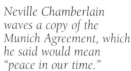

Hitler salutes his troops at a 1934 parade in Nuremberg.

The League of Nations headquarters in Geneva, Switzerland.

Neville Chamberlain waves a copy of the Munich Agreement, which he said would mean "peace in our time."

An Ailing Peacekeeper

The League of Nations had no armed forces and had already shown itself to be powerless in the face of international aggression. Germany and Japan had left the League in 1933, and Italy joined them in 1937, to form an alliance against the Soviet Union. The Munich Agreement, signed by League members Britain and France, showed the organization's weakness against aggression.

Munich Agreement

In September 1938, British prime minister Neville Chamberlain met Hitler at Berchtesgaden, Bad Godesberg and finally Munich. They were joined in Munich by the Italian leader Benito Mussolini and French premier Edouard Daladier. Hitler wanted to take over the German-speaking region of Czechoslovakia called Sudetenland and give other Czechs the right to join the Third Reich. Britain and France wanted peace, and the agreement on Sudetenland was signed.

World War II Breaks Out

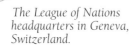

As Hitler expanded his Third Reich, Britain and France became increasingly alarmed. After Austria fell to Germany, the British and French premiers tried to appease Hitler in order to avoid war. Six months later, Hitler broke that agreement and took Czechoslovakia. In September 1939, the Germans continued their aggressive expansion by invading Poland. This time Britain and France felt they had to defend their ally and respond. They declared war on Germany.

Night of Broken Glass

On November 7, 1938, a Jewish student from Poland shot a German diplomat in Paris. The German Propaganda Minister Joseph Goebbels used this as an excuse to encourage stormtroopers to take revenge on the Jewish communities of Germany and Austria. Two days later, Nazis smashed the windows of Jewish businesses and burned down synagogues. Thousands of Jews were terrorized throughout a night of persecution called Kristallnacht ("Crystal night").

Passers-by survey the damage of Kristallnacht in Nuremberg.

Invasion of Poland

Despite an existing non-aggression pact, Hitler invaded Poland in 1939. Britain issued an ultimatum, and when Hitler ignored it, the British and French declared war on Germany. The Second World War in Europe had begun, and British prime minister Neville Chamberlain spoke of "evil things that we shall be fighting against, brute force, bad faith, injustice, oppression, and persecution." The German form of war, later called Blitzkrieg ("lightning war"), using fast mobile ground forces with air support, overwhelmed the Polish armies.

WORLD WAR II BREAKS OUT

1938
In February, Hitler demands that Austrian chancellor Kurt von Schuschnigg admit Nazis into his cabinet; Schuschnigg resigns. In March, the forced union with Austria (Anschluss) takes place. In October, Sudetenland becomes part of the Third Reich.

1939
Germany invades Czechoslovakia in March, and makes most of the country a German protectorate. In August, the Soviet Union signs a non-aggression pact with Germany. On September 1st, Hitler attacks Poland. On September 3rd, Britain, France, Australia, and New Zealand declare war on Germany. The Soviet Union joins the attack on Poland on September 17. German air raids on Britain begin in October. In December, the League of Nations expels the Soviet Union for its attack on Finland.

Polish troops in Warsaw resisted the Germans until the end of September. The photograph below shows Polish generals signing a ceasefire agreement and surrendering to German General Johannes Blaskowitz.

Left: *Jewish children in the Warsaw ghetto in 1941. Polish Jews in large cities were rounded up and locked in enclosed areas. In Warsaw there were more than 400,000 people living in the ghetto. In 1943, they organized the first armed uprising against the Nazis.*

The Growing Third Reich
By September 1939, Germany had already taken over Austria and Czechoslovakia. Its attack on Poland from the west was joined by a Russian invasion from the east. This was the situation at the start of World War II (see map, right). The defeated Polish government fled first to Romania and then to Britain.

GERMANY, SEPTEMBER 1939

- Allies
- Germany (including Czechoslovakia)
- Soviet Union
- Poland — German aggression
- Poland — Soviet aggression

GREAT BRITAIN

SOVIET UNION

POLAND

GERMANY

FRANCE

HITLER'S WAR TO THE WEST AND EAST

1940
In April, Germany invades Denmark and Norway; in May, Germany invades the Netherlands and France; in June, Italy declares war on Britain and France; 12 days later, France signs an armistice with Germany. In October, German U-boats sink 32 British ships in the Atlantic in a week.

1941
In April, Germany invades Greece and Yugoslavia, and in June invades the Soviet Union. German troops blockade Leningrad in September. In December, Hitler declares war on the United States.

1942
In August, Hitler orders his army to capture Stalingrad. October 23 sees the start of the Battle of El Alamein, in Egypt, which the British win.

1943
41 German U-boats are destroyed in the Atlantic in May. In September, Italy surrenders to the Allies.

1944
Allies land troops at Anzio, Italy, in January. June 6th is D-Day, the Allied invasion of German-occupied Normandy.

Hitler's War to the West and East

The Second World War began as a European conflict between the Allies (Britain and France) and Nazi Germany (in a non-aggression alliance with the Soviet Union). The Germans were joined by Italy and gained France, and by 1942 much of mainland Europe was under their control. But the situation changed dramatically when Hitler turned on Stalin. This left the Axis Powers (Germany and its partners) facing hostility to the west and the east in Europe, while the Allies were also making progress in North Africa.

Winston Churchill (1874–1965), prime minister of Britain during World War II.

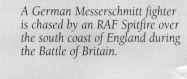

A German Messerschmitt fighter is chased by an RAF Spitfire over the south coast of England during the Battle of Britain.

The German pocket battleship Admiral Graf Spee *sank in the Atlantic, off Uruguay, in December 1939.*

Battle of the Atlantic

The struggle for control of the Atlantic supply routes from America went on from 1940 to 1944. German U-boats were the main threat to British merchant ships. One of the most important battles took place in May 1941, when British ships and aircraft eventually sank the Bismarck, a powerful German battleship that was intended to raid the sea lanes.

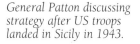

General Patton discussing strategy after US troops landed in Sicily in 1943.

Nazi-Soviet Pact

In August 1939, foreign ministers Vyacheslav Molotov of the Soviet Union and Joachim von Ribbentrop of Germany signed a military agreement in Moscow. Each side promised not to attack the other, to remain neutral if the other was attacked, and not to join any alliance against the other. They also agreed how to divide Poland after its capture. The pact gave Hitler the confidence to attack in September 1939.

Von Ribbentrop stands behind Molotov, as he signs the Nazi-Soviet Pact. Stalin (right), who was pleased with the pact's terms, looks on.

WAR IN EUROPE, 1942–44

Battle of Stalingrad, 1942–43

Fall of Berlin, May 1945

D-DAY June 6, 1944

BERLIN   STALINGRAD

Invasion of south of France, Aug. 1944

Invasion of Italy, Sept. 1943

Invasion of Sicily, July 1943

Battle of El-Alamein, Nov. 1942

Open Torch invasion of NW Africa, Nov. 1942

EL-ALAMEIN

Advances and Gains
When Hitler broke with Stalin and invaded Russia, he committed Germany to war on two fronts. The map shows how the territory controlled by the Axis Powers expanded in the first three years of the war. But Germany itself was squeezed between the advancing Allies.

- Maximum extent of Axis Powers, Nov. 1942
- Unoccupied Allied Powers
- Neutral states
- Soviet advances
- Allied advances

Battle of Britain

Journalists called the period up to spring 1940 the "phoney war," because Britain and France did little fighting. In August, Göring's Luftwaffe (air force) started trying to destroy the British RAF (Royal Air Force). Hitler's idea was to follow this with an invasion of Britain. Despite being outnumbered and losing about 900 planes, the RAF destroyed about 1,700 German aircraft and won the battle. Hitler changed his plans in October 1940 and turned to bombing British cities.

General Montgomery in the desert in North Africa.

North African Campaigns

During 1940, British troops fought the Italians in North Africa for control of Egypt, the Suez Canal and routes to the oil fields of the Middle East. In 1941, Hitler sent over tank divisions led by Field Marshal Erwin Rommel, known as the "Desert Fox." Rommel came up against the British commander Bernard Montgomery, who stopped the German advance at the Egyptian port of El Alamein. The Allies used their strength in North Africa to invade Sicily, southern Italy, in July 1943.

Operation Barbarossa

Germany and the Soviet Union were uneasy, distrustful partners. Before the end of 1940, Hitler drafted plans to invade Russia, code-naming the secret operation Barbarossa. The unexpected attack began in June 1941 and at first was successful, but the Russians showed great resistance in the siege of Leningrad. In the winter of 1942–43, German troops were beaten by Soviet forces and freezing temperatures at Stalingrad, and were forced to surrender.

German tanks were successful in the early months of the campaign on the Eastern Front. But the starving German troops (below) were finally defeated.

Britain's Home Front

British civilians were prepared for war as soon as it was declared. A blackout was introduced, evacuation was ordered and air-raid routines become the norm. In London and other major cities, bombing took a heavy toll, and by May 1941 more than 43,000 civilians had been killed. While men were away in the armed services, women took their place in farms and factories.

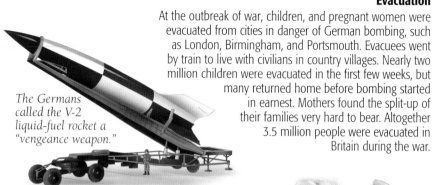

The Germans called the V-2 liquid-fuel rocket a "vengeance weapon."

Evacuation

At the outbreak of war, children, and pregnant women were evacuated from cities in danger of German bombing, such as London, Birmingham, and Portsmouth. Evacuees went by train to live with civilians in country villages. Nearly two million children were evacuated in the first few weeks, but many returned home before bombing started in earnest. Mothers found the split-up of their families very hard to bear. Altogether 3.5 million people were evacuated in Britain during the war.

Like all evacuees, this youngster wore an identity label.

Rationing

The Ministry of Food issued ration books with coupons for restricted foods. A weekly ration allowed small amounts of bacon, butter, cheese, lard, margarine, meat, sugar, and tea. In addition, a person could have up to 8 ounces of jam and a packet of dried egg every month, plus an egg every fortnight. Children were allowed daily orange juice and cod liver oil, and infants got an extra allowance of milk.

Families got used to the routine of going into their shelter when they heard an air-raid siren.

Air-raid Shelters

Public air-raid shelters were built in schools and parks, most holding about 100 people. In London, people sheltered in underground railway stations. At home, families with gardens were issued with corrugated-iron Anderson shelters that could be half-buried under earth. Indoors, people put rigid-steel cages (Morrison shelters) under tables. Curtains with black linings "blacked out" all windows after dark, so that German planes could not spot targets.

A 1941 ration book. There were spaces to enter the names of approved shops.

A Home Guard volunteer stands on a London rooftop on the lookout for enemy planes.

The Home Guard

Local Defense Volunteers guarded against parachute landings by German troops. In June 1940, the force changed its name to the Home Guard. Most volunteers were too young or too old to serve in the armed forces. They were issued with a basic uniform, tin hat and rifle, and by 1943 the force numbered about two million. At the same time, more than one million women joined the Women's Voluntary Service (WVS).

Helping the War Effort

One of the most successful slogans of the war was "Dig for victory." This was part of a programme to get people to turn their gardens into mini-allotments and grow their own food. Housewives were also encouraged to "make do and mend," recycling and repairing their clothing, especially after clothes rationing was introduced in 1941. Metal was collected for recycling in factories.

WVS volunteers collected pots, pans and even old railings, for use in munitions factories.

Inspection of St John Ambulance volunteers in 1939.

Women's Work

Women were needed to take on essential jobs. One advertising slogan read, "For a healthy happy job, join the Women's Land Army." Volunteers worked on farms to keep agriculture going. Other women worked in munitions factories, and some became mechanics, plumbers, fire-engine or ambulance drivers. Many took on night jobs, and nurseries were set up to provide childcare by day.

The Blitz

On September 7, 1940, 348 German bombers attacked East London. This was the start of the Blitz, a series of 127 large-scale air raids on London and other cities over a period of nine months. People spent most nights in their shelters. There were 71 raids on London alone, in which 20,000 people were killed and 1.4 million made homeless. Barrage balloons were put up to stop low-flying aircraft and force the bombers higher.

London's St Paul's Cathedral was surrounded by fire but suffered little damage.

Air-raid damage in Battersea, in south London, in 1940.

BRITAIN'S HOME FRONT

1939
The Military Training Act calls for all British men aged 20–21 to do military service. Identity cards are introduced.

1940
Food rationing is introduced. The Local Defense Volunteers force is created, as proposed by War Minister Anthony Eden.

1941
Conscription is introduced for all men aged 18–50, except those in reserved occupations, and for unmarried women aged 20–30 (for non-fighting service).

1942
In April, heavy bombing raids are made on Bath, Exeter, Norwich and York in retaliation for raids on Germany.

1944
So-called "Baby Blitz" bombings on London and southern England; on June 13, the first V-1 "doodlebug" flying bomb hits Hackney, East London; on Sep 8, the first V-2 rocket hits London.

1945
The Family Allowances Act gives mothers a tax-free cash payment for each of their children.

Many people lost all their possessions in the conflict, as well as their homes.

The Battle for the Pacific

This poster shows Japanese tentacles grasping Southeast Asia, including the Dutch East Indies. It reads: "The Indies must be free! Work and fight for it!"

In an effort to discourage Japanese expansion by force into China and French Indo-China, a number of western powers stopped selling oil, iron ore and steel to Japan. Japan saw this embargo as an act of aggression and responded by attacking the US fleet at Pearl Harbor. The attack immediately brought the United States into the war, and Japanese territorial gains were short-lived.

A US front-page report on Pearl Harbor (above). Many Japanese-Americans were immediately put into makeshift US resettlement camps.

Japanese Conquests

In 1942, Japanese forces swept across much of Southeast Asia, including Burma, Malaya, the Philippines, the Dutch East Indies, northern New Guinea, and the Solomon Islands. Following the lightning capture of Malaya, three Japanese divisions took the British stronghold of Singapore island in a week. Prime Minister Winston Churchill described this loss as the "greatest disaster and capitulation in British history."

POWs at Japanese camps were kept on starvation rations. Japanese commanders took the view that captives had dishonored their country.

Prisoners of War

The fall of Singapore to Japan led to many thousands of Allied servicemen being captured. Many were taken to a prisoner-of-war camp at Changi, in the east of the island. Conditions there were brutally harsh. Inmates were used as forced labour and only those strong enough to work were fed properly. There was poor medical treatment, and one in three prisoners of war died in Japanese camps.

Struggle for Naval Supremacy

The USA had an important base at Midway Island, to the northwest of Hawaii. When a Japanese fleet approached the island atoll in June 1942, US planes responded at once. They sank four Japanese aircraft carriers and one cruiser, destroying more than 200 planes. This was a decisive victory for the Americans. It crippled Japan's naval air power and was a turning point in the overall battle for control of the Pacific.

In the later years of the war, Japan used kamikaze suicide pilots, who flew aircraft packed with explosives into target ships.

US marines storm ashore from their landing craft at Guadalcanal. The battle for the island lasted 6 months and ended in an Allied victory.

Island Battles

US marines fought famous battles to take Japanese-held islands. In 1942, they invaded Guadalcanal in the Solomon Islands. This was followed by a successful island-hopping campaign. By early 1945, the Americans were ready to invade Iwo Jima, a tiny island 745 miles (1,200 km) south of Japan, defended by Japanese troops in fortified caves and tunnels. The fighting lasted almost a month. The US victory allowed them to use the island as a base against Japan.

This still from the 2001 film Pearl Harbor *shows a Japanese dive-bomber flying over damaged US ships.*

WAR IN THE PACIFIC AND FAR EAST, 1941–45

USSR
MANCHURIA
CHINA
JAPAN
Aleutian Islands
HIROSHIMA
NAGASAKI
IWO JIMA
MIDWAY ISLANDS
INDIA
BURMA
HONG KONG
HAWAIIAN ISLANDS
MARSHALL ISLANDS
MALAYA
SINGAPORE
PHILIPPINES
DUTCH EAST INDIES
GUADALCANAL
AUSTRALIA

 Maximum area occupied by Japan 1942
→ Allied advances
➤ Soviet advances

Gains and Losses

Following Pearl Harbor, the Japanese expanded their empire. They captured the mainland of Southeast Asia (including the important British crown colony of Hong Kong) and the Pacific islands. From mid-1942, the US and their Allies slowly regained this territory, but with enormous loss of life on both sides.

Pearl Harbor

The Japanese surprise air attack on the US naval base in Hawaii came without any previous declaration of war. Japanese aircraft carriers launched 350 planes to attack the US fleet, and the attack lasted just two hours. The Japanese destroyed or damaged 21 American ships, including 8 battleships, and more than 300 planes, killing more than 2,300 people. President Roosevelt called December 7 "a date which will live in infamy."

The Path to Victory

In June 1944, Allied forces landed on the north coast of France and began the liberation of Europe. At the same time, the Russians pushed the German army back on the Eastern Front. Having lost Italy to the south, Germany had effectively lost the war, but Hitler refused to accept this until April 1945. After finally gaining victory in Europe, the Allies used the world's first atomic bombs to force Japan's surrender and end the World War.

On June 6 1944 (D-Day), Allied troops landed on the coast of German-occupied Normandy, France.

D-Day

The Germans expected the Allies to invade France near Calais, the narrowest point of the English Channel. But Normandy, further west, was chosen for Operation Overlord. On D-Day, US, British and Canadian troops took the Germans by surprise as they landed on the beaches. They were backed by naval bombardments and air attacks.

By the end of the month, about a million Allied soldiers had reached France and were gradually fighting their way south.

Operation Bagration

Towards the end of June 1944, the Russians launched a massive four-prong offensive against the Germans' Eastern Front. Stalin code-named the operation Bagration, after a great Russian general of the Napoleonic Wars. In four weeks, the huge Soviet army re-conquered Byelorussia (Belarus), destroying thousands of tanks and inflicting huge losses on the German army. Hitler's forces were now being squeezed from both west and east.

A Soviet infantry scout with his well-trained dog.

US and Free French forces liberated Paris on 25 August 1944. Hitler had ordered his commanders to destroy the city, but instead they surrendered.

The End of Hitler

By the end of 1944, the war was going disastrously for Germany. But Hitler still refused to give in. In his bunker beneath Berlin, the Nazi leader still seemed to believe the hopeless situation could be turned around. When Soviet troops entered the capital, Hitler at last accepted the truth. On 30 April, in his underground bunker, he finally killed himself; his body was burned by one of his personal guards. The Nazi regime was at an end.

EXTRA THE STARS AND STRIPES EXTRA

HITLER DEAD

Fuehrer Fell at CP, German Radio Says; Doenitz at Helm, Vows War Will Continue

Daily Mail

HITLER DEAD — DOENITZ APPOINTED FÜHRER

The front page of a British newspaper, 2 May 1945, tells of Hitler's death.

German-Jewish girl Anne Frank (1929–45) kept a diary that was later published. She died in Belsen. The Nazi slogan on the camp gates means "Work makes you free."

The Holocaust

The Holocaust (meaning "complete destruction by fire") is the name given to the mass murder of Jews by the Nazis. Many millions of Jewish people—men, women and children—were sent to concentration camps. They were starved, tortured, and forced to work. Many were murdered in gas chambers and their bodies incinerated, in death camps such as Auschwitz and Belsen. About six million Jews died in the Holocaust.

The "Big Three" leaders, Winston Churchill (UK), Franklin D. Roosevelt (USA) and Joseph Stalin (USSR).

Yalta Conference

In February 1945, Allied leaders Churchill, Roosevelt and Stalin—representing the "Big Three" nations—met at Yalta, in the Crimea. They discussed strategy for finishing the war, the proposed occupation of Germany and its division into four zones. The leaders also agreed to the formation of a new peacekeeping organization (the United Nations).

Victory in Europe

May 8, 1945, the day after the full German surrender, was called VE (for Victory in Europe) Day. Churchill appeared with King George VI and his family on the balcony of Buckingham Palace in London, waving to enormous, cheering crowds. Churchill said, "In all our long history we have never seen a greater day than this." In the United States, President Harry Truman dedicated victory to the memory of President Roosevelt, who had died only a few weeks earlier.

President Truman said: "We have used [the atomic bomb] to shorten the agony of war."

Victory over Japan

In 1945, US bombers increased their raids on Japan. On August 6 and 9, they dropped atomic bombs on the cities of Hiroshima and Nagasaki. The bombs killed at least 110,000 people immediately, and many thousands more later from burns and radiation. On September 2, Japan formally surrendered.

A watch found at Hiroshima, showing the time of the blast, 8:15 in the morning.

PATH TO VICTORY

1944
On July 20, a bomb plot to assassinate Hitler is unsuccessful, and leading conspirator Colonel Claus von Stauffenberg is executed. On September 4, Antwerp and Brussels are liberated by the Allies.

1945
In March, US incendiary bombs destroy central Tokyo.
On April 25, Dachau concentration camp is liberated.
On May 2nd, German troops in Italy surrender. May 7 sees the unconditional surrender of all German forces. The following day is VE (Victory in Europe) Day. On May 23, Heinrich Himmler (head of the SS) commits suicide. The Potsdam Conference declaration (July 26) demands that Japan surrender or face "utter destruction." August 15 is VJ (Victory over Japan) Day (also celebrated on Sept. 2, the day of formal surrender).

In Britain there were huge celebrations on VE Day, with singing, dancing and parties in the streets.

After the end of the Second World War, a political divide quickly opened up between the Allied victors. Distrust and suspicion led to hostility between the United States and the Soviet Union, along with their respective allies. This came to be known as the Cold War, which led to involvement in various conflicts around the world but never to direct military confrontation. The fear of nuclear war was felt everywhere and increased during periods of heightened tension. The situation altered during the 1980s, when reforms and political uprisings led to great changes in the Eastern bloc.

This chapter tells the story of the Cold War from its beginnings in 1945 to the break-up of the Soviet Union in 1991. It covers events around the world, including wars in Korea and Vietnam, changes in newly independent India and Mao's China, struggles in Africa and the Third World, and the development of peace and human rights movements.

Jawaharlal Nehru (1889–1964) a leader in India's independence movement. India became independent from the United Kingdom in 1947. Many other countries also regained their indeoendence during this time.

TIMELINE

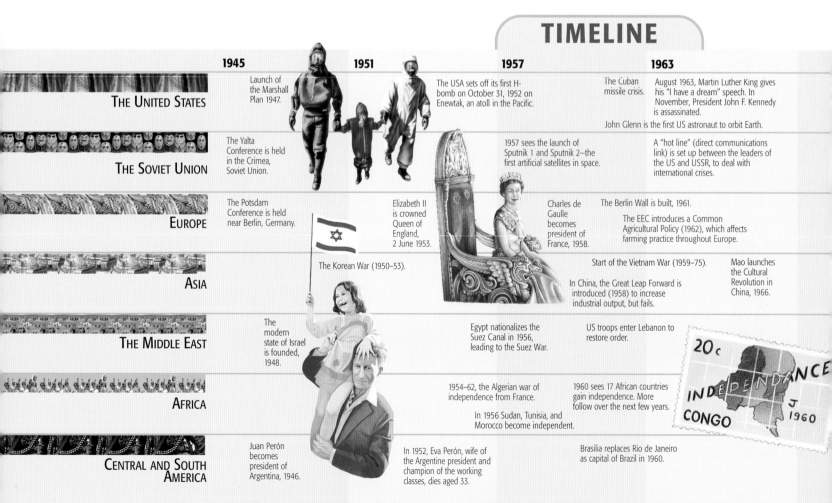

	1945	1951	1957	1963
THE UNITED STATES	Launch of the Marshall Plan 1947.		The USA sets off its first H-bomb on October 31, 1952 on Enewtak, an atoll in the Pacific.	The Cuban missile crisis. / August 1963, Martin Luther King gives his "I have a dream" speech. In November, President John F. Kennedy is assassinated. / John Glenn is the first US astronaut to orbit Earth.
THE SOVIET UNION	The Yalta Conference is held in the Crimea, Soviet Union.		1957 sees the launch of Sputnik 1 and Sputnik 2–the first artificial satellites in space.	A "hot line" (direct communications link) is set up between the leaders of the US and USSR, to deal with international crises.
EUROPE	The Potsdam Conference is held near Berlin, Germany.	Elizabeth II is crowned Queen of England, 2 June 1953.	Charles de Gaulle becomes president of France, 1958.	The Berlin Wall is built, 1961. / The EEC introduces a Common Agricultural Policy (1962), which affects farming practice throughout Europe.
ASIA		The Korean War (1950–53).	In China, the Great Leap Forward is introduced (1958) to increase industrial output, but fails.	Start of the Vietnam War (1959–75). / Mao launches the Cultural Revolution in China, 1966.
THE MIDDLE EAST	The modern state of Israel is founded, 1948.		Egypt nationalizes the Suez Canal in 1956, leading to the Suez War.	US troops enter Lebanon to restore order.
AFRICA			1954–62, the Algerian war of independence from France. / In 1956 Sudan, Tunisia, and Morocco become independent.	1960 sees 17 African countries gain independence. More follow over the next few years.
CENTRAL AND SOUTH AMERICA	Juan Perón becomes president of Argentina, 1946.	In 1952, Eva Perón, wife of the Argentine president and champion of the working classes, dies aged 33.		Brasilia replaces Rio de Janeiro as capital of Brazil in 1960.

20c INDEPENDANCE CONGO J 1960

From 1945 to the Cold War

The first artificial heart was implanted by American surgeon William DeVries in 1982. It was made of plastic and aluminium.

Monument to the Vietnamese Communist leader Ho Chi Minh (1890–1969), who became president of North Vietnam.

1969	1975	1981	1987	1993
The Apollo 11 mission lands the first men on the Moon.	The Watergate scandal of 1972 leads to the resignation of President Nixon in 1974.	A US Apollo spacecraft docks with a Soviet Soyuz craft in space (1975).	Ronald Reagan is 40th President of the USA (1981–89).		In the Gulf War (1990–91), the US leads a coalition force that forces Iraq to leave Kuwait.

Cold War tensions begin to ease.

The Sino-Soviet split reaches a peak. There are armed border clashes between China and the USSR.

In December 1979, Soviet troops invade Afghanistan. Fighting continues for 9 years.

The Chernobyl nuclear disaster, 1986.

In December 1991, Mikhail Gorbachev resigns as Soviet president and the Soviet Union breaks up.

Start of the Troubles in Northern Ireland.

Margaret Thatcher is first female Prime Minister of the United Kingdom (1979–90).

1989, the Berlin Wall is knocked down.

Death of Ho Chi Minh, president of North Vietnam.

1978, Vietnamese forces invade Cambodia, driving out Pol Pot and the Khmer Rouge.

The Vietnamese leave Cambodia after an 11-year occupation.

1976, North and South Vietnam unify into a single nation.

Tiananmen Square protest and massacre in China (1989).

October 1973, the Yom Kippur War is fought between Israel and a coalition of Arab states led by Egypt and Syria.

The first Intifada—a popular uprising of Palestinian refugees living in Israel—starts in 1987.

The Gulf War, 1990–91.

In Uganda, a military coup brings Idi Amin to power in 1971. His brutal regime lasts for 8 years.

Drought causes terrible famines in Ethiopia in 1984–85, killing about 1 million people.

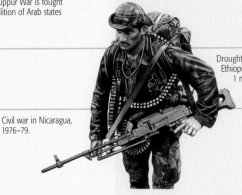

Civil war in Nicaragua, 1976–79.

The International Court of Justice decides that the US acted illegally in aiding the Contras in Nicaragua (1986).

Augusto Pinochet steps down as president of Chile, 1990.

Communists Versus Non-Communists

The post-war creation of two Korean states—the Communist Democratic People's Republic in the north and the non-Communist Republic of Korea in the south—led to a real "hot" war by 1950. The Korean War (see page 142) included the first use of United Nations troops in battle, on the side of the South Koreans.

Korean children walk beside an American M-26 tank in 1951.

A Divided World

During the Cold War the world was divided by political aims and ideologies. The United States and its allies viewed Communism as a threat to democracy. They accused the Soviet Union of trying to spread Communism throughout the world. The Soviets, on the other hand, accused their opponents of practising imperialism and stopping popular revolution. The rift widened until the downfall of the Soviet system led to a form of unity between East and West.

East German police talk to West Berliners across the wall that was put up by the Soviet-backed Democratic Republic in 1961.

Boom Years

The economic difficulties of the immediate post-war period in the United States were followed by growth and prosperity in the 1950s. The boom, which created a predominantly affluent American society, spread to western Europe. Later it also transformed Japan and the region of Southeast Asia (see pages 122–123), while the Soviet Union concentrated on rebuilding heavy industry.

By the late 1950s, British grocers, like other shopkeepers, had many more goods to offer their customers.

Connecting People

During the 1950s, the growth of television led to the world becoming a smaller place to many people. In the 1960s, the launch of communications satellites gave people instant access to global events. America's Telstar satellite transmitted the first live transatlantic television signals in 1962. This led to enormous progress in telecommunications, a fashionable term in the 1970s, though people in the Soviet bloc were not allowed the same access.

A TV guide from the 1950s. The television set quickly became the focal point of many families' lives.

Divided World

During the Cold War period the world split into three groups. The first two worlds were those directly involved in the Cold War: the United States, western European industrial nations and Japan on the one side; the Soviet Union and other Communist nations, especially in eastern Europe, on the other. The so-called Third World was made up of developing countries in Africa, Asia and Latin America.

Into the Computer Age

Computers of the 1950s were huge, complicated machines. They were gradually introduced into large businesses, mainly for accounting purposes, but were of little interest to smaller companies or ordinary people until the 1970s. Then the introduction of smaller, more user-friendly personal computers (PCs) led to the launch of a revolution in information technology (IT). Word processing, simple data operation and games programs made computers much more desirable by the beginning of the 1990s.

By the 1980s, personal computers were being used in schools and by many young people at home.

The three leaders at Yalta: Winston Churchill (UK), Franklin D. Roosevelt (USA) and Joseph Stalin (USSR).

The Post-War World

The end of the Second World War led to the occupation of Germany by the four major powers. German war criminals were tried, and as reconstruction began, the United States made plans to help economic recovery throughout Europe. At the same time, the Soviet Union helped Communist governments take power in Eastern European countries such as Czechoslovakia, Hungary, and Poland. The new United Nations organization was formed to address the kind of tensions that were already developing.

Decisive Meetings

The post-war occupation of Germany was discussed by the "Big Three" nations at the Yalta and Potsdam conferences in 1945. By the end of the second conference, the nations were led by British Prime Minister Clement Attlee, US President Harry S. Truman, and Soviet Premier Joseph Stalin. By this time the Soviet Union had helped establish Communist governments in the Eastern European countries that it had liberated from German rule. The other two nations resented and criticized this.

Controlled Zones

After the war, Germany was divided into four zones controlled by Britain, France, the Soviet Union and the United States. The Soviet Union also controlled East Prussia, and territory east of the Soviet zone came under Polish administration. Berlin, in the Soviet zone, was divided into four sectors.

British zone	American zone
Soviet zone	French zone
Polish admin.	Soviet admin.

OCCUPIED GERMANY

DENMARK · NETHERLAND · EAST PRUSSIA · HAMBURG · BREMEN · HANNOVER · BERLIN · WARSAW · DÜSSELDORF · LEIPZIG · POLAND · BONN · FRANKFURT · PRAGUE · CZECHOSLOVAKIA · FRANCE · STUTTGART · MUNICH · VIENNA · AUSTRIA · HUNGARY · SWITZERLAND

Legacy of Destruction

The war had caused devastating destruction throughout Europe. Cities across the continent lay in ruins. The Polish capital of Warsaw, which had been captured by the Germans at the very beginning of the war, was almost completely destroyed. The German capital of Berlin was left in ruins by Allied bombing raids and a land battle at the end of the war. Children of many nationalities were orphaned, and surviving soldiers returned from battle to search in vain for their homes and families.

The Marshall Plan

In 1947, US Secretary of State George C. Marshall proposed a European Recovery Program, agreed by Congress the following year. The Marshall Plan invited European nations to list their requirements for economic recovery, to be met by financial grants, loans, food and machinery. Seventeen countries formed the Organization for European Economic Cooperation, but the Soviet Union stayed out. In the first two years nearly $12 million were distributed, mainly to Britain, France, Italy and West Germany.

A German poster urges free passage for the Marshall Plan.

A woman wheels her few belongings through a Berlin street in 1946. About a third of the city was completely destroyed.

United Nations

The former League of Nations, which had not operated during the war, was replaced in 1945 by a new United Nations organization. The UN Charter created a Security Council of five permanent members—China, France, the Soviet Union, the UK and the USA—and ten non-permanent members elected to two-year terms by a General Assembly. Importantly, the Security Council was given the power to ask UN members to provide military peacekeeping forces to settle international disputes.

The UN flag and an Indian member of a UN peacekeeping force.

Nuremberg Trials

From November 1945, leading Nazis were tried at Nuremberg for war crimes and crimes against humanity. There were eight judges, two each from the powers occupying Germany. Twelve military leaders were sentenced to death by hanging, and others received long prison sentences. Hitler, Goebbels, Goering, and Himmler had committed suicide. Later, Nazi party officials and others were tried.

In this painting, the Nuremberg defendants are surrounded by the destruction they caused.

THE POST-WAR WORLD

1945

Feb 4–11: The Yalta Conference is held in the Crimea, Soviet Union.
April 12: US President Franklin D. Roosevelt dies.
Jun 26: All 50 nations present at a conference in San Francisco vote to accept the UN Charter.
Jul 17–Aug 2: The Potsdam Conference is held just outside Berlin, Germany.
Oct 24: The UN Charter is ratified at a meeting in London (and the date becomes the annual United Nations Day).

1946

Jan 3: William Joyce (known as Lord Haw Haw), who broadcast on behalf of Nazi Germany, is hanged in Britain for treason.
April: Tokyo War Crimes Trial begins in Japan.
October: End of the first trial conducted by the International Military Tribunal at Nuremberg.

1947

March: President Truman declares that the US will help any nation resist Communist aggression (the Truman Doctrine).
June: The US proposes to provide aid to Europe via the European Recovery Program. George C. Marshall says the policy is directed at "hunger, poverty, desperation and chaos."

Start of the Cold War

The United States and the Soviet Union were the world's two major powers after World War II, in which they had been allies. Yet as the Soviets expanded their Communist influence throughout Eastern Europe, they quickly made enemies of the Americans in what became known as the Cold War. Though this never turned into open warfare, there was always the threat of nuclear devastation as the arms race escalated.

The US/UK Berlin airlift of 1948–49 prevented the city being cut off during a Soviet blockade (see Timeline, left).

Red Scare Period

From 1950 to 1954, Republican Senator Joseph McCarthy ruthlessly pursued his claims that Communist spies and sympathizers had found their way into all parts of American life. During this age of so-called McCarthyism, many academics, artists, entertainers, and journalists came under suspicion and were investigated by the Un-American Activities Committee. Many employees were required to take oaths of loyalty to the US government in order to keep their jobs.

Senator McCarthy waves his list of supposed Communist sympathizers in the State Department in 1950. The US Army Information Division poster (above) appeared six years later.

By the 1950s, some people were investing in anti-radiation suits.

Iron Curtain

In 1946 the former British war leader Winston Churchill said in a speech that a shadow had fallen across the Allied victory. "From Stettin in the Baltic to Trieste in the Adriatic, an iron curtain has descended across the Continent," Churchill went on. He was referring to the militarized border between the newly developed Communist bloc and western Europe. The Iron Curtain prevented free movement of people and ideas.

Russia gets the A-bomb

In August 1949, four years after the US dropped the world's first atomic bombs on the Japanese cities of Hiroshima and Nagasaki, the Soviet Union exploded its own atomic bomb. It was a test explosion in Kazakhstan of a plutonium bomb called First Lightning, which was similar to the Nagasaki device. The successful Soviet test came much earlier than US scientists and politicians expected, and in many people's minds it raised for the first time the horrendous possibility of nuclear war.

Scientists watched the nuclear tests from a distance with only sunglasses for protection.

Nuclear Arms Race

The first Soviet test explosion triggered a nuclear arms race between the US and its allies and the Soviet bloc. The race included both the number of bombs and their individual power. In 1955, three years after the US, the USSR set off its own H-bomb.

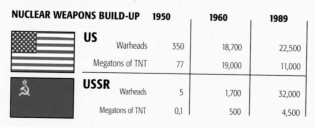

NUCLEAR WEAPONS BUILD-UP		1950	1960	1989
US	Warheads	350	18,700	22,500
	Megatons of TNT	77	19,000	11,000
USSR	Warheads	5	1,700	32,000
	Megatons of TNT	0,1	500	4,500

Joseph Stalin (1879–1953), the Soviet dictator who led his country into the Cold War.

Internal Hostility
As the Cold War progressed, there were internal tensions within the Soviet Union and the Communist bloc. In 1952 several important Jewish Czech politicians were charged with being traitors to the USSR and hanged. Then Stalin investigated an alleged conspiracy by Jewish doctors to poison the Soviet leadership. After Stalin died, in March 1953, Soviet repression and the Cold War eased slightly.

This was the mushroom-shaped cloud produced by the first American H- (for hydrogen) bomb, tested at Enewetak atoll in the South Pacific in 1952. It was hundreds of times more powerful and destructive than earlier A-bombs.

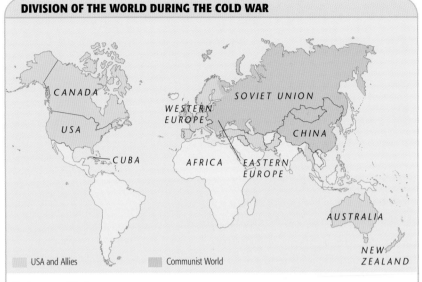

DIVISION OF THE WORLD DURING THE COLD WAR

CANADA

USA

CUBA

WESTERN EUROPE

SOVIET UNION

CHINA

AFRICA

EASTERN EUROPE

AUSTRALIA

NEW ZEALAND

USA and Allies

Communist World

East versus West
The Soviet Union and China dominated the Communist world during the Cold War. Their allies were the Eastern European states, which were satellites of the USSR, and Cuba, placed conveniently close to the USA. Australia, New Zealand, Canada, and the Western European NATO countries were all on the American, non-Communist side.

Independence for India

The Indian subcontinent underwent huge changes during this period. The independence movement gathered pace swiftly at the end of the Second World War. The ruling British handed over power and by 1947 India was independent, along with a new Muslim state of Pakistan. Religious differences and mass migrations between the partitioned states led to violence. There was further unrest between Hindus and Sikhs, and between Muslims until the creation of Bangladesh.

Partition

Pakistan became independent on 14 August 1947, and India followed the next day. Pakistan (meaning "land of the pure" in Urdu) was itself divided, with India between West and East Pakistan. More than 10 million people became refugees, as Muslims fled to Pakistan and Hindus and Sikhs to India. Hindu–Muslim riots cost about half a million lives during this partition period.

Muslim refugees pack a train as it leaves Delhi for their new homeland in 1947. Others travelled on bullock carts, and millions went on foot.

Charismatic Leaders

Jawaharlal Nehru was Prime Minister of India from independence until his death in 1964. Two years later, Nehru's daughter Indira Gandhi came to power. In Pakistan, the first leader was Muhammad Jinnah. In 1988 Benazir Bhutto became the first female leader of a Muslim country.

Indira Gandhi (1917–84) was Indian leader for a total of 16 years.

Jawaharlal Nehru (1889–1964) had been a leader in India's independence movement.

The 17th-century Badshahi mosque in Lahore, which became capital of the Pakistani province of West Punjab in 1947.

The Muslim–Hindu Divide

The president of the Muslim League, Muhammad Ali Jinnah, had been demanding a self-governing Muslim homeland since 1940. By 1946 the League feared that an independent India would be dominated by the Indian National Congress and the Hindu majority. Jinnah called for a Day of Direct Action, in which Muslims demonstrated for a separate state. This was followed by violent riots between Muslims and Hindus in Calcutta and other Indian cities.

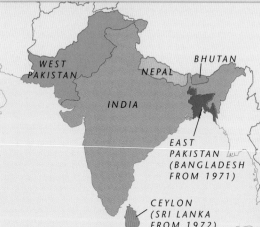

THE NEW SUBCONTINENT

WEST PAKISTAN

NEPAL

BHUTAN

INDIA

EAST PAKISTAN (BANGLADESH FROM 1971)

CEYLON (SRI LANKA FROM 1972)

Pakistan and Bangladesh

The people of West Pakistan and East Pakistan (later Bangladesh) spoke different languages (officially Urdu and Bengali respectively) and had different cultures. Though the eastern population was higher, the West contained the capital (Karachi and then Islamabad) and controlled the economy. Tensions grew and civil war broke out in 1971, killing thousands and making millions more refugees. Bangladesh (the "Bengal nation") became independent later that year.

Benazir Bhutto (1953–2007), daughter of the founder of the Pakistan People's Party, herself led the Party.

Celebrating crowds wave the flag of the Indian National Congress, which became the national flag of India. The orange stripe stood for Hindus, the green for Muslims, with a "wheel of law" at the center.

The Golden Temple in Amritsar, center of the Sikh faith.

Attack on the Golden Temple

In the early 1980s, an extreme group of Sikhs increased their demands for an independent state of Punjab, in northwest India. Prime Minister Indira Gandhi saw this as a threat to Indian unity and ordered troops to attack armed Sikhs in their holiest temple, the Golden Temple in Amritsar. Many hundreds of Sikhs were killed. Five months later, Mrs Gandhi was assassinated by two Sikh members of her bodyguard. Her son Rajiv succeeded her as prime minister.

The Foundation of Israel

Since the late 19th century, Zionists had sought to establish a Jewish homeland and nation in Palestine. After the Second World War, many Jewish survivors of the Nazi Holocaust migrated to Palestine. In 1947 the United Nations proposed that a Jewish nation should exist alongside an Arab state. In 1948 the modern state of Israel was founded. This caused the first of the Arab-Israeli conflicts that were to go on until the present day.

This man was released from Buchenwald concentration camp when it was liberated in 1945.

A New Jewish State

In 1947 the UN recommended creating separate Jewish and Arab states in Palestine, but Arab leaders refused to accept this. Fighting broke out and Zionist forces secured control of their intended lands and captured positions in Arab areas. On 14 May, 1948, the new state of Israel was proclaimed under the leadership of David Ben-Gurion, and was immediately recognized by the United States and the Soviet Union. The next day, the British ended their mandate in Palestine.

The new Israeli flag showed the Star of David and the colors of the Jewish prayer shawl.

The Holocaust

The Nazi program of mass murder, which killed six million Jewish people, led to greater demands for a separate Jewish state after the war. The British had supported this at the end of the First World War, yet they still limited Jewish immigration to Palestine while it was under their control. Other countries also resisted immigration, increasing the despair of Holocaust survivors who did not wish to return to their pre-war homes, now under Communist rule.

Occupied Territories

The lands gained by Israel throughout the Arab-Israeli conflict are usually referred to as "occupied territories." They include the Golan Heights, Sinai Peninsula (1973–79), West Bank and Gaza Strip. Throughout the period the possession of these territories was disputed, since they were originally part of the Arab state proposed by the UN.

ISRAEL 1948–82

CYPRUS

South-Central Lebanon 1982 only

South Lebanon, occupied 1982

LEBANON

Kuneitra Strip 1967, returned to Syria 1974

SYRIA

JERUSALEM

Gaza Strip, occupied 1967

Suez Perimeter 1973 only

Golan Heights, occupied 1967

West Bank, occupied 1967

East Jerusalem, annexed 1967

Sinai 1967, returned to Egypt 1982

Gulf of Suez

Gulf of Aqaba

EGYPT

Red Sea

■ State of Israel as proclaimed 1948

■ Subsequent acquisitions

■ Temporary acquisitions

■ Occupied territories

War in Palestine

In 1948, Arab forces from surrounding countries immediately attacked the new state of Israel. The forces came mainly from Egypt, Syria, Lebanon, Iraq and Transjordan. By early 1949, the Israelis had gained about half the land intended for the new Arab state of Palestine. Egypt and Jordan controlled the rest of Palestine. The UN intervened and by mid-1949 Israel had agreed an armistice with its neighbors, who would not sign peace treaties because they did not officially recognize Israel.

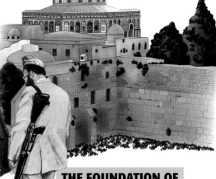

In times of conflict, some Israelis carried weapons as they went about their daily business.

THE FOUNDATION OF ISRAEL

1947
The UN agrees to divide Palestine into Arab and Jewish states and to place Jerusalem under international control.

1948
Foundation of the state of Israel; David Ben-Gurion becomes the nation's first prime minister.

1953–55
Moshe Sharett is Israeli prime minister, until Ben-Gurion takes over again.

1956
Egypt nationalizes the Suez Canal, leading to the Suez War, in which Britain and France help Israel.

1959
Israel starts a National Water Carrier Project to divert the River Jordan from the Sea of Galilee to the Negev region.

1967
The Six-Day War (June 5–10) between Israel and the Arab forces of Egypt, Iraq, Jordan and Syria; a UN resolution calls for the return of territory seized by Israel, recognition of Israel by the Arab states, free navigation, and future peace and stability.

The PLO

The Fatah organization was founded in 1958 by Yasser Arafat to fight for an Arab Palestinian state. Six years later, Fatah joined other groups to form the Palestine Liberation Organization (PLO). Arafat persuaded the UN to recognize the PLO as the official representative of Palestinian Arabs. In 1988, the PLO recognized Israel's right to exist alongside a Palestinian state in Gaza and the West Bank, both of which Israel occupied.

Originally a Palestinian guerrilla soldier, Yasser Arafat (1929–2004) eventually received the Nobel Peace Prize.

Invasion of Sinai

After Egypt closed the Suez Canal and the entrance to the Gulf of Aqaba to Israeli shipping, relations between Israel and Egypt worsened. In October 1956, Israeli forces invaded Egypt's Sinai peninsula. Britain and France also responded to Egyptian nationalization of the Suez Canal by attacking Egypt. The UN stepped in, ending the fighting, arranging for foreign troops to leave Egyptian territory and setting up a peacekeeping force.

Egyptian president Gamal Abdel Nasser (1918–70) became leader of the Arab world after taking full control of the Suez Canal.

The Six-Day War

In 1967 Egypt again blocked Israeli shipping. Israel launched a surprise air attack on Egypt. Syria, Jordan and Iraq joined in on behalf of the Egyptians. Israel won the war in the air and on the ground, and six days later the UN arranged a ceasefire. Israel had again shown its military power and gained control of Sinai and the West Bank of the River Jordan.

In 1967 Israel took control of East Jerusalem. Israeli troops were able to parade in front of the Tower of David citadel.

Europe Rises from the Ashes

Europe was at the center of the power struggle between the United States and the Soviet Union. The Cold War (see pages 130–131) resulted in the continent being strictly divided into West and East, and differences grew stronger throughout the 1950s. The new West Germany developed a strong economy under calm leadership. East Germany and the other Soviet satellite states did less well and were treated harshly whenever they rose up against their rulers.

A New Beginning

For Germany, the end of the war was a "zero hour"–time for a new beginning. By 1955, just six years after it was officially formed, the new West German republic had made remarkable progress. Chancellor Konrad Adenauer helped create an "economic miracle," which allowed ordinary Germans to improve their standard of living. Ruins had been cleared away and all the major cities were rebuilt, including Berlin. West Germany quickly became a successful consumer society, respected and integrated in post-war Western Europe.

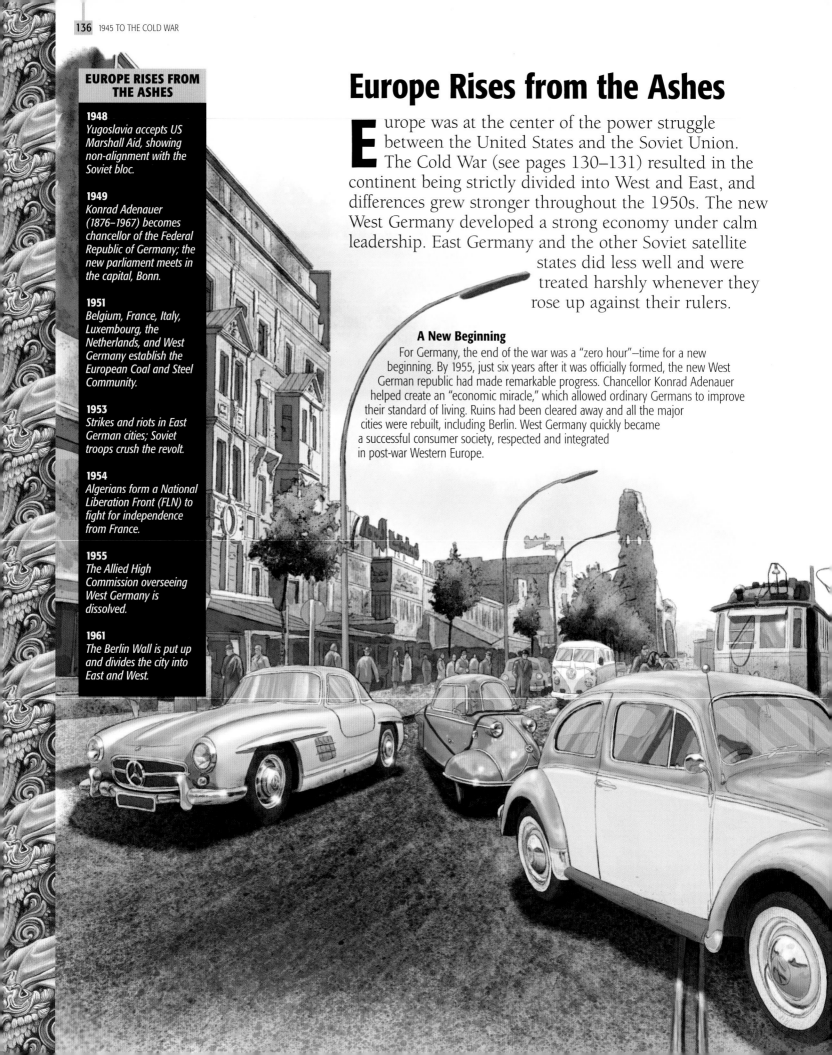

Farming methods and foods such as milk products (right) were affected by the new policies.

Decolonization

Britain, France, the Netherlands and Portugal all had to come to terms with losing their overseas colonies. Between 1954 and 1962, there were bloody battles in Algeria, which fought for independence from France. In 1958 the former leader of the Free French, Charles de Gaulle, became president of France when there was almost civil war in his country over Algeria. He negotiated with nationalist leaders and ended French rule in Algeria four years later.

Creating a Common Market

In 1951, West Germany and five other nations (see Timeline, left) created a common market for coal, iron and steel. Seven years later this developed into the European Economic Community (EEC), which promoted economic cooperation among the six member countries. This included the free movement of workers between these countries, as well as joint policies on social welfare and foreign trade. In 1962 the EEC introduced a Common Agricultural Policy, which affected farming practice throughout Europe.

General Charles de Gaulle (1890–1970) became a symbol of France during his presidency (1958–69).

By the mid-1950s, Berlin was a bustling city again. The German motor industry was successful, and many people could afford their own family car.

NATO AND THE WARSAW PACT

West versus East

The North Atlantic Treaty Organization was formed in 1949 to resist any aggression by the Soviet Union. West Germany joined NATO in 1955. In response, in 1955 the Soviet Union set up a military alliance, the Warsaw Pact, with Albania, Bulgaria, Czechoslovakia, East Germany, Hungary, Poland, and Romania. It gave the Soviet Union even tighter control over its allies.

- NATO nations
- Other US allies
- Warsaw Pact nations
- Other USSR allies

The Soviets sent in tanks to put down the attempted revolution in Hungary.

Divided Continent

During the 1950s, Europe was divided into the capitalist West (including the Federal Republic of Germany) and the Communist East (including the German Democratic Republic). Western Europe was becoming more prosperous, but there were tensions in the Eastern bloc, where there were uprisings against strict Soviet rule. In Hungary, there was an attempted revolution by the people in 1956. When this was unsuccessful, the Hungarian prime minister and others were convicted of treason by the Soviets and executed.

中国
东方红

In 1956 the government simplified the characters of the Chinese written language.

Communist China

The Communists formed the People's Republic of China, uniting the country under a powerful central government. The defeated Nationalists were forced to form their own republic on the island of Taiwan. Mao Zedong introduced massive economic projects, some of which proved disastrous. Nevertheless, he was a strong leader with a cult following. After his death, economic conditions improved as China modernized and became more open to the world.

Students reading Mao's "Little Red Book." They and young Red Guards were encouraged always to carry a copy with them.

Mao Zedong (1893–1976) announced the birth of the People's Republic of China on 1 October 1949, in Beijing.

Chairman Mao

Mao Zedong, Chairman of the Communist Party, established the People's Republic of China in 1949. The new republic was run on similar political and social lines to the Soviet Union, with Mao and his party keeping a tight grip on people's lives. However, economic policies were not successful, and the collectivization of farming led to terrible famines in the late 1950s, in which millions starved.

Cultural Revolution

In 1966 Mao launched the Great Proletarian Cultural Revolution. Its stated aims were to get rid of bureaucracy and revive revolutionary attitudes. Leading officials were dismissed, universities were closed, and many intellectuals were sent to labor camps to be "re-educated." Many young people joined the Red Guards and attacked party officials who disagreed with Mao. The result was massive civil unrest, as the revolution turned into a reign of terror.

SPREAD OF COMMUNISM

AREAS CONTROLLED BY CHINESE COMMUNISTS:

- 1934
- 1936–1949
- By April 1947
- By July 1948
- By December 1949
- By 1950
- North Korea, occupied by Russia, 1945–48
- South Korea, occupied by US and UN, 1945–49
- Area controlled by Russia, 1945–48

SOVIET UNION
MONGOLIA
MANCHURIA
BEIJING
SHAANXI
CHINA
JIANGXI
TAIWAN

Nationalist Defeat

The map shows the steady growth of Communist control. Mao gained the support of vast numbers of peasants, as his army pushed the opposing Nationalists further south. At the end of 1949, Chiang Kai-shek and his Nationalist followers fled to Taiwan (previously called Formosa). There they set up a rival government for their own Republic of China.

Occupation of Tibet

Chinese forces moved in and occupied Tibet in 1950. The Tibetans surrendered their sovereignty to the Chinese government but kept their right to self-government and became an autonomous region of the People's Republic, called Xizang. An uprising in 1959 was suppressed, and Tibet's Buddhist spiritual and political leader, the Dalai Lama, fled to India. The Communists then repressed Tibetan culture.

COMMUNIST CHINA

1946–49
Civil war between the Nationalists and Communists.

1958
The Great Leap Forward is introduced to increase industrial output, but fails.

1966–67
About 350 million copies of Quotations from Chairman Mao (the "Little Red Book") are published.

1971
The UN expels the Nationalists and admits the People's Republic as China's representative.

1972
US President Richard Nixon visits China and meets Mao and premier Zhou Enlai (1898–1976).

1979
China and the US establish normal diplomatic relations. Chinese border war with Vietnam.

1984
China reaches agreement with the UK for the return of Hong Kong in 1997.

1989
Tiananmen Square protest and massacre.

1991
China's first McDonald's burger restaurant opens in Beijing.

New Beginning

In the early 1970s Mao's health failed, and he died in 1976. His widow Jiang Qing joined others in a so-called Gang of Four, but they failed to seize power. In 1977 the more moderate Deng Xiaoping became vice-chairman of the Communist Party and effectively leader of the republic. Deng was more liberal in running the economy and gave farming land back to the peasants. He also increased trade and contact with other countries.

The Dalai Lama has continued to oppose Chinese oppression. In 1989 he was awarded the Nobel Peace Prize.

Left: Deng Xiaoping (1904–97) is shown on this poster as a leader of economic reforms.

Right: A brave protester tries to stop the tanks rolling into Tiananmen Square on 4 June 1989.

Planned Birth Policy

The government controlled all aspects of society. In 1979, it introduced a policy of limiting population growth. Couples were encouraged to have only one child; in some towns and cities this was a strict requirement. Later, rules were changed, so that families could have a second child if the first was a girl at least 3 years old. Offenders faced penalties, and many people considered this a violation of human rights.

Tiananmen Square

During the 1980s there were calls for a more democratic form of government, but attempts at political reform failed. In 1989 university students led crowds in large demonstrations in several Chinese cities. The biggest was in Tiananmen Square, in the capital, Beijing. Protesters called for more democracy and less corruption in government. Army tanks were sent in, and the peaceful protest was brutally put down. Hundreds of demonstrators were killed, and many more were arrested.

Posters promoted the two-parent, one-child family as ideal. Chinese authorities say the policy reduced the possible population by 300 million.

The Developing World

Prime Minister Nasser of Egypt arrives at Bandung for the 1955 conference.

D uring the Cold War period, commentators often referred to the United States and other Western industrialized democracies as representing the First World. The Soviet Union and its satellites made up the Second World. The Third World referred to developing nations, most of which were former colonies of European nations. These poorer countries contained about three-quarters of the world's population.

Famine regularly struck millions of African children.

Poverty

There was an enormous divide between the "haves" of rich nations and the "have-nots" of the developing world. In the poorest countries, there was widespread hunger and disease, with a shortage of clean water and adequate shelter. There were few sources of energy, and illiteracy and poor equipment kept production down in agriculture and industry. Many people depended on a single crop, and if this failed, there was famine.

Nigerian troops on their way to fight supporters of an independent Biafra, in 1967. Three years later, Biafran resistance ended.

Revolutionary Shock Waves

Revolutions shook the world. A military coup in Egypt in 1952 led to the nationalization of the Suez Canal and an invasion by Israeli and Anglo-French forces. The UN settled the issue in Egypt's favor. Seven years later, Fidel Castro gained power in Cuba. Relations with the US quickly deteriorated, and the following year Cuba signed an economic pact with the Soviet Union.

The Suez Canal was extremely important to developed trading countries. The Egyptians decided to use the money it raised from the canal for an enormous hydroelectric dam.

Bandung Conference

In 1955, India and four other nations organized a conference in Bandung, Indonesia. It was attended by 29 Asian and African countries, representing more than half the world's population. The developing countries expressed concern over tensions between the US and China, and dislike of colonialism. Over the next ten years, rich countries did give up some of their colonies, but the solidarity shown at Bandung gradually disappeared.

World Politics

The United States and the Soviet Union competed for influence in the developing world. Both superpowers wanted their political system to be the model for development in African countries. In 1972, for example, army leaders set up a Marxist-Leninist republic in Benin (then called Dahomey). In 1967, when Biafra tried to break away from Nigeria, the federal government was supported by the Soviet Union and Britain, while France helped the Biafran region.

THE DEVELOPING WORLD

1948
Mother Teresa starts her work for the poor of Calcutta.

1950
The Office of the United Nations High Commissioner for Refugees is established to resolve refugee problems worldwide.

1956
The US and UK withdraw financial support for the Aswan High Dam in Egypt, leading to the Suez Crisis; the Soviet Union later provides finance.

1956–75
Civil war rages in Angola, until final independence from Portugal.

1962
The UN World Food Program is established to provide food aid to people in need.

1968
Drought in the Sahel (Africa); 250,000 die.

1980
The World Health Organization announces the eradication of smallpox after mass vaccinations.

1991
Aung San Suu Kyi wins the Nobel Peace Prize for her efforts to restore democracy to Myanmar (Burma).

International Assistance

Charitable agencies were formed to provide relief and development aid for disaster-stricken communities. OXFAM (founded in 1942) worked on improving farming and food production in famine-stricken regions. Médecins Sans Frontières ("Doctors without borders") was set up in 1971 to provide emergency medical assistance. Unfortunately, the work of these and other agencies was often hampered by the governments of the countries in need.

Above: Mother Teresa (1910–97) founded a charity dedicated to helping the poor of Calcutta and other Indian cities.

Live Aid

Drought caused terrible famines in Ethiopia in 1984–85, killing about 1 million people. To raise money for the starving people of the region, rock singers and songwriters Bob Geldof and Midge Ure organized an all-day concert held at the same time in Philadelphia and London. The Live Aid concert was seen by an estimated 1.5 billion television viewers in 100 countries. It raised awareness of problems in the developing world, especially those caused by natural disasters.

Bob Geldof, lead singer of the Boomtown Rats, visited this Ethiopian famine-relief camp in January 1985.

AIDS Epidemic

The fatal disease AIDS (Acquired Immune Deficiency Syndrome) was first identified in 1981. It soon became epidemic throughout many developing regions, especially in Africa. According to the World Health Organization, by 1991 ten million people had AIDS, and a large proportion were in developing countries. Many were young adults, causing an overall decrease in life expectancy across Africa. By then the disease was being taken much more seriously in the US and other parts of the developed world.

In 1987, President Reagan described AIDS as "public enemy number one." The red ribbon was introduced in 1991 as a symbol of the fight against AIDS.

The Struggle for East and Southeast Asia

Communism and nationalism fuelled independence movements in the region. The tense Cold War atmosphere led to Soviet and China-backed regimes fighting those supported by the US and its allies. By the 1950s, France had lost control of Indo-China, and Vietnam became another battleground. The Vietnam War eventually led to massive anti-war demonstrations in the US and Europe, and the Americans were forced to withdraw.

Children throughout the region were forced to flee war.

Flashpoint Korea

After World War II, the Allies divided Korea. In 1950 North Korea, backed by China, invaded South Korea. The USA and UN countries came to the defence of the South. The Korean War lasted until 1953 without victory to either side and with more than 3 million people dead. The war also left the two countries separated by the world's most heavily fortified frontier.

American general Douglas MacArthur led South Korean, American, and United Nations troops in Korea.

WARTORN ASIA

1948
Foundation of North and South Korea.

1953
Cambodia and Laos gain independence from France.

1954
The Viet Minh take Dien Bien Phu from the French.

1963
Sabah, Sarawak and Singapore join Malaya to form the Federation of Malaysia.

1966
In Indonesia, Raden Suharto outlaws the Communist Party.

1967
The Association of Southeast Asian Nations (ASEAN) is founded to promote economic, cultural, and social cooperation.

1975
The Vietnam War ends.

1990
In Burma (Myanmar), the State Law and Order Restoration Council arrest Aung San Suu Kyi, leader of the National League for Democracy.

French Indo-China

France regained control of Indo-China—the region covering Cambodia, Laos and Vietnam—after World War II. But in 1946 war broke out between the French and revolutionary Vietnamese nationalists called the Viet Minh. By the time it ended, in 1954, Cambodia and Laos were already independent. According to the Geneva Agreements, Vietnam was temporarily divided at the 17th parallel, until national elections were held.

Monument to the Vietnamese Communist leader Ho Chi Minh (1890–1969), who became president of North Vietnam.

Vietnam War

The elections planned for Vietnam in 1954 never took place, and civil war broke out in South Vietnam. The United States sent military aid to the South Vietnamese government, while North Vietnam intervened on the side of the insurgents. US ground troops arrived in 1965, and the Soviet Union provided war materials for the North. Amidst growing opposition at home, the US withdrew its troops and North Vietnam eventually unified the country.

Cambodia

In 1975, Communists of the Khmer Rouge organization, led by Pol Pot, took control of Cambodia. Their ruthless policies were aimed at depriving people of their property and eliminating all opposition. Around 2 million Cambodians were executed or starved to death. An invading Vietnamese force overthrew Pol Pot in 1978, but the Khmer Rouge continued its guerrilla tactics. The Vietnamese left in 1989, but internal disagreements continued until 1991, when UN-led peace talks created a new coalition government.

Pol Pot (1925–98) was the brutal leader of the Khmer Rouge and prime minister of Cambodia 1976–79.

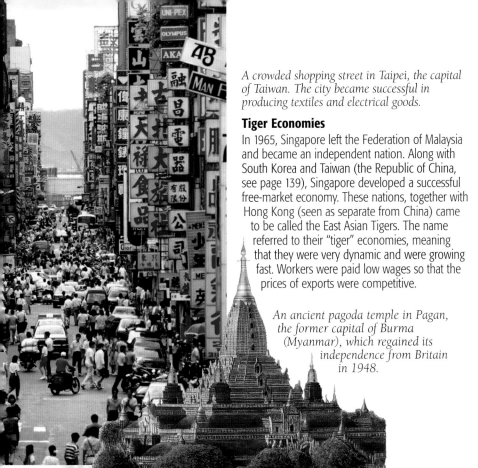

A crowded shopping street in Taipei, the capital of Taiwan. The city became successful in producing textiles and electrical goods.

Tiger Economies

In 1965, Singapore left the Federation of Malaysia and became an independent nation. Along with South Korea and Taiwan (the Republic of China, see page 139), Singapore developed a successful free-market economy. These nations, together with Hong Kong (seen as separate from China) came to be called the East Asian Tigers. The name referred to their "tiger" economies, meaning that they were very dynamic and were growing fast. Workers were paid low wages so that the prices of exports were competitive.

An ancient pagoda temple in Pagan, the former capital of Burma (Myanmar), which regained its independence from Britain in 1948.

SOUTHEAST ASIA, 1946–75

INDIA 1947
BHUTAN
PEOPLE'S REPUBLIC OF CHINA
MYANMAR (BURMA) 1948
BANGLADESH (EAST PAKISTAN) 1947
NORTH VIETNAM, 1954
PHILIPPINES 1946
LAOS 1954
SOUTH VIETNAM 1954
SRI LANKA (CEYLON), 1947
CAMBODIA 1954
MALAYA, 1957
SINGAPORE, 1965
INDONESIA 1949

Divided Nations

The map shows Southeast Asian dates of independence. In Burma, civil war ended when a bloodless coup set up a ruling revolutionary council of military leaders in 1962. In 1976, North and South Vietnam unified into a single nation, the Socialist Republic of Vietnam, with its capital at Hanoi.

US marines on a "search and destroy" ground mission near the village of Tam Ky in South Vietnam in 1968.

Algerian Conflict

France had governed much of Algeria since 1830. Many French and other European citizens had settled there, and Algerians were subjects of France. It was a most important colony, four times the size of the mother country. Independence was gained only after an 8-year long conflict between Algerian nationalists and France (see page 137), where there were many differing attitudes toward colonialism.

Women were recruited to fight for Algerian independence by the National Liberation Front (FLN).

Winds of Change in Africa

During the early 1950s, African political parties increased their demands for freedom for their nations. Rapidly growing nationalism took the colonizing countries by surprise. In 1960 alone, 17 new independent countries came into being. By the 1970s there were few colonies left, mostly in the southern region. There, white colonial governments found it increasingly difficult to resist the black African majority.

Kenya and the Mau Mau

Kenya had been a British colony since 1920. In the 1950s a secret independence movement of the Kenyan Kikuyu people led a revolt against the colonial government. Members of this nationalist movement, called the Mau Mau by Europeans, were considered terrorists by the British. Thousands of nationalists were put in detention camps, and more than 13,000 Africans were killed during the conflict.

Jomo Kenyatta (1891–1978), leader of the Kenya African Union, is led to trial in 1952. He was jailed for 7 years for his part in the Mau Mau rebellion.

Apartheid in South Africa

Apartheid (Afrikaans for "separateness") was a system of racial segregation introduced by the ruling National Party in 1948. The system classified South Africans in four groups—white, black, colored, (mixed race) and Asian. The groups were segregated in education, housing and transport. The African National Congress (ANC) fought for equal rights for blacks, but was declared illegal, and some leaders, including Nelson Mandela, were jailed. Apartheid finally ended in 1991.

ANC members demonstrated against apartheid and demanded the release of Nelson Mandela, who spent 27 years in jail.

This poster captured African feelings of the 1950s.

South of the Sahara

In 1957, the Gold Coast was the first black African colony to become independent, leaving the British Commonwealth and taking the name Ghana. Three years later, all its immediate neighbors gained independence from France—Burkina Faso (formerly French West Africa), Côte d'Ivoire and Togo (French Togoland). By the mid-1960s, many sub-Saharan nations had gained their independence without conflict, and Belgium, Britain, and France had given up most of their African colonies.

A military band in Gabon (formerly French Equatorial Africa) celebrates independence in 1960.

The Belgian Congo became independent Congo in 1960 (renamed Zaïre in 1971).

20c
INDEPENDANCE
CONGO
J 1960

This Ghanaian woman was proud of her first president, Kwame Nkrumah.

FREEDOM AND JUSTICE

Coups and Civil War

A number of newly independent countries soon faced internal conflicts. Five years after independence, a military coup overthrew the government of the Central African Republic. In Nigeria, the region of Biafra attempted to break away in 1967. In Uganda, a military coup brought Idi Amin to power in 1971. His brutal regime lasted for 8 years, until he was overthrown by Ugandan exiles and Tanzanian troops.

After his coup, Idi Amin (1925–2003) had himself sworn in as president of Uganda.

ALL MEN ARE BORN EQUAL

1951 *Libya (from Italy).*

1956 *Morocco (France), Sudan (UK), Tunisia (France).*

1957 *Ghana (UK).*

1958 *Guinea (France).*

1960 *Benin (France), Burkina Faso (France), Cameroon (France, UK), Central African Republic (France), Chad (France), Congo (France), Côte d'Ivoire (France), DR Congo (Belgium), Gabon (France), Madagascar (France), Mali (France), Mauritania (France), Niger (France), Nigeria (UK), Senegal (France), Somalia (Italy, UK), Togo (France).*

1961 *Sierra Leone (UK), Tanzania (UK).*

1962 *Algeria (France), Burundi (Belgium), Rwanda (Belgium), Uganda (UK).*

1963 *Kenya (UK).*

1964 *Malawi (UK), Zambia (UK).*

1965 *Botswana (UK), Gambia (UK).*

1966 *Lesotho (UK).*

1968 *Equatorial Guinea (Spain), Mauritius (UK), Swaziland (UK).*

AFRICAN INDEPENDENCE, 1974–90

1. Guinea-Bissau (1974)
2. Angola (1975)
3. Mozambique (1975)
4. Cape Verde (1975)
5. Comoros (1975)
6. Sao Tome & Principe (1975)
7. Djibouti (1977)
8. Zimbabwe (1980)
9. Namibia (1990)

Liberation Movements

Determined liberation movements at last achieved independence for large parts of southern Africa during the 1970s. There was civil war in Angola and a long period of guerrilla warfare in Mozambique before freedom was gained. South Africa's control over Namibia was finally ended, just 4 years before the South Africans themselves enjoyed majority rule.

Civil Rights and Confrontation

In the 1950s, southern states still practised racial segregation.

While the Cold War continued, racial discrimination became a controversial issue in the United States. The civil rights movement grew dramatically throughout the 1950s, as leading African Americans became more influential. There were riots and shootings, but new laws in the 1960s led to greater integration. By then the Vietnam War had become another major issue for students and other protesters, who wanted an end to violence and warfare.

John F. Kennedy (1917–63) (below), with his wife Jacqueline. Front-page report (right) of the assassination.

THE DALLAS MORNING NEWS

KENNEDY SLAIN ON DALLAS STREET

JOHNSON BECOMES PRESIDENT

JFK Assassinated

President John F. Kennedy was killed by an assassin's bullet on 22 November 1963, at a very tense period of the Cold War. At the time some people suspected that the Cubans or Russians must have been involved in the murder plot. If that had been the case, the next president, Lyndon B. Johnson, might well have come to the conclusion that a nuclear war was inevitable.

Martin Luther King (1929–68) in Washington in 1963, when more than 200,000 people staged a freedom march.

Struggle for Civil Rights

Baptist minister Martin Luther King was an activist in the US South who became a national leader of the civil rights movement. In 1963 he made a famous speech, in which he said he had a dream that his children "will one day live in a nation where they will not be judged by the color of their skin but by the content of their character."

Protests and Demonstrations

In the 1960s, students and others staged bigger and better organized boycotts, demonstrations, marches and sit-ins for civil rights and against war. Folk singers wrote protest songs, and the youth movement included hippies, who believed in "flower power" and a world based on love and peace. Different groups were brought together by their opposition to the Vietnam War (see page 142), which they felt showed the United States in its worst light.

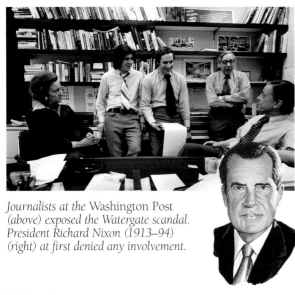

Malcolm X (1925–65), born Malcolm Little in Nebraska, was assassinated while addressing a rally in New York.

Journalists at the Washington Post (above) exposed the Watergate scandal. President Richard Nixon (1913–94) (right) at first denied any involvement.

Malcolm X

The civil rights leader Malcolm X was originally an influential member of the militant Black Muslims, or Nation of Islam movement, which believed in black power and aimed to establish an Islamic state. In 1964 Malcolm X (whose initial stood for the unknown name of his African ancestors) visited Mecca and then founded his own Organization of Afro-American Unity. He was condemned as a hypocrite and shot by Black Muslim militants.

MAI 68

DÉBUT D'UNE
LUTTE,
PROLONGÉE

Watergate

In 1972, Republican Party employees were found to have broken into Democratic Party headquarters at the Watergate building in Washington DC. This was part of a secret and illegal campaign to help Richard Nixon win the 1972 presidential election. The break-in was covered up, as the White House denied all knowledge of the affair. It eventually became clear that Nixon had been involved, and the president resigned in August 1974. He was pardoned by the next president, Gerald Ford.

So-called "flower children" preached gentleness and love, but they were also prepared to speak out against war and racial discrimination.

END THE WAR IN INDOCHINA VIETNAM NOW

CONFRONTATION AND CIVIL RIGHTS

1954
The Supreme Court declares that school segregation is unconstitutional.

1955
Rosa Parks, an African-American woman, is arrested in Montgomery, Alabama, for refusing to give up her seat on a bus to a white person.

1959
Vice-President Nixon and Soviet leader Khrushchev exchange strong words about the merits of capitalism and communism at a Moscow trade fair.

1963
Kennedy makes it clear that "race has no place in American life or law." The US, Soviet Union and UK sign a treaty banning nuclear testing in the atmosphere.

1964
Civil Rights Act outlaws discrimination in employment, voter registration and public accommodation.

1968
Martin Luther King is assassinated. Civil Rights Act ends discrimination in the sale and renting of housing.

1970
Four students are killed by national guardsmen during an anti-war protest at Kent State University, Ohio.

International Superstars

The biggest star of the new rock 'n' roll music that appeared in the 1950s was Elvis Presley, who had a string of chart-topping hits on both sides of the Atlantic. He was followed by a number of American and, in the 1960s, British singers and groups. The new superstars also made films, just as some film stars made records.

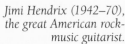

Elvis Presley (1935–77) had his first big hit in 1956 with "Heartbreak Hotel."

Jimi Hendrix (1942–70), the great American rock-music guitarist.

Film star Marilyn Monroe (1926–62) became a famous sex symbol.

The Beatles, from Liverpool, shot to fame in 1962 with "Love Me Do."

New Look

French fashion designer Christian Dior (1905–57) introduced his first collection in 1947. Called the New Look, it included narrow waists and extravagantly full, long skirts, with elegant accessories. As with other designers, Dior's business expanded into jewelry and perfumes, to complete the "look," which was taken up by American film stars. The short miniskirt came as a complete contrast in the 1960s.

An elegant New Look ball gown of 1949.

Pop Art

The movement known as pop art originated in the 1950s in Britain, and then developed in the United States. Artists such as Andy Warhol and Roy Lichtenstein were inspired by mass media images of television, comics, and advertising to break down the barriers between high art and popular culture. The movement was also a reaction to the earlier abstract expressionism of artists such as Jackson Pollock.

Andy Warhol (1928–87), pop artist and film-maker (right), and one of his most famous creations, Campbell's Soup (1968).

Spy Thrillers

The realities of World War II and the Cold War led to an interest in fiction set in the world of espionage, intelligence agencies and secret services. The dangerous, violent aspects of spying were mixed with a fascination for secret codes and false identities. The fictional character of James Bond, created by writer Ian Fleming (1908–64), became an international icon through a series of books and films.

James Bond appeared first in the book Casino Royale (1953) and on screen in the film Dr No (1962).

Icons, Idols, and Trends

The post-war consumer boom brought massive changes in popular culture. Rock 'n' roll and other forms of modern music spread from the United States. Successful pop and film stars became global idols, influencing the way young people dressed and behaved. Pop artists also reacted against the past, as the rich countries of the world entered the "swinging sixties." At the same time, feminists rebelled against women's traditional, conventional roles. Pop culture became a search for freedom.

Hippie Culture

The hippie movement of 1960s America, which included non-violent protest against war and nuclear arms (see pages 146–147), spread to Europe and elsewhere. Hippie culture, associated with drugs such as marijuana and LSD, influenced pop music and street fashion and promoted a liberal attitude towards "free love." It coincided with the rise of the "women's lib" movement, which sought equal opportunities for women, free contraception, and abortion on demand.

Carnaby Street, London West End.

Religious Cults

Several new religious groups gained popularity during the 1960s. The International Society for Krishna Consciousness, popularly known as the Hare Krishna movement, spread from India. Members wearing orange robes were often seen chanting in the streets. Transcendental Meditation also came from India, and gained in popularity after the Beatles met its guru, Maharishi Mahesh Yogi, in 1967. In the 1970s, members of the Unification Church, called Moonies after their founder Sun Myung Moon, tried to spread belief in a global struggle between good and evil.

A Hare Krishna member with the group's 16-word mantra, which is supposed to bring about a higher state of spiritual awareness.

Carnaby Street, in London's West End, became famous for its fashionable shops and represented trendy life in the "swinging sixties."

The Space Race

The United States and the Soviet Union both used their developments and successes in space technology as Cold War propaganda tools. The wish to demonstrate superiority became more intense after the Soviet launch of the first satellite, causing a genuine "space race." After early Soviet successes, the US won the competition to land a man on the Moon, before putting its efforts into reusable shuttle technology.

THE SPACE RACE

1958
The US launches its first satellites and establishes the National Aeronautics and Space Administration (NASA).

1961
A month after Yuri Gagarin's space flight, US astronaut Alan Shepard travels in space for 15 minutes in Mercury 3.

1962
John Glenn is the first US astronaut to orbit Earth.

1971
The first space station, Salyut 1, is launched by the Soviet Union.

1972
Apollo 17 is the last Apollo mission to the Moon.

1975
A US Apollo spacecraft docks with a Soviet Soyuz craft in space.

1983
A Pioneer 10 probe becomes the first manmade object to leave the solar system.

1986
Space shuttle Challenger explodes soon after launch, killing all 7 crew.

1987–88
Russian cosmonauts spend nearly a year in the Mir space station.

1989
Voyager 2 probe reaches Neptune after 12 years.

Into Orbit

In 1957, the Soviet R-7 rocket sent the first artificial satellite into space. *Sputnik 1* orbited the Earth for three months. While it was in space, the Soviets launched *Sputnik 2*, which carried a dog. The Soviet Vostok and US Mercury programs raced to get a human into space. On 12 April 1961, the Russian Yuri Gagarin made the first successful orbit in *Vostok 1*.

The first animal in space was Laika the dog. Sadly, she did not survive the flight.

G-2, the first Soviet intermediate range ballistic missile (IRBM), launched in 1949.

Guided Missiles

The superpowers raced to produce guided missiles for military purposes. In 1957, the Soviets tested their R-7, the first intercontinental ballistic missile (ICBM). Four months later, the US had a similar Atlas-A. ICBMs could send a nuclear warhead more than 15,000 km (9,300 mi). During the 1960s, as the number of attacking missiles increased, both superpowers developed anti-ballistic missile systems.

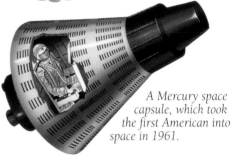

A Mercury space capsule, which took the first American into space in 1961.

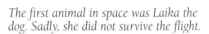

A 1956 UNIVAC (Universal Automatic Computer).

Bill Gates, who founded the Microsoft Corporation in 1975.

Computer Age

Developments in the field of computers helped space travel. Early machines filled whole rooms, but in 1959 IBM introduced its first transistorized computer. This led to the introduction of minicomputers. As computers got smaller, they also became more powerful, until the first personal computer (PC) was launched in 1975.

A 1980s virtual reality headset.

Shuttles

In 1981, NASA launched its first space shuttle, named *Columbia*. It was able to travel in space and land on Earth again many times. By 1991 there had been a further 43 flights by four different shuttles. They were used to deploy satellites, probes, the Hubble space telescope and the Spacelab station. In 1984, shuttle astronauts captured and repaired a satellite in space.

Space shuttle Atlantis is carried back to Kennedy Space Center after landing in California.

A giant Saturn-5 rocket (left) blasts off from Kennedy Space Center, sending three astronauts on a three-day journey to the Moon.

Apollo Program

In 1961 President Kennedy committed the United States to "landing a man on the Moon and returning him safely to the Earth" before the end of the decade. The Apollo program was launched to achieve this, and manned test flights were followed in 1968 by *Apollo 8* astronauts orbiting the Moon. The following year, the goal was achieved, when *Apollo 11* landed safely on the Moon's surface. Two astronauts spent more than 21 hours there, before returning safely.

Apollo 11 *mission badge. The lunar module was code-named Eagle, and is represented here by a real bird landing on the Moon.*

Buzz Aldrin is photographed by Neil Armstrong as he climbs down to the Moon's surface from the lunar module on 20 July, 1969.

Revolts in Central and South America

A South American guerrilla fighter (the Spanish word means "small war").

US capitalist interests and Communist ideology had a profound influence on many Latin American countries during the Cold War. Nationalism added tension to this dangerous mix, leading to army-backed dictatorships in the largest countries—Brazil and Argentina—as well as many others. Repression of any form of opposition led to enormous numbers being tortured and killed, or going missing. Democratically elected governments returned toward the end of the period.

Monument in Grenada to the successful US invasion of 1983.

Grenada

Former British colony Grenada, in the West Indies, was taken over by a rebel Marxist leader in 1979. Four years later there was another uprising by left-wing forces. The US, contending that the island was becoming a Communist outpost, invaded and installed a new government. Elections were held the following year.

A computer generated image of the Panama Canal.

Civil War in Nicaragua

For more than 40 years Nicaragua was dominated by the Somoza family. Opposition to this regime finally brought civil war in 1976–79, forcing the exile of President Somoza Debayle. The new government was headed by the Sandinista National Liberation Front. From 1981 to 1990 the US backed a coalition of anti-Sandinista forces, called the Contras, while the Soviet Union supported the government. The Sandinistas lost power in elections in 1990.

Panama Canal

In the 1970s, there was a movement in Panama to end US control of the Canal. In 1977 the two countries signed a treaty, agreeing a transfer of the Canal Zone in 1979 and full Panamanian control of the Canal itself 20 years later. The US was very concerned at the actions of General Noriega, head of the Panamanian forces. After Noriega forced his president from office and declared elections invalid, the Americans sent in a force to capture him. A convicted drug-trafficker, he was imprisoned.

A soldier in the Nicaraguan civil war. It has been estimated that 60,000 died in the struggle in the 1980s.

CENTRAL AND SOUTH AMERICA, 1982

- USA and allies
- American military assistance
- Soviet ally
- Soviet military assistance
- Other Western military assistance
- French military presence

Cold War Struggles

The two superpowers struggled to gain the upper hand in this region. In the early 1960s, there was a series of crises surrounding Cuba, which took the US and the USSR to the brink of nuclear war. In the 1970s, US neighbor Mexico decided to improve relations with Cuba and Chile despite US opposition. The map shows the situation in 1982.

REVOLTS IN CENTRAL AND SOUTH AMERICA

1946–55
Juan Perón is president of Argentina. He follows a path between communism and capitalism.

1954
General Alfredo Stroessner seizes power in Paraguay and becomes president (until 1989).

1961
The left-wing Sandinista National Liberation Front is formed in Nicaragua.

1967
Argentinean revolutionary Che Guevara is captured and killed while leading a revolt in Bolivia.

1974
Grenada gains independence from UK.

1983
General Manuel Antonio Noriega becomes head of Panama's military and the country's leader.

1986
The International Court of Justice decides that the US acted illegally in aiding the Contras in Nicaragua.

1990
The new Nicaraguan government is formed by a US-backed coalition.

Argentinean Nationalism

After Juan Perón's second period as president of Argentina (1973–74), the economic situation got worse. Military juntas took over the running of the country from 1976 to 1983, a period of authoritarian rule and political terrorism. Around 20,000 Argentineans may have been killed in the so-called "dirty war." Having lost the Falklands War against the UK in 1982, Argentina democratically elected a new president the following year.

Eva (Evita) Perón (1919–52), second wife of the Argentinean president, introduced many reforms. She famously addressed the crowds from the balcony of the Casa Rosada (Pink House), the country's presidential palace.

The cathedral in the modern city of Brasilia, which replaced Rio de Janeiro as Brazil's capital in 1960.

Brazil's Military Rule

South America's largest republic came under military rule after a coup in 1964. Over the next 21 years, a series of authoritarian regimes failed to improve the economic situation, which included high inflation and labor unrest. Towards the end of the period, there were calls for political rights for ordinary people, and in 1985 a civilian president was elected.

Changes in Chile

In 1970 Salvador Allende, a Marxist, was elected president of Chile and started a socialist program, including nationalization of the country's copper mines. He was overthrown by a military coup three years later, which led to violent struggles, causing thousands of deaths and the emigration of many. General Augusto Pinochet ruled over a repressive regime until 1990, when civilian, democratic government was at last restored.

Augusto Pinochet (1915–2006), right, on a visit to Santiago, Paraguay, in 1974 to visit another president and military dictator, Alfredo Stroessner (1912–2006), seated.

US–Soviet Stand-Off

Relations between the two world superpowers changed throughout the Cold War. Tensions rose and fell after the death of Stalin, as one side responded to actions—or intended actions—by the other. The Cuban missile crisis of 1962 led the superpowers and the world to the brink of nuclear war. The policy of brinkmanship was an extremely dangerous one. Events in Hungary and Czechoslovakia also showed that the Soviets would not tolerate a weakening of the Communist system.

Nikita Khrushchev (1894–1971) denounced Stalin in 1956 for his "intolerance, brutality and abuse of power."

Post-Stalin Thaw

Soviet leader Khrushchev believed in the superiority of the Communist system and felt that it would overtake western capitalism in time. Nevertheless, he and President Eisenhower agreed at a meeting in Geneva in 1955 that a nuclear war would be disastrous for everyone. The following year, Khrushchev began a program of "destalinization," discrediting the former leader and calling for peaceful coexistence between East and West. Yet just six years later, there was a missile crisis (see page 155).

Soviet–China Split

Relations between the Soviet Union and China worsened in the late 1950s. The Chinese felt the Russians were becoming soft towards the West. The Soviets were alarmed by the failed campaign of China's "Great Leap Forward." In 1961, Chinese prime minister Zhou Enlai left the 22nd Communist Party Congress in Moscow abruptly. Eight years later, fighting broke out between the two countries over a border dispute.

A Soviet poster of 1950 shows Stalin greeting Mao Zedong. This apparent solidarity was a great worry to the United States.

ПУСТЬ ЖИВЁТ И КРЕПНЕТ НЕРУШИМАЯ ДРУЖБА И СОТРУДНИЧЕСТВО СОВЕТСКОГО И КИТАЙСКОГО НАРОДОВ!

Prague Spring

Alexander Dubcek became secretary of the Czechoslovak Communist Party in 1968. During a period known as the Prague Spring, he introduced liberal reforms. The Soviets were unhappy at this, fearing that it weakened their control in Czechoslovakia and their position in the Cold War world. Soviet and other Warsaw Pact troops invaded Czechoslovakia and occupied Prague. Dubcek was ousted and his reforms were reversed. US President Johnson called the invasion "tragic news."

A Soviet tank crashes into a building in the centre of Liberec, north of Prague, in 1968.

A Cuban exile in the USA watches news of the developing missile crisis.

Cuban Missile Crisis

In 1962, the US discovered that Soviet nuclear missiles were being installed in Cuba. President Kennedy demanded that Khrushchev remove the missiles and dismantle the bases, and the US blockaded Soviet shipments to Cuba. For six days the world was on the brink of a possible nuclear war, until the Soviet leader accepted Kennedy's demands in return for a US undertaking not to attack Cuba.

Signs of Détente

By the mid-1970s, after the first Strategic Arms Limitation Treaty, there was a slight relaxation in Cold War tensions. At a Conference on Security and Cooperation in Europe (CSCE), the two superpowers and 33 other nations agreed to recognize the European boundaries that had been set up after World War II. These included the Baltic states annexed by the Soviets. All parties also agreed to respect human rights and improve cultural and economic cooperation.

Soviet leader Leonid Brezhnev (1906–82) signs the CSCE Final Act in Helsinki, 1975.

Signs such as this became increasingly common in the 1970s.

The Reagan–Thatcher Years

Margaret Thatcher was the longest serving British prime minister of the 20th century. During the 1980s, her period in office coincided with that of US President Ronald Reagan. The two leaders' shared economic beliefs meant that Reaganomics, as they became known, were not very different from Thatcherism. There were differences of approach and opinion—over the Falklands War and the US invasion of Grenada, for example—but the president and prime minister were seen by the world as allies and friends.

Ronald Reagan and Margaret Thatcher at Camp David, Maryland, in 1986.

Economic problems

Both the US and UK suffered economic difficulties throughout the 1970s. There were growing problems of inflation, strikes and fuel shortages. In 1973, the member states of the Organization of Petroleum Exporting Countries (including Iraq, Saudi Arabia, and Venezuela) disagreed with major oil companies. OPEC raised crude oil prices by up to 200 percent, causing a sharp rise in petrol and other prices in the USA and the UK, and triggering an economic recession.

The Prince and Princess of Wales rode in an open-topped state landau from the cathedral to Buckingham Palace.

The Royal Wedding

On 29 July 1981, hundreds of thousands of people lined the streets of London to see Prince Charles, heir to the British throne, and Lady Diana Spencer on their wedding day. The marriage took place at St. Paul's Cathedral, watched by a television audience of 750 million people around the world. The bride became the Princess of Wales.

Conservative Policies

Ronald Reagan's Republican administration and Margaret Thatcher's Conservative government had similar aims and policies. Reagan wanted to cut taxes, reduce welfare benefits and increase spending on defense. His economic program became known as Reaganomics. Both leaders believed in free enterprise and opposed the state regulation of business, but economic downturns in the late 1980s prevented them from carrying through all their policies. In foreign affairs, they both took a hard line on the Soviet Union.

Iraqi forces set fire to oil wells outside Kuwait City before withdrawing from the region. They also dumped oil into the Persian Gulf.

War in the Falklands

In April 1982, Argentinean troops invaded the Falkland Islands, a British overseas territory in the South Atlantic. Attempts by the United Nations and the US to find a peaceful solution to the differences failed, and Britain sent ships, planes and 6,000 troops to the islands. By June the UK had won the war, but more than 900 soldiers died in the conflict.

A British Royal Navy commando in the Falklands (left). The reputation of Margaret Thatcher (right) was boosted at home by patriotic sentiment and a sense of victory.

From Punks to Yuppies

Punk rock of the late 1970s was an aggressive, rebellious form of popular music that influenced youth culture and fashion. It encouraged extreme hair-dos and body piercing. In the 1980s, rap music became more popular. The consumer boom also produced so-called yuppies (young urban professionals)— who were earning a lot of money and enjoyed spending it.

In 1983, consumers queued to buy "adoptable" Cabbage Patch Kids dolls.

Piercings and wild hair-dos were part of punk style.

Mobile phones were an innovation.

Yuppies had plenty of money to spend.

The Gulf War

After Iraq—led by Saddam Hussein—invaded Kuwait in August 1990, a coalition force of the US and UN countries (including the UK) launched Operation Desert Storm in January 1991. This included massive air attacks from Saudi Arabia, followed by a ground offensive. The Iraqis left Kuwait at the end of February 1991 and were forced to agree to comply with UN resolutions. Nevertheless, tensions continued between Iraq and the US.

THE REAGAN-THATCHER YEARS

1973
UK joins the European Economic Community.

1976
A Soviet newspaper calls Margaret Thatcher the "Iron Lady."

1979–90
Margaret Thatcher is the first female Prime Minister of the United Kingdom.

1981–89
Ronald Reagan is 40th President of the USA.

1981
Race riots in Britain. Reagan is shot in a failed assassination attempt.

1983
Reagan announces the Strategic Defense Initiative (SDI or "Star Wars").

1984
Miners' strike in Britain, as coal mines are closed.

1987
On Black Monday (Oct 19), world stock market prices show the biggest single-day drop (23 per cent in US).

1990
Anti-poll tax riots in UK.

1991
Margaret Thatcher is awarded the US Presidential Medal of Freedom.

Soviet Collapse

By the mid-1980s, the cost of maintaining a massive military machine was ruining the Soviet economy. Mikhail Gorbachev brought in reforms, but they were too few, too late. The Soviets were forced to allow non-Communist governments to come to power in their Eastern European satellites. Their own republics started declaring independence and, at the end of 1991, the Soviet Union ceased to exist.

A Russian doll shows the figures of Lenin, Stalin, Brezhnev, Gorbachev, and Yeltsin.

Everyday goods were often in short supply in the Soviet Union in the 1980s. People had to queue outside shops.

War in Afghanistan

In December 1979, Soviet troops invaded Afghanistan, which bordered on its three southernmost republics. They did so in order to support the Marxist revolutionary council that had taken over against its many opponents. Opposition rebel guerrillas called mujahedin ("holy warriors") believed that the new government's policies went against the teachings of Islam. The Soviets fought for nine years, before withdrawing in 1988–89.

An Afghan rebel soldier. The mujahedin were supplied with US arms via Pakistan.

Economic Problems

The Soviet economy did not make any progress under Brezhnev in the late 1970s. The government invested huge sums in farming and agricultural equipment, but output went down. This meant the Soviets had to import large amounts of grain, which they could only afford because of an expansion in their oil and gas industries. The US protested against the invasion of Afghanistan by limiting supplies of its wheat to the Soviet Union, which made matters worse.

People of all ages helped knock down parts of the Berlin Wall in 1989. Some kept pieces as souvenirs.

Fall of the Berlin Wall

The Berlin Wall had stood since 1961 as a symbol of the political conflict between East and West. In 1989, Hungary opened its border with Austria, allowing thousands of East Germans to move through Austria to West Germany. Anti-government demonstrations broke out in East Germany, and it was finally announced that East Germans could travel freely. Thousands of people flooded the checkpoints and the Berlin Wall was opened.

Soviet Republics

The USSR was made up of 15 socialist republics, of which Russia was by far the biggest, followed by the Kazakh and Ukrainian republics. The three Baltic republics were annexed in 1940, when the Moldavian republic was also created. In 1990 Lithuania was the first republic to declare its independence.

An Uzbek man.

Cotton is an important crop in the Central Asian republics.

LITHUANIA is KUVEIT 1940!

A Lithuanian protester.

A Kyrgyz man celebrates independence.

Soviet passports skewered on Lithuanian railings.

Street scene in a Moscow suburb during the 1980s. The new reforms did not have an immediate effect on most people's everyday lives.

Glasnost and Perestroika

When Gorbachev became head of the Soviet Communist Party in 1985, he set about trying to improve the economy through a policy of *perestroika* ("restructuring") aimed at increasing efficiency. Gorbachev's *glasnost* ("openness") policy tried to make Soviet society freer and more flexible. These initiatives were not popular with old-fashioned Communists. The reforms, though many failed, nevertheless encouraged freedom movements within many of the 15 republics that made up the Union.

INDEPENDENT STATES, 1991

1 Lithuania	3 Estonia	6 Moldova
2 Latvia	4 Belarus	7 Georgia
	5 Ukraine	8 Armenia

RUSSIAN FEDERATION

9 Azerbaijan	11 Uzbekistan	13 Kyrgyzstan
10 Turkmenistan	12 Tajikistan	14 Kazakhstan

End of the USSR

In December 1991, Russia, Belarus, and Ukraine announced that the Soviet Union was no more and formed a new Commonwealth of Independent States. Eight other newly independent states quickly joined this loose confederation, but the Baltic States (1, 2 and 3 on the map) did not. On 25 December, the Soviet flag was lowered in Moscow and the USSR ceased to exist.

SOVIET COLLAPSE

1982–84
Yuri Andropov (1914–84) is president.

1984–85
Konstantin Chernenko (1911–85) is president.

1985
Chernenko is succeeded by Mikhail Gorbachev.

1987
Boris Yeltsin (1931–2007) is dismissed as Moscow party chief for criticizing the slow pace of reforms.

1989
First openly contested elections are held for the newly created Congress of Peoples' Deputies.

1990
The Soviet government votes to permit non-Communist political parties.

1991
In July, Gorbachev and President Bush sign START (the Strategic Arms Reduction Treaty). In August, Boris Yeltsin opposes a conservative coup against Gorbachev. On 25 December, Gorbachev resigns as Soviet president. On 26 December, the Russian government takes over offices of the former USSR.

Chernobyl

On 26 April 1986, a reactor failed in a run-down nuclear power station at Chernobyl in the Ukrainian republic. The reactor should have shut down automatically, but a safety device had been switched off. There was a massive explosion that blew the top off the reactor, causing the world's worst nuclear accident. Many thousands were killed or made seriously ill by the nuclear fallout in Ukraine, neighboring republics and much further afield.

The Chernobyl disaster convinced many people that nuclear power is dangerous.

Japan on the Rise

Japan suffered complete devastation and a large loss of territory during World War II. The end of the war was followed by seven years of foreign occupation. Political democracy was established, but some anti-American feeling soon developed. As their independence was regained, Japanese business and industry went from strength to strength, adopting modern methods of high-quality mass production. Manufacturing companies, especially of cars and electronics, came to dominate world markets during a long economic boom period.

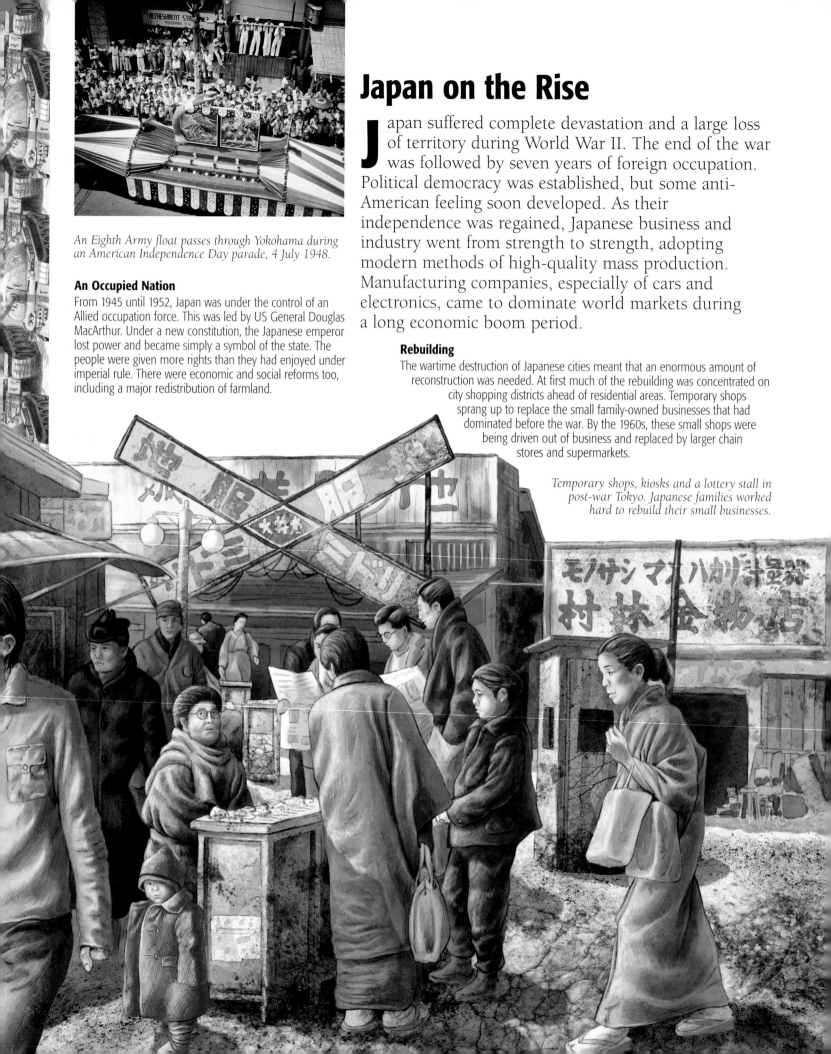

An Eighth Army float passes through Yokohama during an American Independence Day parade, 4 July 1948.

An Occupied Nation

From 1945 until 1952, Japan was under the control of an Allied occupation force. This was led by US General Douglas MacArthur. Under a new constitution, the Japanese emperor lost power and became simply a symbol of the state. The people were given more rights than they had enjoyed under imperial rule. There were economic and social reforms too, including a major redistribution of farmland.

Rebuilding

The wartime destruction of Japanese cities meant that an enormous amount of reconstruction was needed. At first much of the rebuilding was concentrated on city shopping districts ahead of residential areas. Temporary shops sprang up to replace the small family-owned businesses that had dominated before the war. By the 1960s, these small shops were being driven out of business and replaced by larger chain stores and supermarkets.

Temporary shops, kiosks and a lottery stall in post-war Tokyo. Japanese families worked hard to rebuild their small businesses.

For a long time Japan was quite closed to Western influences. That gradually changed and young people especially adopted many aspects of European and American fashion and culture.

Civil Unrest

Many Japanese people opposed the US-Japan Security Treaty of 1952, which allowed continued American use of bases in Japan and possible intervention in disturbances within the country. A new treaty was signed in 1960, giving Japan more say in its own affairs and committing the US to defend Japan in case of attack. Some Japanese political activists still opposed any form of military alliance with the US.

TERRITORIAL LOSSES

Post-War Japan

During the Second World War, Japan occupied large parts of Southeast Asia. After the war, it basically lost all lands gained in the 20th century, including all territory on the mainland of Asia. Japan was reduced to its four large main islands and small offshore islands.

- Allies
- Territory lost by Japan to the Allies prior to August 1945
- Japanese territory in August 1945

Learning from the West

By the mid-1950s, Japanese industry was recovering well. Japanese businessmen and engineers studied Western industrial methods and then applied them in the new, modernized factories that had replaced old-fashioned workshops. This led the way by the 1970s to the development and mass production of high-tech electronic equipment, such as hi-fi products and computers. Japanese goods soon gained a reputation for high standards and affordable prices.

The pioneering Walkman first went on sale in Japan in 1979. It was soon a huge hit around the world.

By 1990, advertising like this was common on the high-rise buildings of Tokyo and other Japanese cities.

JAPAN ON THE RISE

1946
The Allied occupation force draws up a new Japanese constitution.

1951
The Treaty of Peace with Japan is formally signed.

1954
Japan introduces the world's first transistor radio.

1955
The Liberal Democratic Party (LDP) comes to power and dominates for the rest of the period.

1956
The first Japanese car is sold in the USA.

1964
The Shinkansen (bullet train) is launched.

1975
Japan joins France, Italy, UK, USA and West Germany in the G6 forum of industrialized nations.

1982
Sony launches the compact disc (CD).

1989
Emperor Hirohito dies and is succeeded by his son Akihito. Japan joins the Asia-Pacific Economic Cooperation (APEC).

Booming Economy

The Japanese economy continued to grow at an enormous rate. It weathered the problems caused by sharply rising oil prices in the 1970s. Exports continued to increase as Japanese steel, cars, television sets, and other electronic products proved lastingly popular. Japan became a model for the developing nations of Southeast Asia. By the late 1980s, however, rising prices caused Japanese exports to slide from their high position.

With the ending of the Cold War, a collective sigh of relief went up. For the West, whose way had prevailed, this was a time to celebrate. One American thinker even proclaimed the "end of history." Threats to peace and stability had not gone away, however. The rising menace of Islamic radicalism was horrifically brought home on 11 September 2001.

Meanwhile, the astonishing achievements of technology were being undermined by the unforeseen consequences of development—from climate change to population movements. At the same time, the Internet and other "smart" technologies offered hope for new solutions to global problems, while transforming people's working routines and personal lives. This chaper tells the exciting story of an era that gave us the problems and possibilities we live with today.

Nelson Mandela led the battle that ended the apartheid system in South Africa (see pages 182–183 and 232–233). Mandela died at the age of 95 on 5 December 2013. Deeply respected within South Africa, where he was often known affectionately as Tata (father), it was a mark of his international standing that representatives of more than 90 foreign nations traveled to South Africa for his state funeral.

TIMELINE

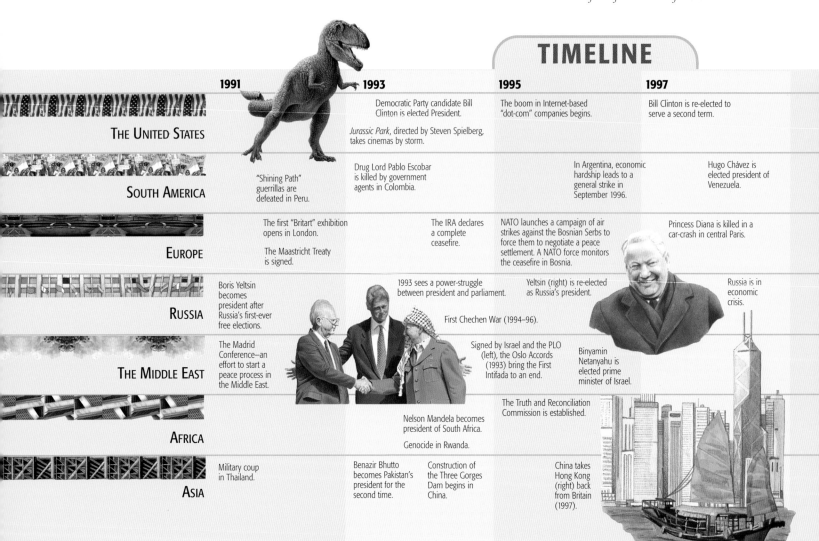

	1991	1993	1995	1997
THE UNITED STATES		Democratic Party candidate Bill Clinton is elected President. / *Jurassic Park*, directed by Steven Spielberg, takes cinemas by storm.	The boom in Internet-based "dot-com" companies begins.	Bill Clinton is re-elected to serve a second term.
SOUTH AMERICA	"Shining Path" guerrillas are defeated in Peru.	Drug Lord Pablo Escobar is killed by government agents in Colombia.	In Argentina, economic hardship leads to a general strike in September 1996.	Hugo Chávez is elected president of Venezuela.
EUROPE	The first "Britart" exhibition opens in London. / The Maastricht Treaty is signed.	The IRA declares a complete ceasefire.	NATO launches a campaign of air strikes against the Bosnian Serbs to force them to negotiate a peace settlement. A NATO force monitors the ceasefire in Bosnia.	Princess Diana is killed in a car-crash in central Paris.
RUSSIA	Boris Yeltsin becomes president after Russia's first-ever free elections.	1993 sees a power-struggle between president and parliament. / First Chechen War (1994–96).	Yeltsin (right) is re-elected as Russia's president.	Russia is in economic crisis.
THE MIDDLE EAST	The Madrid Conference—an effort to start a peace process in the Middle East.		Signed by Israel and the PLO (left), the Oslo Accords (1993) bring the First Intifada to an end. / Binyamin Netanyahu is elected prime minister of Israel.	
AFRICA		Nelson Mandela becomes president of South Africa. / Genocide in Rwanda.	The Truth and Reconciliation Commission is established.	
ASIA	Military coup in Thailand.	Benazir Bhutto becomes Pakistan's president for the second time. / Construction of the Three Gorges Dam begins in China.	China takes Hong Kong (right) back from Britain (1997).	

1991 to the 21st Century

A symbol of the "Millennium Bug," which caused great concern in the years leading up to the new millenium in 2000. Fears were unfounded as most computer systems switched effortlessly to the new dates.

On 20 January 2009, Barack Obama was sworn in as the 44th President of the United States. He is the first African-American to hold that position. Obama was re-elected for a second term in November 2012.

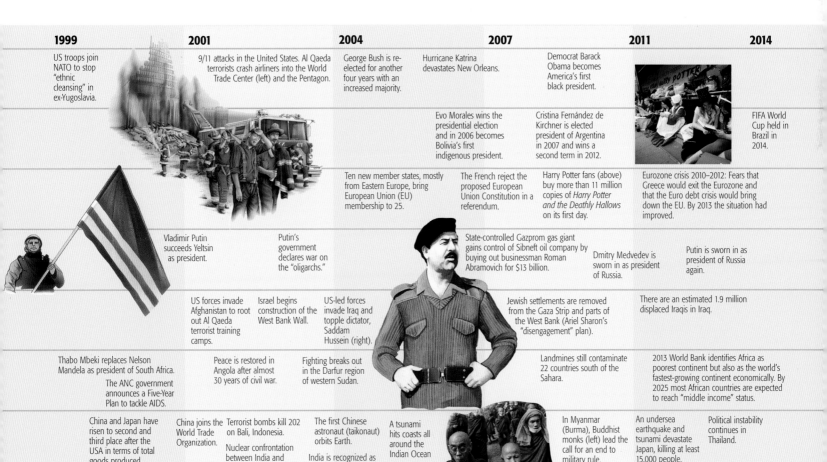

1999	2001	2004	2007	2011	2014
US troops join NATO to stop "ethnic cleansing" in ex-Yugoslavia.	9/11 attacks in the United States. Al Qaeda terrorists crash airliners into the World Trade Center (left) and the Pentagon.	George Bush is re-elected for another four years with an increased majority.	Democrat Barack Obama becomes America's first black president.		
		Evo Morales wins the presidential election and in 2006 becomes Bolivia's first indigenous president.	Cristina Fernández de Kirchner is elected president of Argentina in 2007 and wins a second term in 2012.		FIFA World Cup held in Brazil in 2014.
		Ten new member states, mostly from Eastern Europe, bring European Union (EU) membership to 25.	The French reject the proposed European Union Constitution in a referendum.	Harry Potter fans (above) buy more than 11 million copies of *Harry Potter and the Deathly Hallows* on its first day.	Eurozone crisis 2010–2012: Fears that Greece would exit the Eurozone and that the Euro debt crisis would bring down the EU. By 2013 the situation had improved.
	Vladimir Putin succeeds Yeltsin as president.	Putin's government declares war on the "oligarchs."	State-controlled Gazprom gas giant gains control of Sibneft oil company by buying out businessman Roman Abramovich for $13 billion.	Dmitry Medvedev is sworn in as president of Russia.	Putin is sworn in as president of Russia again.
	US forces invade Afghanistan to root out Al Qaeda terrorist training camps.	Israel begins construction of the West Bank Wall.	US-led forces invade Iraq and topple dictator, Saddam Hussein (right).	Jewish settlements are removed from the Gaza Strip and parts of the West Bank (Ariel Sharon's "disengagement" plan).	There are an estimated 1.9 million displaced Iraqis in Iraq.
Thabo Mbeki replaces Nelson Mandela as president of South Africa. The ANC government announces a Five-Year Plan to tackle AIDS.	Peace is restored in Angola after almost 30 years of civil war.	Fighting breaks out in the Darfur region of western Sudan.		Landmines still contaminate 22 countries south of the Sahara.	2013 World Bank identifies Africa as poorest continent but also as the world's fastest-growing continent economically. By 2025 most African countries are expected to reach "middle income" status.
China and Japan have risen to second and third place after the USA in terms of total goods produced.	China joins the World Trade Organization.	Terrorist bombs kill 202 on Bali, Indonesia. Nuclear confrontation between India and Pakistan over Kashmir.	The first Chinese astronaut (taikonaut) orbits Earth. India is recognized as a "tiger economy."	A tsunami hits coasts all around the Indian Ocean	In Myanmar (Burma), Buddhist monks (left) lead the call for an end to military rule.	An undersea earthquake and tsunami devastate Japan, killing at least 15,000 people.	Political instability continues in Thailand.

Yeltsin Defends Democracy

In the Soviet Union, Mikhail Gorbachev's post-Cold-War policies of openness (*glasnost*) and economic reconstruction (*perestroika*) made many Russians hanker after the certainties of old times (see pages 172–173). In August, 1991, a group of hard-line Communists attempted a coup. Boris Yeltsin defied the coup, and within six months the USSR had ceased to exist and Yeltsin was president of an independent Russia.

Above: Leading from the front, Boris Yeltsin stands on top of a tank in front of Moscow's parliament building, condemning the Communist conspirators inside.

Below: Russia's president Boris Yeltsin in Washington in September 2004 with US president Bill Clinton. Their talks led to a considereble improvement in relations between the two countries and an agreement to limit the nuclear arms race for a period of time.

Conflicts and Crime

Local conflicts and ethnic rivalries erupted in many places after the Cold War was over. Wealthy Western countries became a magnet to refugees fleeing these conflicts, or simply escaping poverty at home. The newly opened borders also made it easier for drugs gangs to become multinational operations.

An Iraqi child plays at driving, but his refugee family has nowhere to go (Iraq, 2003).

A New World Order

The Big Mac came to Moscow on 31st January 1990— a sign of new times.

With the ending of the Cold War, an era of peace and democracy appeared to beckon, but people felt a degree of nervousness. For half a century, the world had been divided into Capitalist and Communist camps, and everyone knew how things stood. Now, there was no knowing what conflicts might flare up or where. New dangers ranged from Islamic radicalism to global warming.

Climate Change

During the early years of the 21st century, the world woke up to the impact of industrial development on the environment. Governments began to agree that action was needed to combat global warming. But the United States was reluctant to acknowledge the problem, while the newly emerging industrial giants, China and India, did not see why they should jeopardize their own hard-won prosperity because of a problem created by other countries.

Stability Gone

The collapse of Communism brought an end to what the West regarded as an enslaving system and removed the threat of nuclear war. But in Russia many people felt adrift, and unemployment soared as the old "collective" farms—which had been overmanned and inefficient —were privatized.

In Minsk, Belarus, workers on a former collective farm spread hay before winter.

"An Old Order Passes"

"Today, as an old order passes," said US President Bill Clinton in 1993, "the new world is more free but less stable." The Cold War rivals now faced the challenge of forging a new, more co-operative relationship. This was successful at first, with the easy-going Boris Yeltsin as Russia's president. But as Russians tried to cope with the changes brought about by a free market economy, and as authoritarian president Vladimir Putin rose in influence, much of the old suspicion between East and West began to return.

The spring of 2008 saw vast cracks appearing in the usually solid Arctic ice. Global warming is happening far faster than many scientists anticipated.

Pakistani protesters demonstrate against Western policies in the Middle East and Iraq in 2003. Young Muslims worldwide are united in their anger.

Islamic Radicalism

The world's Muslims have a proud history. Today, many Muslim countries are angry with the West, particularly the United States, for interfering in their affairs. In what is as much a political as a religious movement, increasing numbers are coming to feel that Islam has to reassert itself and take back its rightful place in the world—by force, if necessary.

All-Powerful America

With the collapse of Communism in 1989, American power and prestige was at an all-time high. The United States had finally seen off the Soviet threat. Rich and successful as America had been in the postwar era, its influence had always been held in check by the might of the USSR. Now, with no significant rival remaining, the ascendancy of the American way was assured. There was nothing the world's sole superpower could not do, it seemed.

The national flags of the NAFTA member-states.

George Bush was president of the United States from 1989 to 1993.

The New Economy

Dot-com companies (so-called for their Internet domain names) revolutionized the business and consumer markets of the 1990s. They offered everything from books to financial services on-line. It was possible to start a dot-com business in the living-room, and often they were not properly thought-through. In 2001 there was a stock-market crash as the "Dot-com Bubble" burst, and many of the weaker companies had to cease trading.

Shelving, computer-terminals, and furniture are up for sale as the assets of another "Dot-Bomb" company are auctioned off after the collapse of 2001.

The President is Impeached

Scandal came to the White House in 1998, when President Clinton's relationship with a young assistant, Monica Lewinsky, was revealed. To the American people it was bad enough that Clinton had deceived his high-profile wife, Hillary. But worse still, he had denied doing so. This came at a time when issues of private morality were coming to the fore in American public life. Clinton was forced to admit sexual relations with Lewinsky and was impeached by the US Congress. He was acquitted by the Senate, however, and served out the rest of his second term.

On 17 August 1998, President Bill Clinton finally admitted in a televised address that he had had an affair with a young assistant, Monica Lewinsky, in the White House.

US Globalization

Before the 1990s, restrictions on trade made it difficult for individual countries to buy and sell goods to each other. The restrictions were designed to protect home-grown industries. But US economists argued that they just impoverished everyone, and that their removal would benefit both rich and poor countries alike. In 1994, NAFTA (the North America Free Trade Agreement) brought down trading barriers between the USA, Canada and Mexico. This was an important first step towards achieving a global economy, in which trade could flow freely across national boundaries.

Environmental Politics

Awareness of pollution and global warming increased during the 1990s. It became an electoral issue in 2000, when Ralph Nader ran for president as the candidate for the Green Party. His campaign caused a major stir. In the event, though, he got less than 3 percent of the vote overall: Americans were not yet ready to make sweeping lifestyle changes.

The Bush Campaign

Military strength and moral values were the two main thrusts of George W. Bush's presidential campaign. He forged a new link with the "Religious Right." Previously, the Republican Party had believed in a powerful and law-abiding America, but had felt that private moral choices were for individual men and women to make. Bush's supporters believed that the US government had a duty to uphold the Christian religion and its institutions—especially marriage.

Rush-hour in the United States, and the consumption of fossil fuels continues unchecked.

George W. Bush's victory as president of the US in 2000 was decided by just a handful of votes. This led to long discussions about voting methods. The ballot box (right) is from Palm Beach, one of the counties in Florida where votes were recounted.

In August 2004, on the eve of the Republican National Convention in New York, Bush supporters shrug off the jeers of protesters who oppose the war in Iraq.

ALL-POWERFUL AMERICA

1991
Operation Desert Storm: US forces lead international action to remove Iraq's invading army from Kuwait.

1992
The world's largest McDonald's restaurant opens in Beijing, China.

1993
Democratic Party candidate Bill Clinton is elected president.

1995
The boom in Internet-based "dot-com" companies begins.

1997
Bill Clinton is re-elected to serve a second term.

1999
US troops join NATO effort to stop "ethnic cleansing" in former Yugoslavia.

2000
The "Dot-com Bubble" bursts. Billions of dollars are wiped off share-values in the "New Economy."

2001
George W. Bush becomes US President.

2008
Financial crisis caused by US housing bubble and sub-prime lending leads to worst global recession in decades.

2009
Barack Obama sworn in as president of the US.

2013
Obama elected for second term.

Western Europe: The Benefits of Peace

After the Second World War, great efforts were made to promote peace and co-operation between the countries of Western Europe. But America's ascendancy in the 1990s made the need for European cooperation seem still more pressing. Even the richest European nations were dwarfed economically and politically by the United States. Only by working together could they compete on equal terms.

To Western consumers, these Trabant cars were scrap metal the moment they rolled off the East German production lines.

Eastern Europe a Burden

Scenes of celebration had accompanied the tearing down of the Berlin Wall in 1989 and the formal reunification of the two Germanys in 1990. But there was a difficult economic hangover: the German Democratic Republic (GDR) in the east had fallen far behind the Federal Republic in the west. Cushioned from competition in the decades of Communism, the GDR's industry was poorly-equipped and inefficient, and its workers were unskilled. The East was more a burden than an asset to the new Germany.

WESTERN EUROPE: BENEFITS OF PEACE

1992
The Maastricht Treaty is signed, paving the way for a single currency. But the UK and Denmark opt to keep their own currencies.

1994
The IRA declares a complete ceasefire. Norwegians reject EU-membership.

1997
Britain hands Hong Kong back to China. Princess Diana is killed in a car-crash in central Paris.

2002
Twelve EU states abolish their currencies and adopt euro notes and coins.

2004
A wave of formerly-Communist countries joins the European Union.

2005
French reject proposed European Union Constitution.

2007
The EU's 27 member-nations approve the Lisbon Treaty, which re-shapes the EU.

2013
Croatia becomes 28th member of the EU. Latvia adopts the Euro.

The Maastricht Treaty

The Maastricht Treaty on European Union was signed in 1992 in the Dutch town of Maastricht, and it came into force the following year. The treaty gave the European Union (EU) its own political and legal institutions and foreign policy. In 1995, the EU's 12 member-states were joined by Austria, Finland and Sweden. The ex-Communist Czech Republic, Estonia, Hungary, Latvia, Lithuania, Poland, Slovakia and Slovenia, among others, joined in 2004; Bulgaria and Romania followed in 2007.

When Europe's leaders came together (above) to sign the Maastricht Treaty (right) in 1992, many people worried that a new European "superstate" would override the rights of member nations.

Launch of the Euro

The French franc, the German mark, the Spanish peseta, the Portuguese escudo, the Greek drachma, the Irish punt... All these and more ceased to exist on 31 December, 2001. It was not easy for proud nation-states to give up their traditional currencies, but at the same time the rewards of EU membership were great. The "Eurozone" was an immensely rich and powerful free-trade area, potentially a real economic match for the United States.

New coins, new notes, new prices—Europeans had much to adjust to when the euro was introduced.

Princess Diana was given all the ceremony of a state funeral, and millions turned out to mourn her.

One of the terms of the Belfast Agreement called for a gradual reduction in the number of security forces deployed in Northern Ireland.

Peace in Northern Ireland

A quarter of a century of conflict in Northern Ireland came to an end on Good Friday, 1998, when an agreement was reached between the British and Irish governments and paramilitary groups. The Belfast (or Good Friday) Agreement proposed that the fighting in Northern Ireland should end, and power should be shared between the Unionist (Protestant) and Nationalist (Catholic) communities. People in both Northern Ireland and the Republic voted in favor of the agreement. By 2005, the Provisional IRA (Irish Republican Army) had destroyed its weapons.

Death of Princess Diana

On 31 August, 1997, Diana, Princess of Wales, was killed in a car accident in Paris. The world mourned her death, but Britain was convulsed by grief. This extravagantly "un-British" reaction came close to causing a constitutional crisis—the Queen was criticized for not showing enough emotion. Tony Blair, Britain's new prime minister, successfully smoothed things over. He caught the mood of the moment when he spoke of Diana as "the People's Princess."

New Prime Minister Tony Blair, here with his wife Cherie, offered Britain a fresh start in 1997.

New Labour

In Britain, a wave of real enthusiasm welcomed Tony Blair to Downing Street in 1997, although cynics suggested his "New Labour" was less about socialism than "spin"—smart presentation. For all his fluent French and sophisticated European style, Blair moved Britain away from its EU allies into a much closer association with the United States. His support for George W. Bush—and, especially, for the invasion of Iraq—won him American admirers, but placed his relations with his own electors under increasing strain.

Rising Tension

Until 1991, Yugoslavia was a multi-national state. It was made up of Slovenia, Croatia, Bosnia and Herzegovina, Montenegro, Serbia (including the self-governing regions of Vojvodina and Kosovo) and Macedonia. In 1991, Slovenia, Croatia, and Macedonia declared their independence from Serb-dominated Yugoslavia. Bosnia's Muslims also wanted freedom. The Serbs felt threatened and tensions escalated.

YUGOSLAVIA'S BREAK-UP AFTER 1991

AUSTRIA • HUNGARY • SLOVENIA • CROATIA • VOJVODINA • ROMANIA • BOSNIA AND HERZEGOVINA • BELGRADE • SREBRENICA • SARAJEVO • SERBIA • MONTENEGRO • DUBROVNIK • KOSOVO • MACEDONIA • ALBANIA • GREECE

Conflict Between Serbs, Croats, and Muslims

Yugoslavia was home to three very different religious traditions. A lack of mutual respect between them deepened into conflict. The Serbs worshipped in the Eastern Orthodox Church, the Catholic Croats looked to the West, while many people in Bosnia were Muslims—descendants of the Ottoman Turks who had ruled the region in the 19th century.

A boat bursts into flames in the Croatian port of Dubrovnik, where violence flared in 1991.

Yugoslavia: Old Scores

Until 1980, Yugoslavia was held together mainly by the authority (and severity) of its Communist leader, Marshal Tito. After his death, increasing opposition by Yugoslavia's Slovenes, Croats, Montenegrans, Macedonians and Bosnian Muslims to the domination of one ethnic group, the Serbs, led to the breakup of the nation. A series of violent ethnic conflicts took place, lasting from 1991 to 2001.

The Bosnian War

Although Bosnia's Muslim majority were eager for their independence, a Serbian minority in Bosnia still wanted to be part of Yugoslavia. In 1992, war broke out as Serbia tried to prevent a Bosnian breakaway from Yugoslavia. Croatia intervened on behalf of the country's Croats. Terrible atrocities were committed and about 100,000 people were killed, many of them civilians. Finally, in 1995, peace was agreed and Bosnia was recognized as a separate state.

As many as 1.3 million people in Bosnia were forced to leave their homes and settle in makeshift refugee camps.

Some 1,300 of Srebrenica's victims were buried at Potocari. This memorial to them was dedicated in 2003 by US president Bill Clinton.

Ethnic Cleansing

Yugoslavia's troubles introduced an ugly new idea to the world. "Ethnic cleansing" meant ensuring that a place was populated by one particular ethnic group and no other—all "outsiders" would be killed or driven out. Dreadful crimes were committed by all sides, but the Serbs were most systematic in seeking to "cleanse" communities. In 1995, at Srebrenica in eastern Bosnia, Serbian fighters massacred over 8,000 Bosnian Muslim men and boys because they believed the region was theirs by right.

The Siege of Sarajevo

Between April 1992 and February 1996, the Bosnian capital, Sarajevo, was besieged by the Serbs, who had bigger and better-armed forces than the Bosnians. They bombarded Sarajevo with artillery and placed snipers at key vantage points. Over 10,000 civilians were killed, and thousands more were forced to flee. The siege was finally lifted after NATO airstrikes against Serb positions brought the Serbs to the negotiating table.

The Northrop-Grumman B-2 "Stealth" bomber spearheaded NATO airstrikes against the Serbs in Kosovo. It could slip undetected through radar defenses.

The people of Sarajevo struggled on as best they could while all around them high-explosives rained down from Serb positions.

Kosovo War

Although politically part of Serbia, Kosovo was mainly populated by Albanians. When the Bosnians won their freedom in 1995, the Kosovo Albanians were inspired to strike out for theirs. The Serbs responded with massive force and widespread ethnic cleansing. In 1999, NATO intervened, bombing strategic targets to hamper the Serbian war effort. An uneasy peace in 2001 left Kosovo under UN control. In February 2008, Kosovo unilaterally declared its independence from Serbia. The declaration was recognized by the USA, the UK, France, and others, but was rejected by Russia.

On Trial

TV news reports from former Yugoslavia horrified audiences around the world. People were especially shocked at the cruelty of the Serbs to civilian populations. There were calls for the ringleaders to be brought to justice. Slobodan Milosevic, Serbia's president from 1989 to 1997, stood trial before the international war crimes tribunal in The Hague, the Netherlands, but he died before a verdict could be reached. Ratko Mladic, the man behind the Srebrenica massacre, was finally arrested in 2011 and sent to The Hague.

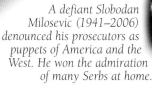

A defiant Slobodan Milosevic (1941–2006) denounced his prosecutors as puppets of America and the West. He won the admiration of many Serbs at home.

Russia After Communism

The collapse of Communism left Russians free— but free to fail as well as to prosper. Embraced in its most ruthless form, Capitalism made a minority of people rich beyond their wildest dreams, but left the majority adrift in poverty, without state help. Not surprisingly, many hankered after the security of Soviet times, and there was a desire for firmer leadership in the country.

To the West, Boris Yeltsin seemed a genial democrat who gave Russia a new and friendly face.

First Free Election

On 12 June, 1991, Boris Yeltsin was elected president of what was still the Russian Republic of the USSR. By the end of the year, the Soviet Union had been wound up altogether. The Russian Federation that replaced it was friendly towards the United States, and agreed to talks on decommissioning nuclear arms. Unfortunately, many weapons were not in Russia, but in the former Soviet republics, now independent states beyond Moscow's control.

Rise of the Oligarchs

"Oligarchy" means "rule by the few," and that was the way "democratic" Russia seemed to be heading. Soviet state monopolies in mining, forestry and energy were sold off to a few individual businessmen who became enormously rich and influential. But their wealth was vulnerable to the cycles of the world market. Demand for commodities slumped and, in 1998, Russia faced financial meltdown.

Shock Therapy for the Economy

After decades of Communist rule, Russians were used to being told what to do. The government had been their employer and provider—although not an especially effective one. State-run factories and offices had been chronically inefficient, while state-owned shops offered little quality or choice. Communism was replaced with unrestricted free-market Capitalism. A few people made spectacular profits, and new shops provided luxuries for them to buy, but many went hungry, with no state support.

A market trader struggles to make a living in post-Communist Russia.

THE FIRST CHECHEN WAR

Russians Invade

The Chechens are a Muslim people in the southwest of the region. After the USSR collapsed, Chechen separatists demanded independence from the Russian Federation. In 1994, Moscow sent troops into Chechnya to prevent the region breaking away. A bloody war was fought until 1996, when a ceasefire was declared.

RUSSIA

RUSSIA

CHECHNYA

The Second Chechen War

Peace between Russia and Chechnya was shortlived. In 1999 Vladimir Putin, prime minister and Yeltsin's intended successor as president, was determined to display his toughness. He blamed a series of bombings in Moscow apartment buildings on the Chechen separatists and sent an overwhelming invasion force to Chechnya. Fighting was ferocious and casualties were high. Russian rule was restored by 2000, but the separatist struggle continued until 2009.

A Chechen fighter flies the flag.

Left. A stretch limousine on Nevsky Prospekt in St. Petersburg. Newly rich Russians were not afraid to show off their wealth.

In 1993, armed soldiers stormed the White House, where Russia's Parliament had set themselves against reform.

In 2004, President Putin took personal charge during the Beslan school siege—but over 300 people were killed when his troops stormed in.

Putin the Dictator?

Voters respected Putin's strength and decisiveness, but critics argued that he was acting as a dictator. Against the background of the global "War on Terror" (see pages 192–193), Russia's Chechen troubles let him boost his own authority at the expense of people's freedom. In 2002, Chechen separatists took hostage the audience inside a Moscow theater; in 2004 they stormed a school in Beslan, southern Russia. Both attacks were violently put down by Russian security forces with great loss of life.

RUSSIA AFTER COMMUNISM

1991
Boris Yeltsin becomes president after Russia's first-ever free elections.

1993
A power-struggle between president and parliament results in a constitutional crisis.

1994–96
First Chechen War.

1996
Yeltsin is re-elected as Russia's president.

1998
Russia in economic crisis.

1999
Start of Second Chechen War. Boris Yeltsin resigns the presidency. Prime Minister Vladimir Putin takes charge, and is elected president in 2000.

2005
The state gains control of Gazprom gas giant. Gazprom gains control of Sibneft oil company by buying out businessman Roman Abramovich for 13 billion dollars.

2013
The Euromaidan protests in Ukraine starting in November unleash violent crackdowns in early 2014. Russia is warned not to step in with its military.

2014
Winter Olympics held in Sochi in February 2014.

Yeltsin in Trouble

Freedom and economic reform in the new Russia might have sounded desirable, but to begin with there were far more losers than winners. Although out-voted in the elections, Russia's Communists had not gone away, and as disenchantment grew, they gained support. In 1993, Communist members of the Congress of Deputies tried to block further reforms and remove Yeltsin. Enraged, the president ordered tanks to surround the Parliament building and crush the coup.

The Arab–Israeli Conflict

Since its creation in 1948, the modern state of Israel has known nothing but conflict, with many Arabs never accepting the existence of the Jewish state. Displaced from their own homeland, some Palestinians turned to violence and the political leadership of the Palestinian Liberation Organization (PLO). In 1993 the Israeli government and PLO agreed to pursue negotiations. But despite plans for a "two-state" solution and George W. Bush's "Road Map for Peace," very little progress was made and the region remained unstable and with frequent flashpoints.

President Clinton with Israeli Premier Yitzhak Rabin and Palestinian leader Yasser Arafat at Oslo in 1993.

The Oslo Accords and First Intifada

In 1993, in Oslo, Israeli and Palestinian leaders met directly for the first time. They agreed that Israel would withdraw partially from the occupied territories in the West Bank and Gaza. There, the rule of a Palestinian Authority would be accepted in return for a Palestinian promise to end attacks on civilians (the First Intifada).

The Second Intifada

By 2000, many Palestinians were pessimistic about the peace process. Then, in September, Israel's opposition leader Ariel Sharon visited Jerusalem's Temple Mount, sacred also to Muslims for its al-Aqsa Mosque. The visit provoked a renewed uprising by the Palestinians (the Second Intifada). The Israelis then restricted Palestinian movement in and out of the occupied territories, creating huge economic problems for the Palestinians.

Lacking guns or grenades, Palestinian youths fought with slings and stones against well-armed Israeli soldiers.

THE ARAB–ISRAELI CONFLICT

1991
President George H.W. Bush meets Middle Eastern leaders at the Madrid Conference in an effort to start a peace process in the Middle East.

1993
Signed by the leaders of Israel and Palestine, the Oslo Accords bring the First Intifada to an end.

1994
The Nobel Peace Prize is awarded jointly to PLO leader Yasser Arafat and Israeli Prime Minister Yitzhak Rabin and Foreign Minister Shimon Peres.

1995
Israel's Labor prime minister Yitzhak Rabin is assassinated by a Jewish extremist.

2000
Disillusion among Palestinians sparks the Second Intifada.

2002
Israel begins construction of the West Bank Wall.

2003
A "Road Map for Peace" is announced by the international Quartet (the US, the UN, the European Union and Russia).

2005
Under Prime Minister Ariel Sharon's "disengagement" plan, Jewish settlements are removed from the Gaza Strip and parts of the West Bank.

2006
Israel' invades Lebanon, starting the Second Lebanon War.
Fighting breaks out in the Gaza Strip between nationalist Fatah supporters and Hamas's Islamist radicals.

2013
US Secretary of State John Kerry attempts to re-start the peace process.

The Road Map for Peace

After the invasion of Iraq (see pages 176–177), the US government returned to the primary concern of many Arab and Islamic states and peoples, the conflict between Israel and Palestine. In 2003, therefore, George W. Bush announced America's commitment to finding a "Road Map for Peace." The Road Map was developed by the United States in cooperation with Russia, the European Union and the United Nations (the Quartet). It called first for an end to the violence, and secondly for the establishment of an independent Palestinian state.

In July 2006, American citizens, including these two boys, were evacuated from Lebanon to the safety of a US ship waiting offshore.

Sharon's Plan for Disengagement

Always previously known as a hardliner, Prime Minister Ariel Sharon surprised everyone when, in 2005, he announced that he was removing all Israeli settlements and army posts from the Gaza Strip and the West Bank. This would give the Palestinians a state of sorts, while the Israelis secured their position in the remaining areas of the West Bank. The plan was controversial. Many of Sharon's supporters felt betrayed, while Palestinians saw it as a way for Israel to strengthen its hold of the West Bank.

The Second Lebanon War

Attacking from across the border in Lebanon, fighters of the Iranian-backed Islamist organization Hezbollah ("Party of God") launched rocket attacks and made incursions into Israel. When, in 2006, Hezbollah took two Israeli soldiers prisoner, Israel invaded Lebanon. Despite severe civilian casualties, the 34-day assault failed to destroy Hezbollah, which was able to claim a victory.

Ten years after the Oslo Accords, America urges Arab leaders to help foster peace between the Palestinians and the Israelis.

Israeli settlers frequently demolished nearby Palestinian homes. Here, children search for salvage in the rubble of a house in Khan Yunis in the Gaza Strip, May 2006.

Iraqi leader Saddam Hussein was notorious for his cruelty.

The Iraq Crisis

The Iran–Iraq War (1980–88) had ended in a stalemate, even though Iraq had received some discreet support from the United States. The US government was aware that Saddam Hussein was a ruthless dictator, but it also saw him as a useful ally against the Islamic radicals of Iran. At the end of the war, Iraq was on the brink of bankruptcy, so Saddam Hussein decided to seize Kuwait. He insisted that the oil-rich sheikdom was rightfully a province of Iraq.

Oil wells in Iraq were set alight by coalition forces during the Gulf War.

Iraq Invades Kuwait

On 2 August, 1990, Iraqi troops occupied Kuwait. The West reacted angrily, and an allied force led by the United States prepared to remove Iraq from Kuwait by force. In January 1991, at the head of an international coalition, the Americans went on the offensive in operation Desert Storm. They expelled the Iraqis from Kuwait, but left Saddam Hussein in power in Iraq.

Weapons of Mass Destruction

In April 1991, Saddam Hussein agreed to the UN's demand that Iraq must destroy its weapons of mass destruction (WMDs). At first he allowed UN inspectors to monitor the disarmament, but in 1998 he put a halt to the inspections. Over the next few years, US and British bombers carried out regular air-strikes to weaken Saddam Hussein. America and its allies claimed that Iraq was still developing chemical gases and harmful bacteria that could be used by the military.

An Iraqi woman toils home carrying a heavy cylinder of cooking gas.

In February 2003, chief UN weapons inspector Hans Blix (centre) met British Prime Minister Tony Blair (right). Blix was reporting to the United Nations on the state of Iraq's compliance with inspections of its weapons programs.

No-Fly Zones

"No-fly zones" were established over Iraq's northern Kurdish areas (1991) and over the southern marshes (1992) to restrict the activities of the Iraqi military. People in both areas had been persecuted and killed by Saddam's regime. The no-fly zones were policed by British and American warplanes. Economic sanctions were also imposed to try to make the Iraqi government co-operate with the UN inspectors. As a result, innocent civilians ended up short of food and medical supplies.

THE IRAQ CRISIS

1990
Saddam Hussein's Iraqi forces invade Kuwait.

1991
Operation Desert Storm – a US-led coalition retakes Kuwait from Iraq.

1994
Iraq drains water from the southern marshlands, home to Muslim Shi'ites who oppose Saddam Hussein's government.

1998
US and British air strikes target Iraqi missile factories and airfields.

2002
US President George W. Bush identifies Iraq, Iran and North Korea as an "axis of evil." The US threatens military action against Iraq if it does not disband its WMD program.

2003
US and Britain lead the invasion of Iraq.

2005
The Iraq Survey Group concludes that Iraq wound up its WMD program in 1991.

2006
Saddam Hussein is executed by hanging.

2010
Parliamentary elections are held in Iraq, confirming Nouri al-Maliki as prime minister.

2011
The last US military forces withdraw from Iraq on 18 December 2011.

ETHNIC AND RELIGIOUS DIVIDES

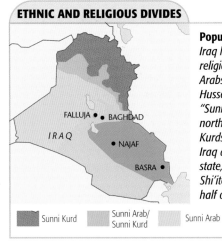

FALLUJA • • BAGHDAD

IRAQ

• NAJAF

BASRA

Population Areas
Iraq has three main ethnic and religious groups. The Sunni Arabs (who supported Saddam Hussein) are based in the "Sunni Triangle" to the northwest. To the northeast, the Kurds want to break away from Iraq and set up an independent state, Kurdistan. The majority, Shi'ite Arabs, live in the southern half of the country.

Sunni Kurd	Sunni Arab/ Sunni Kurd	Sunni Arab	Shia Arab/ Sunni Arab	Shia Arab

An anti-war demonstrator in Washington DC protests against the proposed "surge" of troops in 2007.

"Mission Accomplished"

In March 2003, President Bush formally declared war on Iraq. The US launched a ferocious wave of airstrikes and missile attacks designed to knock out the country's air defenses and communications. Already weakened by years of war and sanctions, the Iraqi armed forces could offer little resistance. By April, the first US troops were in the Iraqi capital, Baghdad. By May, the regime had been brought down and the Americans felt able to declare "Mission Accomplished."

The "Surge" of 2007

Although the war against Saddam was won, Sunni and Shi'ite "insurgents" (rebel groups) quickly began to wage guerrilla campaigns against the occupiers. Amid calls for withdrawal in America, President George W. Bush ordered a "surge," a swelling of troop numbers—one last push that he hoped would bring the conflict to an end.

The toppling of Saddam Hussein's statue in April 2003 was of huge symbolic importance—but the war in Iraq was by no means over.

The Rise of Radical Islam

Many in the West had been almost unaware of Islam's existence, but the terror attacks of September 11, 2001 changed all that. In fact, over the years many Muslims had grown increasingly unhappy at the way the West influenced their societies and exploited their resources. While some Muslims pushed for peaceful reform, others sought revolutionary solutions and extremist groups wanted violent war against the West.

An inspiration to Islamists, Iran's Ayatollah Khomeini helped overthrow the corrupt, US-aligned Shah in 1979. He enforced strict Islamic codes of behavior and dress.

General Grievances

After the collapse of the Ottoman Empire, the Muslim Middle East was divided up by colonial administrators. Interference by the West continued into the 21st century as the United States sought to protect Israel, as well as its own supplies of oil. Western powers were prepared to back tyrants (such as the Shah of Iran and Saddam Hussein), so long as they provided regional stability—and a steady flow of oil.

The "Clash of Civilizations"

Islamic radicals have set themselves against the West not only because of its "bullying" foreign policies, but also because of its ungodliness and free-and-easy morals. Some Western opinion-makers, conversely, have claimed that an enlightened, democratic West is in confrontation with an oppressive, "medieval" Muslim world that is "backward" because it has been held back by Islam, not by decades of Western interference.

Sharia Law

Based on the Qu'ran, the sayings of Muhammad, and on centuries of tradition, Sharia is a code of living that Muslims believe orders life according to God's will. In some countries, Sharia law is enforced by the courts. Problems can arise when Muslim immigrants settle in Western countries that have their own, very different, long-established legal systems. People argue over how far countries with Christian or secular traditions should go to accommodate the rules of Sharia law.

At this pro-Taliban protest rally in 2001, a demonstrator protests at US attacks on Afghanistan.

Saudi Arabia is sacred to Islam as the birthplace of the Prophet Muhammad. To the West it is the country with the world's richest oil reserves.

Al Qaeda Origins

When the Russians invaded Afghanistan in 1979, the local Afghan resistance, the mujahedin, were joined by idealistic Muslims from other countries. After the Soviet invasion collapsed, a highly-trained, highly-motivated Islamic force, Al Qa'eda, remained. Al Qa'eda looked beyond Afghanistan to Saudi Arabia, outraged that there were US bases in the homeland of the Prophet Muhammad. Attacks were launched on US targets not just in Saudi Arabia, but also in Yemen, Kenya, and Tanzania.

Many Muslim women wear either a headscarf or a veil, because they feel a religious duty to dress modestly. This custom can seem alien and unsettling to people in the West.

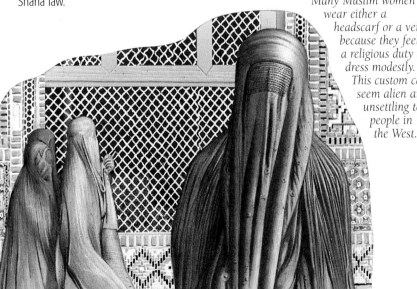

Some former Islamic fighters or mujahedin became members of the Taliban.

The Taliban in Afghanistan

In Afghanistan itself, the Taliban (literally "religious scholars") were determined to build an Islamic state. In 1995 they took the capital, Kabul, and by 2000 they controlled 95 percent of the country. They introduced a harsh version of Sharia law, closing cinemas and barring education for girls. Removed from power by a US-led force in 2001, they withdrew to Pakistan's border territories and regrouped, and by 2006 were on the rise once more.

Suicide bombing

Suicide bombing—a way of waging war mainly against civilians—was developed by the Marxist Tamil Tigers in Sri Lanka. It is a way for a relatively weak force to take on a much larger enemy. Now it is seen as a major weapon of Islamic terror. Muslim suicide bombers, who often wear explosives strapped around their bodies, are motivated by a combination of economic, political and religious goals.

Blasphemy versus Freedom of Speech

In 1989, British novelist Salman Rushdie was condemned to death by Iran's Ayatollah Khomeini because many Muslims believed his award-winning novel *Satanic Verses* contained blasphemous references to Muhammad. He was forced into hiding until the late 1990s. Bangladeshi doctor Taslima Nasreen has also also spent many years in hiding after she criticized the treatment of women under Islam.

Salman Rushdie

Taslima Nasreen

In April 2006, Sunni Muslims set fire to buses and cars following a suspected Shi'ite suicide bomb in Karachi, Pakistan, at a ceremony to mark the anniversary of the Prophet Muhammad's birth.

THE RISE OF RADICAL ISLAM

1991
In the first round of the general elections in Algeria, the Islamic Salvation Front (an Islamist political party) seems set to win, but the army steps in and imposes military rule.

1993
Islamic radicals undertake a series of suicide bombings in Israel.

1996
The Taliban take Kabul, the Afghan capital.

1998
Al Qa'eda bombers target US embassies in Tanzania and Kenya.

2000
Suicide attack on the USS Cole in Yemen.

2001
9/11 attacks in the United States by Al Qa'eda terrorists.

2006
The Shia Islamic organization Hezbollah resists an Israeli invasion of Lebanon.

2007
Hamas takes power among Palestinians in the Gaza Strip.

2013
Most rebel groups in Syria controlled by Islamists.

2014
Planned withdrawal of NATO from Afghanistan leads to growth of Taliban insurgents.

A New South Africa

Realistic rather than idealistic, Frederik Willem de Klerk (b.1936) helped construct the new South Africa.

From 1948, the South African government's policy of apartheid had segregated the races and kept political power in the hands of the minority white population. During the 1980s, opposition to apartheid and the government by the African National Congress (ANC) became increasingly violent. South Africa was isolated internationally and beset by strikes and unrest at home. Dreadful violence and upheaval finally led to major political changes in the 1990s.

Black and white voters line up together during South Africa's 1994 election, the first in which all races were allowed to vote.

De Klerk's Reforms

In 1990, bowing to the inevitable, President F.W. de Klerk legalized the African National Congress (which had been banned in 1960) and released its leader, Nelson Mandela, from prison. He put his plans for new elections, open to all races, to a referendum. At this point, the South African electorate was still all-white, but 68 percent of voters endorsed de Klerk's reforms. From 1990 to 1993, de Klerk held negotiations to end apartheid.

First All-race Elections

At the end of April 1994, South Africa's first-ever universal elections were held. All races, not just white people, were allowed to vote. The enthusiasm of the black majority population was evident: overall, 21.7 million people turned out, of whom some 16 million were voting for the first time. It was no surprise when the African National Congress were swept to power, and Nelson Mandela became South Africa's president.

A former activist shows the Truth and Reconciliation Commission how he was tortured.

Truth and Reconciliation

Founded in 1995 and chaired by the highly respected Archbishop Tutu, the "Truth and Reconciliation Committee" set out to investigate crimes and human-rights abuses committed by South Africa's rulers during apartheid. As its title suggests, its intention was not to deal out punishments to offenders, but to give their victims a voice, establish the facts and allow the process of national healing to begin.

Thabo Mbeki

In 1999, Mandela passed the leadership of the ANC—and of South Africa—to Thabo Mbeki. Mbeki caused controversy abroad with his comments on the AIDS crisis (see below) and his refusal to condemn Robert Mugabe's dictatorial regime in neighboring Zimbabwe, where the economy had collapsed. At home, Mbeki encouraged Africans to solve their own problems rather than to look for help from abroad.

Thabo Mbeki may not be thought such a great statesman as Nelson Mandela was, but his supporters wear his face with pride.

AIDS

South Africa had around 5.6 million people living with HIV and AIDS in 2009, more than any other country. The fight against the syndrome was hampered by President Mbeki's insistence that South Africans were being killed by poverty, not by AIDS. But in 2010, President Zuma's government launched a major HIV counselling and testing campaign.

A NEW SOUTH AFRICA

1990
The ANC is legalized and leader Nelson Mandela is freed after spending 27 years in prison.

1992
South Africa's all-white electorate endorses the dismantling of apartheid.

1994
The ANC comes to power after the first general election open to all races. Nelson Mandela becomes president and remaining sanctions are lifted.

1999
Mandela makes way for Thabo Mbeki as president.

2000
The ANC government announces a Five-Year Plan to tackle AIDS.

2007
An official report finds that South Africa has the second-highest murder rate in the world.

2009
ANC leader Jacob Zuma is elected president.

2010
The FIFA World Cup soccer tournament is held in South Africa.

2013
World mourns the passing of great South African leader, Nelson Mandela.

Poverty and Inequality

South Africa was transformed politically during the 1990s, but economic change has been disappointingly slow. Most of the black population still struggle to get by, and blacks and whites are still segregated—but by income now, rather than by race as such. Crime flourishes in a climate of increasing despair.

A black shantytown in the Johannesburg area in 2001. Black South Africans are still largely confined to such townships, where poverty, crime and infectious disease are major problems.

Health Minister Manto Tshabalala Msimang (1940–2009), shown here in 2005, insisted that AIDS could be treated by traditional folk remedies.

Africa in Trouble

War, famine, natural disaster, disease—Africa has had to contend with all these and more, making prosperity and political stability difficult to achieve. Democracy has all too easily been overthrown by military groups, while impoverished peoples have struggled to survive. International aid has not necessarily helped, fuelling corruption and abuse. However, by the second decade of the 21st century there was record economic growth in some countries and the future, for some Africans at least, seemed much brighter (see pages 232–233).

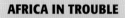

AFRICA IN TROUBLE

1992
Mozambique's 17-year civil war ends. A military coup in Sierra Leone sparks a civil war.

1995
UN troops are forced to leave Somalia as the country collapses into anarchy.

1998
War breaks out between Ethiopia and Eritrea. Civil war is fought in the Democratic Republic of the Congo.

2000
Widespread floods wreak havoc in Mozambique.

2002
Peace is restored in Angola after almost 30 years of civil war.

2003
Fighting breaks out in the Darfur region of western Sudan.

2008
Zimbabwean dictator Robert Mugabe is voted out by his people, but refuses to acknowledge the results of the election.

2010
Drought causes a major famine in the Sahel region south of the Sahara Desert.

Africa's Nightmare

Around 70 percent of the world's AIDS sufferers are in Africa, and nearly 15 million African children have lost parents to the disease. Families and whole communities have been devastated. Developing countries are further held back by war and civil unrest. Famine has been a recurrent problem, made worse by political conflict, as in Sudan and Somalia, or by tyranny, as in Zimbabwe.

A US soldier helps Rwandan Hutu refugees in the Democratic Republic of the Congo, 1994.

Genocide in Rwanda

In April 1994, Rwandan dictator General Juvénal Habyarimana was killed when his plane was shot down by rebels. His Hutu people turned on the smaller Tutsi population. The two ethnic groups had been at odds for decades, but now violence broke out on an unprecedented scale – almost a million people were killed. Hundreds of thousands more from both ethnic groups fled the fighting and became refugees.

Civil War in the Dem. Rep. of the Congo

In 1997, the dictator of Zaire, Joseph-Desiré Mobutu, was expelled by the rebel army of Laurent Kabila. Kabila restored the nation's earlier name, the Democratic Republic of the Congo, but peace was shortlived. His former allies, Rwanda and Uganda, turned against him. At stake were some of Africa's richest mineral reserves. By the time it ended in 2003, the fighting had claimed more lives than any conflict since the Second World War.

In Zimbabwe, veterans of the 1970s independence struggle have become members of President Robert Mugabe's paramilitary forces.

Left: This "wanted" poster was issued by the US government. It offered a reward for the capture of Rwandan killers.

A scene from a 310-foot-long (95-m-long) mural near the airport in Maputo, Mozambique, depicting the civil war.

Re-Building Ravaged Lands

Mozambique, Angola, Sierra Leone, Liberia, Côte d'Ivoire... All these African countries were, until recently, being torn apart by civil war. Such conflicts left millions dead or injured. Often children were recruited as soldiers in the fighting. Economic development has suffered because of the fighting, and roads, railways and port facilities have been destroyed. Recovery is likely to take many years.

WAR IN DARFUR

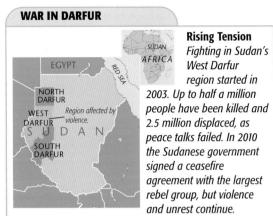

Rising Tension

Fighting in Sudan's West Darfur region started in 2003. Up to half a million people have been killed and 2.5 million displaced, as peace talks failed. In 2010 the Sudanese government signed a ceasefire agreement with the largest rebel group, but violence and unrest continue.

Rock star and outspoken fundraiser Bono talks with President Bush about his aid package to Africa.

International Aid

Aid is not always as helpful as it sounds. In many of the poorest countries of Africa, the aid received has failed to promote development. The providing country may not have development as its goal, but may seek to achieve peace, fight drugs or terrorism, or promote its own culture. The US is known to reward countries that introduce democratic reforms with aid packages.

China: The Market Revolution

During the 1990s, under the leadership of Premier Deng Xiaoping, China's market-based economic reforms (begun in 1978) began to have a real impact on the economy. Many state-owned enterprises were either restructured or closed down. With 1.3 billion people turning to Capitalism, China's rapid economic rise seemed unstoppable, but there were problems with developing a "free market" economy while political freedoms were limited. China faces both the possibility of increased global power and the tensions of internal development (see pages 226–227).

Hong Kong is Returned to China
The British colony of Hong Kong was only leased from China, so it was always due for "return" to the mainland in 1997. While it formally became part of the Communist state, China adopted a "One Country, Two Systems" policy, which maintained Capitalism in the offshore islands.

Economic Reforms
Before introducing economic reforms to the whole of China, Deng Xiaoping first tested them in the southern region of Guangdong (Canton). Doing a U-turn on established Communist policies, he encouraged new businesses, reduced taxation and restricted state interference. In 1992, on a tour of the south, Deng saw how successful his reforms had been, and so he promoted them to the rest of China. Foreign firms were encouraged to invest, and Chinese entrepreneurs were praised, not denounced, for setting up new businesses.

In 1992, Beijing's first McDonald's, the largest in the world, opened to customers. By 2002, China had nearly 400 McDonald's outlets.

IIn 2010, China had an estimated 420 million Internet users, but harsh government censorship (known as the Great Firewall of China) restricts what people can view on-line.

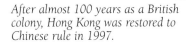

After almost 100 years as a British colony, Hong Kong was restored to Chinese rule in 1997.

Freedom of Ideas
Although successful reforms were made to China's economy, political repression continued. In the 21st century, China's new and fast-growing middle classes are well-paid, and can spend their money on a bewildering range of goods. But the limitations of life in a one-party state may make them increasingly frustrated with their government.

CHINA: THE MARKET REVOLUTION

1992
Deng Xiaoping promotes his economic reforms to the whole of China.

1994
Construction of the Three Gorges Dam begins.

1997
China takes back control of Hong Kong from Britain.

1998
Flooding along the Yangtze River kills over 3,000 people and leaves 14 million homeless.

2001
China joins the World Trade Organization (WTO).

2003
The Shenzhou V spacecraft carries the first Chinese astronaut (taikonaut) into orbit around the Earth.

2005
A special version of the Internet search-engine Google made for China.

2008
Olympic Games in Beijing.

2010
Shanghai Expo celebrates "next great world city."

China's Shenzhou VI spacecraft and Long March 2F rocket blast off on 12 October 2005 in China's second manned space mission. In 2008, Shenzhou VII's taikonauts performed spacewalks.

Flagship Projects

The Beijing Olympics (2008) and the Shanghai Expo (2010) showed Chinese excellence to the world. China has many new projects, including its ambitious space program. In 2003, China became the third country in the world to send a human into space. It plans to complete its first space station and manned Moon mission by 2024.

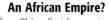

An African Empire?

China first began to invest in Africa during the Cold War. By the 21st century, business was soaring—it did more than $175 million worth in 2005 alone. By 2006 China had overtaken the World Bank as a lender to African governments. But its no-questions-asked approach to some of the continent's most oppressive regimes has caused mounting concern in the West.

A Chinese foreman directs a local laborer in Guinea-Bissau—a country with no oil and little industry.

The Three Gorges Dam, shown above under construction, blocks the flow of the Yangtze River, once home to the now extinct Yangtze River dolphin (right).

Ecological Implications

In 2007, just a few years after the construction of the Three Gorges Dam on the Yangtze River, the extinction of the Yangtze River dolphin was announced. Before China began to industrialize, the river was home to thousands of these freshwater dolphins, but mass shipping, overfishing and pollution have wiped out an entire evolutionary line of mammals. While many countries have criticised this environmental damage, Chinese officials have noted that China is only seeking the development pursued by other nations in the last century.

India and Pakistan

On the flag of the Tamil Tigers, the tiger represents agressiveness, the guns armed force.

Tamil Terror

India's Congress president and former prime minister, Rajiv Gandhi, was assassinated in 1991 by Sri Lanka's Tamil Tigers. They were angry at India's support for the Sri Lankan government, which they felt represented only the majority Sinhalese population. Pioneers of suicide bombing, the Tamil Tigers have fought relentlessly, hoping to create a breakaway Tamil state.

A Hindu stands defiant on the site of Ayodhya's demolished Babri Mosque.

Rivalry between India's Hindus and Muslims led to India being divided into separate countries (India, West Pakistan and East Pakistan, later Bangladesh) at Partition in 1947. The majority of India's Muslims moved to their new homelands. But tension has persisted between the two religious groups. India blames Pakistan for promoting Islamic terrorist attacks in India. There have also been long-running separatist disputes in Assam and Kashmir.

Communal Violence

Built in the 16th century, the Babri Mosque in Ayodhya, India, was sacred to India's Muslims and was an important historical monument. In 1992, however, following a prearranged plan, 150,000 Hindus converged on the building and demolished it stone by stone, believing it to have been built on top of an earlier Hindu shrine. Violence broke out between Muslims and Hindus in towns and cities across India, and more than 3,000 people were killed in the fighting.

INDIA AND PAKISTAN

1993
Benazir Bhutto Pakistan's prime minister for the second time.

1999
From May to July, the Kargil War is fought in Kashmir between India and Pakistan.

1998
Pakistan successfully tests its nuclear weapon, the "Islamic Bomb."

2002
Nuclear confrontation between India and Pakistan over Kashmir.

2004
Manmohan Singh first Sikh prime minister of India.

2007
July: Occupied by Islamic militants, Islamabad's Red Mosque is stormed by Pakistani security forces after a week-long siege. December 27: Benazir Bhutto is assassinated.

2013
Nawaz Sharif 18th prime minister of Pakistan.

Nuclear Nightmare

India acquired nuclear weapons as early as 1974, Pakistan in 1998. Four years later, a nuclear stand-off over Kashmir caused Asia and the world to hold its breath. Since then, the arms race has continued. Pakistan has a much smaller population and military manpower than India, and is comparatively weak in conventional weapons, but is thought more likely than India to resort first to the use of nuclear weapons.

A demonstrator in Karachi with a replica nuclear missile. Being a member of the "nuclear club" is a matter of Islamic pride to Pakistan.

Power Struggle in Pakistan

During the 1990s, power in Pakistan passed between Nawaz Sharif's Pakistan Muslim League (PML) and Benazir Bhutto's Pakistan People's Party (PPP). Bhutto's Westernized, secular outlook appealed internationally, but she repeatedly faced charges of corruption. Sharif, meanwhile, was criticized for his handling of the Kargil War (see map). Following Pakistan's defeat in the war, army Chief of Staff Pervez Musharraf mounted a coup. Both Bhutto and Sharif went into exile. They returned in 2007, after Musharraf promised free elections, but Sharif was arrested on corruption charges and Benazir Bhutto was assassinated. Sharif was returned to power as prime minister in 2013.

Benazir Bhutto, seen here at a PPP election rally in Rawalpindi campaigning for the restoration of democracy. As she left the rally on 27 December 2007, she was assassinated.

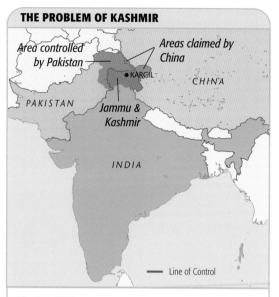

THE PROBLEM OF KASHMIR

Area controlled by Pakistan — Areas claimed by China — KARGIL — CHINA — PAKISTAN — Jammu & Kashmir — INDIA — Line of Control

The Kargil War

At Partition, Kashmir's maharajah (prince) wanted his princely state of Jammu and Kashmir to belong to India, but the largely Muslim population wanted it to be part of Pakistan. A long and bitter separatist struggle followed, and in 1999 war broke out between India and Pakistan in the Kargil region. India, backed by international diplomatic support, forced Pakistan to retreat behind the Line of Control.

The southern city of Bangalore is lit up in 2003 with signs of India's new wealth. But in rural areas, millions still face poverty.

India's Booming Economy

As the 1990s began, India was poor and underdeveloped. Then the government liberalized the economy, cutting taxes and bureaucracy. Soon India was second only to China in terms of economic growth. A new, wealthy middle class was created. In 2000, only 3 million Indians used mobile phones; by 2010, the figure was 525 million. Building for the future, India produces 750,000 engineering graduates a year—many times the figure for Europe and the United States combined.

Colombia's National Police Elite Force search for drug activities in Pablo Escobar's territory, 1990.

Drug Wars

Of all the deaths recorded in the Colombian city of Medellín in 1991, 42 percent were murders. The country was being destroyed by its drug "cartels." But the authorities fought back, and in 1993 drugs boss Pablo Escobar was killed. Five years later, "Plan Colombia" was launched—a major offensive (with US backing) to tackle the cocaine producers.

Argentina in Crisis

At the end of the 20th century, Argentina was facing a major economic crisis. After a decade of mounting debts, by 1989 inflation had reached 3,000 percent. During the 1990s, foreign debt, rampant corruption (e.g. tax evasion) and high unemployment made things worse. By 2001 people were panicking. Many withdrew their money from the banks, which then faced bankruptcy. So the government froze all bank accounts, and thousands of middle-class families lost all their savings.

South America in Turmoil

"Poor old Mexico," lamented Mexico's president, Porfirio Díaz, a century ago: "So far from God, so close to the United States." All Latin American countries have to balance their relationship with their giant neighbor to the north against nationalist policies. Today Venezuela is an example of a country opposing the political leadership of America; Brazil, on the other hand, maintains co-operation with the US.

A campaign poster of Fujimori is carried through a Peruvian shantytown to an electoral rally in April 2000. Fujimori gained much support in Peru's poorest areas.

Fujimori's Peru

The Sendero Luminoso guerrillas promised Peru a "shining path" to a revolutionary future. In reality they caused the deaths of thousands of innocent people. After years of terror, they were defeated by the authorities under Japanese-Peruvian president, Alberto Fujimori. But Fujimori's official crackdown itself involved serious human-rights abuses.

Lula addresses a 2002 presidential election rally in Rio de Janeiro, Brazil. He won the election, and four years later was re-elected as president.

Middle-class Argentines protest at bank closures in 2002. The banner reads: "Robber banks, give us back our dollars!"

A Reasonable Revolutionary

President of Brazil from 2003 to 2010, Luiz Inácio Lula da Silva spoke up for his country's poor, but he was not a fiery revolutionary. "Each day, even if we advance a centimeter, we are going forward," he said. Rather than break with the Americans and international business, Lula made efforts to work with them and brought about a slow but steady improvement in the conditions of his people. He was followed by Dilma Rousseff, Brazil's first woman president, who took office on 1 January 2011.

Chávez: A Threat to Democracy?

Venezuela's president Hugo Chávez walked a fine line between democracy and tyranny. He was popular with the poor, whom he helped with social programs funded by Venezuela's oil wealth. They elected him as president in 1998. After that, he shut down newspapers and TV stations that were critical of him. In 2002, his enemies overthrew him by force (allegedly with US backing), but he was triumphantly returned to power by the people. He remained president until his death in 2013.

In 1998, a woman waits for a bus—and, says the graffiti, for "a Venezuela without corrupt leaders."

The Peasant President: Evo Morales and Bolivia

Evo Morales, who belongs to the Aymara ethnic group, is the first indigenous head of state in South America. He was elected president in 2005. Morales has campaigned to allow Bolivia's coca growers to continue growing their traditional crop for religious and medicinal purposes. Coca, he argues, is not cocaine. The UN regards even its traditional use as illegal. Morales has also campaigned for the nationalization of Bolivia's oil and natural gas. Multinational companies, he claimed, were taking all the profits.

Bolivia takes a firm line on illicit drug production. Here a cocaine factory is set on fire by soldiers from the Bolivian special forces in 2006.

Asia in Adversity

The 1990s began with the nations of east Asia prospering—they were described as having "tiger economies" (economies with rapid growth rates). But a series of setbacks, including a major financial crash in 1997 and various natural disasters, forced the Asian people to call upon all their resources of endurance and determination. The region gradually recovered, with most countries returning to their previous levels of growth and prosperity.

Singapore weathered the financial storm of 1997 more successfully than the other Asian "tigers." Within a year its recovery had begun.

ASIA IN ADVERSITY

1991
Military coup in Thailand.

1993
Kim Young-sam becomes South Korea's first civilian president for 30 years.

1994
North Korean dictator Kim Il Sung is succeeded by his son Kim Jong Il.

1997
Asian financial crisis.

1998
Unrest prompts Indonesian dictator Suharto to step down.

2000
Thaksin Shinawatra's Thai Rak Thai Party comes to power in Bangkok.

2001
Philippines president Joseph Estrada resigns on corruption charges.

2006
A military coup overthrows the Thai government.

2011
Supreme leader of North Korea Kim Jong-il dies.

2013
North Korean dictator Kim Jong-un declares the US the "sworn enemy of the Korean people," and menaces preemptive nuclear attack.

Waiting for Freedom

Myanmar (Burma's new name since 1989) has been ruled since the 1960s by a succession of military governments. In 1990 elections were held, but the military promptly overturned the results and resumed their reign, defying sanctions imposed by the European Union and the United States. In 2007, the government abolished fuel subsidies, which caused massive price rises for consumers. Widespread unrest followed, and thousands of monks took to the streets of Rangoon and Mandalay in anti-government protests.

Fuel price rises triggered the unrest of 2007 in Myanmar, but soon people grew more ambitious in their demands. Buddhist monks led the call for an end to military rule.

Aung San Suu Kyi's quiet courage has awed the world.

Aung San Suu Kyi

Aung San Suu Kyi won the election in Myanmar in 1990, but the military refused to acknowledge her as prime minister. She then spent most of her life under house arrest, until she was released in 2010. She was awarded the Nobel Peace Prize in 1991. She is now head of the National League for Democracy in Burma.

The Tigers Tamed

South Korea, Singapore, Malaysia, Indonesia, Thailand, Hong Kong, Taiwan—in the 1990s these countries were known as the "tiger economies." In 1997, however, following a currency crisis in Thailand, a wholesale collapse in business confidence took place. So severe was the crisis that for a while a world recession was feared, but this did not materialize, and the "tigers" soon began to recover.

Thaksin Shinawatra greets fans of Manchester City, the English football club he owned in 2007–2008. The Thais saw his more ruthless side.

Ups and Downs for Democracy

In 1991, Thailand's government was overthrown in a military coup. Protests were put down with great bloodshed in the "Black May" of 1992. Civilian government was restored five months later, and survived the financial crisis of 1997. In 2001, Thaksin Shinawatra was elected president. His clampdown on the drug trade worked, but at a considerable cost to human rights. Thaksin Shinawatra was toppled by the military in 2006. Political unrest continued into 2014, with a succession of governments, large popular protests, and harsh military crackdowns.

Right: A North Korean boy scrabbles in the dirt for scraps of food.

A Place Apart: North Korea

North Korea is a Communist country that for decades has been governed by repressive dictators: first Kim Il Sung then, from 1994–2011, his son Kim Jong Il, followed by his son Kim Jong-un. The highly secretive government's aim was to turn the country into a self-sufficient industrialized state. In 1995, a three-year famine broke out, affecting possibly more than 2 million people. In 2007 Kim Jong Il agreed to halt his nuclear weapons program in return for US aid, but in 2009 resumed enriching uranium.

In the Shadow of Suharto

Comprising over 17,000 islands, and hundreds of different peoples, Indonesia was for decades held together by the authority of its dictators. Its founder, Sukarno, inspired loyalty, but his successor, Suharto, enforced it through sheer terror, savagely repressing political dissent and separatist movements. Although Suharto resigned in 1998, after the financial crash, Indonesia's ethnic tensions have continued.

Indonesia's Chinese celebrate their New Year—and the departure of Suharto—in January 2000. This was their first public celebration after 32 years of oppression.

Americans, though deeply disconcerted by the 9/11 attacks, drew inspiration from the heroic rescue-workers.

The Age of Terror

Groups like the Irish Republican Army (IRA) and Spain's Basque separatists (ETA) conducted campaigns of bombing and shooting in the 1970s and 80s. But the 9/11 attacks in the United States in 2001 opened up a new and unprecedented age of terror. A community of Islamic radicals, not based nationally but linked by modern phone and Internet communications, seemed to represent a truly global threat.

In the past, terrorists such as this attacked local, small-scale targets. Now they think globally.

The 9/11 Attacks

Carefully planned and ruthlessly executed, the attacks of 11th September (9/11 in the US dating system), 2001, shocked the world. Two hijacked airliners crashed into the twin towers of the World Trade Center in New York. The towers collapsed, killing more than 3,000 office workers. A third plane hit the Pentagon, the US defence headquarters in Washington DC, and a fourth plane crashed in the countryside after its brave passengers overpowered their Islamic hijackers.

Bush's War on Terror

President George W. Bush responded to the 9/11 attacks by declaring a "War on Terror", to be fought worldwide, potentially over many years. His critics argued that terror was a concept, not a country on which war could be declared, and that the "terrorist" label would be attached to anything of which the US did not approve.

To demonstrate its resolve to fight "terror" in the wake of the 9/11 attacks, the US called-up its reserve units, including these Marines, to active duty.

Osama bin Laden and the Post-9/11 Attacks

After 9/11, Osama bin Laden, the mastermind behind the attacks, was believed to be hiding in the mountains between Afghanistan and Pakistan. The arch-terrorist continued to release video statements against the West, while his followers committed further atrocities. Over 200 people died, 164 of them young Western tourists, in the Bali nightclub bombing of 2002. Further attacks were made on Madrid in 2004 and London in 2005. He was finally killed by US soldiers at his compound in Pakistan in 2011.

Osama bin Laden (1957–2011), sought the withdrawal of US and allied military forces from Muslim countries.

Guantánamo

Guantánamo is a US naval base on the coast of Communist Cuba. The US are using it as a camp in which to imprison terrorist suspects indefinitely. The suspects are branded "enemy combatants," and the US claims that they are not entitled to the rights accorded either to convicted criminals or prisoners of war. President Obama promisd to close the camp in 2009 but at the end of 2013 there were still 155 detainees in the camp.

In January 2008, fresh demands were made in the US for the closure of the Guantánamo camp and the restoration of fair trials.

Moral Cost?

After 9/11, America introduced new laws to tackle the terrorist threat. The Patriot Act gave agencies sweeping powers of search and surveillance, and the right to detain people on suspicion. Britain brought in similar laws, despite opposition from those who felt the West was betraying the principles of freedom for which it claims to stand. Alarming reports suggested that suspects were being secretly shipped to Uzbekistan and Algeria for interrogation under torture.

Increased fears of terrorist attacks have boosted demand for "disaster assistance robots" such as this one, which can go into unsafe areas to try to detect victims and test for bio-weapons.

Four suicide bombers struck in central London on "7/7"—7th July, 2005. Rescue workers helped victims at Aldgate Station, below, following an explosion on a tube train. What most shocked Britons was the fact that the bombers were British-born members of the UK's Pakistani community.

On 26 November 2008 a terrorist group in Mumbai struck in ten different places at the same time. Armed with Kalashnikov submachine guns, hand grenades, and a car bomb, their targets included the Chhatrapati Railway Station, the Oberoi (in the photograph below) and the Taj Mahal and a Jewish study center.

THE AGE OF TERROR

1993
Terrorist bomb explodes under the World Trade Center, New York, killing six and injuring over 1,000.

1996
The IRA breaks 17-month ceasefire, bombing London's Canary Wharf.

2001
9/11 attacks on New York and Washington, DC.

2002
On Bali, Indonesia, Islamic terrorists bomb a nightclub.

2004
191 people are killed when commuter trains are bombed in Madrid, Spain.

2005
Islamic extremists carry out the 7 July suicide bombings in London, UK.

2007
Failed car-bomb attack on Scotland's Glasgow Airport.

2008
Muslim extremists kill 474 people in a series of attacks in Mumbai.

2010
Times Square car bombing attempt foiled.

2013
Boston marathon bombings kill 3 and injure 183 others.

2013
British soldier Lee Rigby hacked to death with cleavers by Islamic extremists in London street.

Global Entertainment

The years after the Cold War saw the entertainment industry transformed as mass-culture gained a truly worldwide audience. Advances in technology meant that simple video games such as Space Invaders made way for an explosion of multi-million-selling, virtual-reality computer games, while music and movies could be downloaded on to portable, personalized players for enjoyment as and when required. With such huge audiences, stars of the entertainment world became globally famous.

Ugandan musicians at a WOMAD festival in 2008 play the embaire, a traditional instrument of their country.

World Music

Ever since the rock 'n' roll era of the 1950s and '60s, US and British pop music had been popular around the world. By the 1990s, though, musicians in developing countries wanted to show what they could do in their own styles and traditions—and Western audiences were eager to find out. CD sales soared and young people flocked to see and hear international artists at WOMAD (World of Music, Arts and Dance) events.

Blockbuster Books

Even as commentators prophesied the "death of the book", J.K. Rowling's *Harry Potter* series (1997 to 2007) and Dan Brown's *The Da Vinci Code* (2003) were being eagerly read by millions. Lavish marketing campaigns and film adaptations gave a huge boost to sales. The first decade of the 21st century saw book sales expand particularly fast among teenagers (sales of teen books were up by a quarter between 1999 and 2005), as libraries and publishers increasingly used the Internet to promote books. Young adult literature has become a global phenomenon.

All over the world, tens of thousands of young fans dressed the part for the launch of the last title in the Harry Potter *series in July 2007. Some 11 million copies were sold in the first 24 hours.*

Highest-grossing Films

From the 1990s, extravagant productions, high-tech special effects and relentless marketing enabled Hollywood to make greater profits than ever before with its blockbusters. *Titanic* (1997), for example, made over $1.8 billion worldwide. But more off-beat films saw huge success, too. The Chinese thriller *Crouching Tiger, Hidden Dragon* (2000) packed in audiences worldwide.

Jurassic Park took cinemas by storm in 1993.

Steven Spielberg directs a scene from Jurassic Park.

The French film Amélie *was the surprise hit of 2001.*

The world's press eagerly reports every action of celebrity icon and fashion designer Victoria Beckham.

The Maracanã stadium, Rio de Janeiro (right). Brazil hosted the World Cup in 2014.

Sporting Spectaculars

The great sporting events such as the World Cup and the Olympic Games are watched by billions on TV. People all over the world become football-crazy during the World Cup, even if their country is not taking part. They want to be part of the global phenomenon created by clever branding and marketing. Countries compete with one another to play host. London hosted the Olympic Games in 2012, while it is Rio De Janiero's turn in 2016, and Tokyo's in 2020.

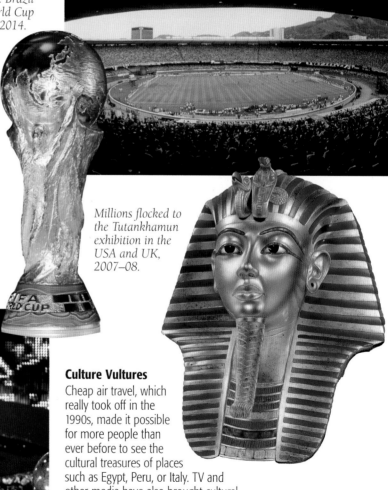

Millions flocked to the Tutankhamun exhibition in the USA and UK, 2007–08.

Cult of Celebrity

The modern age had "stars," revered as actors, singers, or sporting heroes. But post-modernism is fascinated with the surfaces of things rather than impressed by skills or talents. So today we have "celebrities," famous simply for being famous. Soap actors, pop singers, and reality TV contestants live their lives in public, every shopping expedition, sunbathing trip, least sign of cellulite, or drug problem being cruelly reported as news by the media.

The Eurovision Song Contest attracts 300 million TV viewers around the world.

Culture Vultures

Cheap air travel, which really took off in the 1990s, made it possible for more people than ever before to see the cultural treasures of places such as Egypt, Peru, or Italy. TV and other media have also brought cultural events to millions around the globe—from art exhibitions, ballet, and opera on the one hand, to the Eurovision Song Contest on the other.

History is a non-stop process. No-one can tell for sure what will happen next. Surprise events such as the 9/11 terrorist attacks in the USA can at any time change the picture dramatically, out of the blue. Yet around the world, many thousands of experts earn their living by seeking to predict future trends, in everything from the weather to the state of the global economy.

This chapter draws on their predictions and the computer models they draw up to examine some likely developments and to sketch out the major challenges that lie ahead. The first part looks at the major forces currently working to shape the planet and the lives of coming generations. The second half considers the outlook for each of the world's main regions.

Maori children are taught their traditional language and culture by their elders.

TIMELINE

	2005	2006	2007		2008
NORTH, CENTRAL AND SOUTH AMERICA	Hurricane Katrina devastates New Orleans, USA. Evo Morales is the first Native American president of Bolivia.	Evo Morales nationalizes Bolivia's natural gas fields.	President Bush authorizes a troop surge to combat the continuing insurgency in Iraq.	The US plans to expand its missile defenses into Eastern Europe.	The Phoenix mission lands on Mars in search of microbial life.
EUROPE	The European Space Agency launches Venus Express, which is currently orbiting Venus.		Romania and Bulgaria become members. of the European Union.		The 2009 G8 Summit is due to be held in Italy.
RUSSIA		Russia and China agree a deal on the future supply of Russian gas to China.	In St. Petersburg, riot police (left) break up protests by demonstrators accusing President Putin of stifling democracy.		
ASIA AND OCEANIA	In India, Sri Lanka and other countries, aid begins to reach the survivors of the tsunami that struck in December 2004.		Mumbai, India, has an estimated 24 million people in the city and its suburbs.		Beijing hosts the 2008 Summer Olympic Games.
THE MIDDLE EAST			The UN refugee agency (UNHCR) estimates that there are 1.9 million displaced Iraqis in Iraq and over 2 million in neighboring Middle Eastern countries.		The Middle East controls 66 percent of global oil reserves (estimate from the Institute for the Analysis of Global Security).
AFRICA	The Sudanese government signs a peace treaty with rebel groups, but violence continues in Darfur.	Twenty-two countries south of the Sahara are still contaminated by landmines.			
GLOBAL	The Human Genome Project produces a 92-percent complete version of the human genome sequence.	There are estimated to be over 1 billion internet users.	Vietnam is the 150th nation to join the World Trade Organization.		

Issues Today

The Times Square, New York, headquarters of Lehman Brothers. The September 2008 bankruptcy of the fourth largest US investment bank led a meltdown of many more firms.

A Chinese farmer transports vegetables to market in a homemade cart. The prosperity of China's cities has not fed through to the hundreds of millions of people living off the land.

2014	PROJECTIONS:	2020	2025	2050

In 2011, NASA plans to launch the Juno mission to Jupiter (left), arriving in 2016. Messenger is scheduled to go into orbit around Mercury.

The USA plans a manned mission to the Moon by 2020.

In the USA, non-Hispanic whites will represent about 50 percent of the total population (projection by the U.S. Census Bureau).

The 2016 Summer Olympic Games are to be hosted by Rio De Janiero, Brazil.

The European Space Agency hopes to put astronauts on Mars (left) by 2024.

2018 World Cup to be hosted by Russia.

China's government has pledged to keep the population under 1.36 billion by 2010, and under 1.45 billion by 2020.

By 2020, China's gross national product (GNP) is expected to have exceeded the GNP of all Western countries except the USA's. India's GNP will have overtaken (or will be close to overtaking) European economies.

Unless 2007 trends are changed, in 2025 China is set to overtake the USA as the biggest producer of greenhouse gases.

The Arab Spring uprisings begin in North Africa. Civil War in Libya, and then in Syria.

By 2020, the Middle East will control 83 percent of global oil reserves (estimate from the Institute for the Analysis of Global Security).

At the United Nations Millennium Summit in 2000, 189 world leaders made the historic promise to "end poverty by 2015."

World population is projected to be 8 billion.

World population may by now have reached 9 billion.

By 2017, global temperatures may have risen by 0.2°.

Our Changing World

Portable media players such as the iPod make music available anywhere.

This may just be the most exciting time to be alive, ever. Thanks to technological advances, we have greater power than ever before over the world in which we live. In the developed nations at least, people are living longer, fuller lives. Yet there are dangers, too, in the new human potential. If we apply it unwisely, we could end up harming the planet irreversibly.

A medical researcher investigates a recently-discovered virus in the hope of developing a vaccine to combat its effects.

Exciting Times

The 21st century could be a golden age. There are more people alive today than ever before and a greater number are living long and healthy lives, with better education, and a higher standard of living than in previous times. But this places an ever-greater strain on the resources of our planet, so there are harsh new stresses to confront as the world around us becomes more complex and challenging.

Expanding Our Horizons

Technological advances are transforming our daily lives, making travel easier, simplifying housework, and providing non-stop access to entertainment and culture in many different formats. Yet the biggest change may still be growing computerization. The Information Age is still in its early days, and a lot of its applications are yet to come.

The Power of Science

In recent times, science has given us awesome new powers, and the pace of change just keeps getting quicker. Last century scientists learned to split the atom and put humans on the Moon. Now they are unravelling the secrets of the genetic code, giving us the ability to interfere in the processes of life itself. Used wisely, that knowledge could fight disease and aging, improving lifestyles around the globe. Put to the wrong uses, it could create monsters.

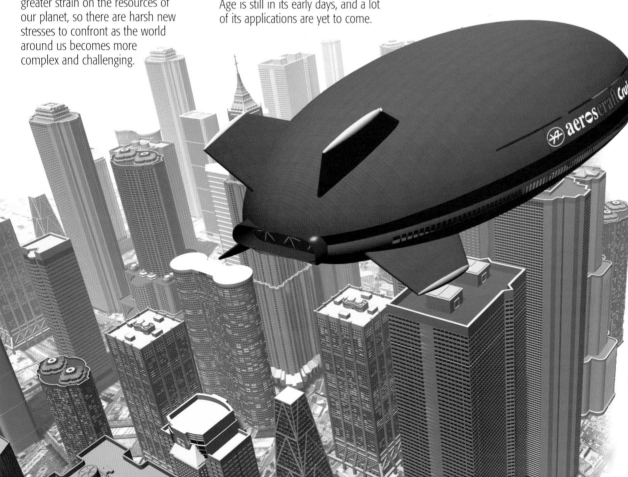

Shown here in an artist's impression is the Aeroscraft, a series of cargo-carrying airships planned for release soon. The futuristic airship uses a combination of helium gas and lift from its propellers to cruise economically and quietly through the skies.

Green Living

No-one now doubts that human activities are profoundly affecting the planet; we are depleting its resources and causing the climate to warm up. Few people want to give up any of the benefits that modern technology and an advanced standard of living can bring. But in an increasingly crowded world, if we want to safeguard the Earth's future, we may have to give up some of our comforts, learn to avoid waste, make the best use of our resources, conserve energy, and live in an eco-friendly way.

Familiarly known as "the Gherkin," London's Swiss Re building—the first skyscraper built in the UK capital after 1980—is energy-friendly, making use of natural light and ventilation.

Responsible for the Planet

People's growing power to shape the planet brings with it huge responsibilities. The more we learn about the Earth's ecosystems, the more we realize that they are interconnected—and sometimes surprisingly fragile. As booming population growth and spiralling energy demands create new stresses, we may have to be prepared to make sacrifices to ease the burden. Otherwise, at the very worst, we could make the planet unlivable—or even blow ourselves up.

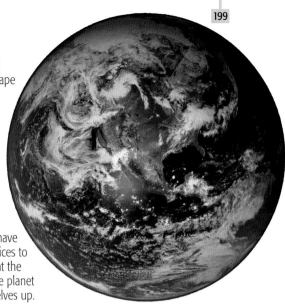

With the expansion of scientific knowledge, world leaders have been forced to take on new responsibilities as guardians and protectors of planet Earth.

Looking Beyond Earth

The Space Age is only 50 years old, and vast new horizons still glimmer. Unmanned probes provide ground-breaking information about the Solar System, while space-based telescopes let scientists spy on distant galaxies. A day may come when people will choose to work and maybe even live in artificially created environments beyond the Earth's surface.

As imagined by a NASA artist, future space explorers use a manned vehicle to explore Mars. The European Space Agency hopes to put astronauts on the planet by 2024.

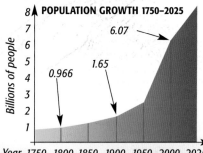

More people around the world means less space for each one. As the number of people grows, wilderness areas shrink.

A World Full to the Brim

The world is more crowded than it has ever been, and it is getting fuller by the minute. Thanks to improved healthcare and better nutrition, more people are living longer than in the past. Pregnant women are also better cared for now than they were in the past, and fewer babies die at birth or in infancy. The good news is that more people around the world can expect to lead long, healthy lives. The challenge in future years will be to provide enough food, water, jobs, and homes for everyone as the world's population continues to grow.

World Population Today

According to the United Nations the world's population reached 7 billion—that's 7,000,000,000 (7,000 million) people on 31 October 2011. Each year the figure increases, and experts predict that by 2060 there will be nearly 10 billion people on the planet. That means billions more mouths to feed, jobs to create, and houses to build.

POPULATION GROWTH 1750–2025

The world's population grew in the 1800s, but the big rise came after 1950 as standards of healthcare improved in less developed regions.

Population Explosion

World population is soaring. Some scientists argue that overpopulation will lead to famine and disease, which will reduce the population again. But both famine and disease result from poverty rather than high population density.

REGIONAL POPULATION GROWTH

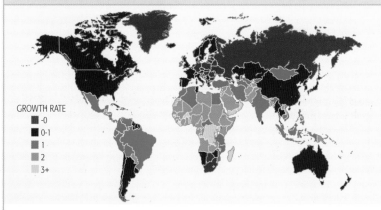

GROWTH RATE
- -0
- 0-1
- 1
- 2
- 3+

Sparse and Crowded Regions

The population is growing at different rates around the world. The biggest increase is in Africa and parts of Asia. In some, mainly northern, regions the population is actually falling. The countries with the highest population growth rates tend to be among the poorest, and have the fewest jobs to offer their new citizens.

Growth rate in percent, as listed in CIA factbook.

Daily Rise in Numbers

The population is currently increasing at a rate of over 200,000 people every day. Experts reckon it will continue to grow at least until the year 2050, although the rate of growth is slowing down. Figures show that mothers in rich countries have fewer children than those in less developed countries, so the best hope for world population numbers is that the rate of growth will fall as the world becomes wealthier. In some European countries there are even worries about falling population numbers.

Throughout the world mothers regularly have their babies weighed, as babies with lower-than-average weights may need special care to ensure their survival.

Living in Peace

Even in the most crowded parts of the world, most people live with their neighbors in peace. Dangers arise when one group of people believes, rightly or wrongly, that it is being treated unjustly by others. In such circumstances, a growing population can mean growing tensions. A major problem people face today is working out how to reduce pressures in crowded areas. The world's only global peacekeeping body, the United Nations, has limited powers.

A wall now separates Israelis from Palestinians who live in lands captured by Israel in 1967, on the West Bank of the river Jordan.

The Hong Kong skyline suggests what a crowded world might look like as more and more people flock to the cities to find jobs.

Making Room for Lots of People

More people to be housed means less space for each one. There are already reckoned to be at least 40 megalopolises (cities with over 5 million people): nine in China, six in India, only one (New York) in North America, and one (London) in western Europe. The increasing number of mouths to feed means that more wilderness land is farmed for food, putting pressure on wild animals, who risk losing their living space.

A Global Economy

Coffee is in high demand in developed countries. To meet the demand, some growers in developing countries use unpaid child labor. Other growers sell their coffee as a Fair Trade product, which guarantees them a fair deal.

Child Labor

Campaigners against globalization sometimes highlight the problem of child labor, which is still common in many developing countries. One recent report puts the numbers involved at 180 million—one in 12 of the world's children. Yet few of the affected young people work in export industries—less than 5 percent, according to a United Nations' report. Many more are employed in agriculture or in street selling. In time the spread of global trade should cut child poverty.

Fair Trade

Launched in Europe in the 1960s, the Fair Trade movement aims to secure a better deal for the poorest workers in world markets. Its backers link up with farmers and other producers to see they get a fair price for their goods. They also work with employers to ensure that their workers enjoy safe and healthy working conditions and do not harm the environment. In recent years the campaign has become big business, giving its seal of approval to goods valued at $5 billion worldwide.

Today's supermarkets source their products from every corner of the globe. Some of the goods in your basket may have been grown locally; others will have been flown in from thousands of miles away.

As improved transport links make the world a smaller place, business has gone global as never before. A single multi-national corporation may employ workers in dozens of different countries and sell its goods in many more. Consumers choose products from all around the world, helping to create jobs in countries they may never have seen. Traders grow rich transporting produce by land, sea, and air and selling it on from shops and warehouses. In theory, everybody benefits—but some people do better than others, and some risk being exploited in the rush for profits.

Organic
Yellow
banana 99¢ lb

2/$3
FRESH
CANTALOUPES
PRODUCE SPECIALS

Jet planes have speeded up links between continents, although most bulk produce is still shipped by sea.

A GLOBAL ECONOMY

6000 BCE
Obsidian is traded widely in the Middle East.

100 CE
Trade flows across Europe under the Roman Empire.

c.650
The Silk Road provides a trade route between China and the West.

c.1520
New trade routes by sea link India and America.

1850
Clipper ships carry trade from China to New York in under 75 days.

1970
Jumbo jets introduce the age of bulk air transport.

1995
The World Trade Organization (WTO) comes into existence.

2008
A severe financial crisis, or credit crunch, hits the global economy.

From China to California

In today's globalized world, a Chinese factory worker may well be making computer parts for use in the Czech Republic or California, while a 'phone call to a local bank in England may be answered from a call center in India. The advantage of outsourcing—sending jobs abroad—is that companies can employ people who are prepared to work for less money than those at home. Workers in the poorer countries benefit by getting jobs that usually pay well by local standards.

Against a backdrop of skyscrapers, one of India's homeless people cooks a meal on an open fire. Wealth from global trading has been slow to trickle down to the world's poor.

Winners and Losers in a Shrinking World

Economists believe widening trade links make the whole world richer. It is true that doing business across international boundaries does create jobs for people who have the skills employers need. Those who do not have these skills, however, can lose out as growing prosperity pushes up prices and raises the cost of living. Whole countries and regions risk getting caught in the poverty trap, without the money to educate their people into employment.

GROSS DOMESTIC PRODUCT

Economic Growth

A map of countries showing Gross Domestic Product (the total value of the goods each country produces) reveals the new economic superpowers of China and India. Brazil and Russia are on the rise. Africa is still behind other continents, but GDP in many African countries is now growing at 6%, faster than most other parts of the world.

US$ BILLION

2000+	1000–2000	500–1000	200–500	100–200
50–100	20–50	10–20	5–10	0–5

Map is based on IMF figures, Purchasing Power Parity (PPP).

Rich and Poor

There are huge gaps between rich and poor countries around the world. The most prosperous nations are now better off than ever before, with car ownership and other signs of wealth surging. Yet some countries have been left behind in the global drive for growth. According to the World Bank, in 2010 1.22 billion people were living on less than $US1.25 a day, and 2.4 billion on under $2.

China and India

The world map of rich and poor nations is changing fast. Between them, China and India are home to one out of every three people on the planet. Both countries are rapidly becoming richer. China today produces six times as much as in 1978, when economic reforms were introduced. India's boom is more recent, but its economy is now growing by leaps and bounds.

High-rise buildings light up the night sky in Shanghai. China is enjoying a dramatic economic boom that has lifted millions of its citizens out of poverty.

An artist performs at a Live 8 concert in 2005. Part of the Make Poverty History campaign, the concerts reached an audience estimated at 3 billion people.

Daily Spending

Developing countries have most of the world's poor. According to recent estimates, there are still at least 10 countries in Africa where most people live on less than $2 a day. In contrast, the average figure for the USA is about $129 (£80) and for Britain $96 (£48).

A rich lady enjoys a glass of wine at a garden party.

New-found Wealth

Over time, poor countries can become rich. In the early 1950s, Japan and South Korea were developing nations with much of the population living below the poverty line. By 2007, both ranked among the top 30 most prosperous nations judged by average income per person.

Poorest and Richest Countries

One way of measuring a country's wealth is to work out how much it earns per person each year. According to International Monetary Fund figures, the richest countries in the world in these terms in 2012 were Qatar, Luxembourg, Singapore, Norway, Brunei, and the USA. In contrast, 24 of the 30 poorest nations, with average incomes below $1,770 (£895), were in Africa.

WORLD HUNGER

DAILY CALORIE INTAKE
more than 3,000   2,000–3,000   less than 2,000

Feeding the Poor

When people are caught in the poverty trap, hunger is a central problem. Even well-off nations can be affected in times of war or famine, but poorer countries are particularly at risk. The greatest concentration of hungry people is in Africa, south of the Sahara Desert. According to United Nations' figures, in the four poorest African countries more than half the population suffers from undernourishment.

Make Poverty History

Campaigners in the developed world have tried to fight poverty by persuading their governments to cancel debts run up by developing nations. They argue that the money put aside to pay off the debts would be better spent on helping poor people in those countries. They had some success in 2005 in encouraging world leaders to announce some debt reductions, but many of the promises made at the time have still to be met. Debt remains a real problem.

Poor Among the Rich

Poverty is not just a problem for developing countries. Some people in rich nations remain poor, too. Even in the USA, a recent study found that one person in 10 is not always sure of being able to afford a healthy meal. Homeless people can be found in many of the world's wealthiest cities, driven onto the streets not just by lack of money, but also by alcoholism, mental illness, or just not being able to get a job. Most developed countries have welfare systems to help the very poor, but some people fall through the net.

A homeless man looks for food scraps in New York City. Poverty is found even in the wealthiest countries.

RICH AND POOR

0 CE
The world's richest countries are India and China, followed by the lands of the Roman Empire.

1000 CE
India and China still lead the way, while Africa also sees a time of wealth.

1600
Spain enjoys a golden age thanks to gold and silver from the Americas.

1870
The British Empire is now the world's economic superpower, replacing China.

1920
The USA takes the lead soon after the end of World War I.

1973
By now the USA accounts for almost a quarter of all world production.

2010
China and Japan have risen to second and third place after the USA in terms of total goods produced.

NOTE
Dates based on estimates by economic historians.

Populations On The Move

People have been on the move ever since prehistoric times. The world would never have been populated if the first humans had not chosen to leave their original home in Africa in search of fresh living space. In recent years, however, the flow of people on the move has increased as travelling has become easier. In 2013 a United Nations report concluded that about 232 million people now live in a country other than the one where they were born. That's about 3.2 percent of world population.

Why People Migrate

Some people are forced to leave their own countries because of religious or political persecution—they risk being tortured or executed if they stay. Many more choose to go because they hope to find a better life abroad, with a job and an improved standard of living. In future years, large numbers may have to move because of climate change, if global warming makes their old homes uninhabitable.

Above: Since the mid 1980s, thousands of miners have moved in to the Amazon rain forest in search of gold. The effects on the traditional way of life of the Yanomami people of Brazil have been devastating.

Winners and Losers

Some parts of the world see their numbers grow through immigration, while others lose people. The most popular destinations for new arrivals are North America, western Europe, and Australia. Regions from which people are leaving include Africa, eastern Europe, Central Asia, and Central and South America. Young people of working age are most likely to emigrate, though these are the people that developing countries can least afford to lose.

Above: First-generation immigrants arriving in Europe often prefer to keep all or part of their traditional dress.

Different worlds come together when a gap-year student visits Sudan.

The Transportation Revolution

People are able to move between countries because traveling has become easier. Even remote regions are now mostly connected to the rest of the world by roads, and air travel between continents is cheaper than ever. For illegal immigrants, though, the journey can be dangerous. Since 1988, more than 10,000 people are thought to have died seeking to enter Europe alone, most of them drowned when the leaky boats carrying them sank.

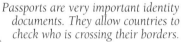

People flock to cities such as Madhapur in the Indian state of Hyderabad, where software companies provide many new jobs.

The Pull of the City

Huge numbers of people around the world are moving within their own country, as well as to different ones. Most travel from villages to the cities, where there are more jobs to be found. In 2010, just over half the world's population lived in cities, up from 13 percent a century before. According to the same UN report, that figure is likely to rise to 60 percent by 2030—an estimated 5 billion people.

French police detain illegal immigrants. Many countries are now debating how many newcomers to allow in, and how best to integrate them into the host society.

Controlling Immigration

According to United Nations rules, people fleeing religious or political persecution in their own countries are refugees and should not be subject to immigration law. However, it is up to individual governments to decide exactly who qualifies as a refugee. Some immigrants are allowed to become full citizens of their new country. Illegal immigrants may be sent back to where they came from.

Unwilling Hosts?

Some countries are more willing than others to accept immigrants. No state in the world currently allows unrestricted movement across its borders. In general, those with free-market economies and democratic governments are most welcoming to immigrants. Yet even those nations sometimes restrict the number allowed in per year or use other means to limit the number of people who can settle there. Once admitted, immigrants may have to take language tests or complete community service programs before they can become full citizens.

Passports are very important identity documents. They allow countries to check who is crossing their borders.

Fear of Immigration

Some migrants are treated unfairly by people in the host country that allows them in. They may be accused of taking work from people born in that country, or of forcing down wages by accepting low pay. Some people in host countries worry that too many immigrants will change their culture and language, or fear overcrowding. Yet immigrants are vital to the economies of most developed countries. They do the jobs other people don't want, and provide some of the basic services on which society depends.

A road sign on the Mexican–US border warns families that they may not enter the USA without permission.

The Information Revolution

In the wake of the agricultural and industrial revolutions, the world now faces a third historic change: the Information Revolution. New digitized media, conveyed through computers over the internet, has transformed how we think, study, work, and have fun. The revolution is still in its early days, and no-one knows exactly how it will shape up. If all goes well, people will be better informed, better educated, and better entertained. If not, we could end up controlled and spied on in a Big Brother society.

Mobile phones and tablets have become everyday accessories.

The Internet

The revolution began with the invention of computers, but really got under way with the spread of internet use in the 1990s. The net is a worldwide grid of interconnected computer networks, giving anyone with a linked computer access to more information than the world's biggest libraries could ever contain. Suddenly anyone can find out almost anything, virtually at the click of a button. But how should we best use the information, and check if it is accurate?

Images taken by press photographers can be digitized and sent around the world in minutes.

Too Much Information?

As internet use spreads around the world, people are becoming more concerned about the content it carries. Some countries such as China use political censorship on the internet to ban minority views. In the West, there are worries about sexually explicit material and information that could be of use to terrorists. Then there is the question of personal privacy. Should we have the right to stop unflattering pictures of ourselves from appearing on the web? And what is the right response to unfair or untrue comments?

New Frontiers for Schooling

Electronic learning is growing around the world. By 2003, almost 2 million students were studying online in the USA alone, and the figure is growing by 25 percent each year. E-learning is particularly useful for people working from home, often far from the schools and colleges that sponsor the courses. But there are drawbacks. Students not only need access to computers; they also must want to learn. Teachers are needed not only to encourage students, but also to assess the results of on-line learning.

The internet can promote education. Here a mother helps her daughter with homework on a laptop computer.

Identity Theft

Increasingly, Western companies are "outsourcing" work to developing countries where the work can be done more cheaply (see pages 230–231). This helps keep their costs down and provides a better income for the workers in the developing countries. But it has led to a new crime—identity theft. More and more people are finding that their personal details have been stolen and used to open bank accounts or obtain credit cards, loans and important documents such as passports. Among those who obtain stolen identities are terrorists, who use them to provide funds to pay for their activities and conceal their whereabouts.

A woman pays for goods by 'phone using her credit card, which contains valuable personal information.

New Ways to Keep in Touch

Between them, e-mails, online chat, video phones, and text messaging have revolutionized the way people keep in touch. It is now possible at any time to see and talk to a loved one travelling on the far side of the world or a business contact living in a different continent. Individuals can have long-distance online friendships with people in distant places whom they would otherwise never have seen. By providing instant connections across the globe, the new media have helped make the world a smaller place. Now the worry is that by spending too much time online, people may be losing the skills of communicating face to face.

"Silver surfers" enjoy exploring the web as a leisure activity. The internet can be vitally important for older people who often live alone, allowing them to stay in touch with family and friends, and ask for help if they need it.

THE INFORMATION REVOLUTION

1943
Scientists at Bletchley Park in England invent the world's first fully electronic computer to crack German military codes.

1946
U.S. engineers J. Presper Eckert and John Mauchly launch ENIAC, the world's first general-purpose computer.

1973
Motorola develops the first US analogue hand-held mobile phone.

1981
IBM puts the Personal Computer (PC) on sale for home computing.

1991
The World Wide Web becomes freely available. Kodak introduces the first commercially available digital camera.

1994
Sony releases the first Playstation in Japan.

2012
There are estimated to be over 2.4 billion internet users worldwide.

The Surveillance Society

One worry about the sheer amount of information now available is that some of it is about us. Security cameras watch us in the streets, computers note everything we download, and computerized records increasingly store details of our lives, from the state of our health to what we buy in shops. Much of this data is used for our welfare. It can reduce crime and enable better medical treatment. In the wrong hands, though, it could become a form of spying, used by the state to keep people in line.

Communications masts are the flagpoles of the Information Age. Some people are concerned that some types of mast may emit microwave emissions that are bad for our health.

Confronting Climate Change

The world's climate has always been changing, but now it is getting warmer at a dangerously fast pace. According to scientists, human activities are at least partly to blame. Unless action is taken, the results are likely to include more extreme weather conditions that will affect much of the globe, expand deserts, and cause sea levels to rise as the polar ice cap melts.

New Forms of Energy

Burning coal and oil—so-called "fossil fuels"—contributes to global warming, so governments are looking to develop cleaner forms of energy. Efforts are being made to put nature itself to use. Wind power is used to generate electricity on wind farms, and the energy from waves can be converted using turbines. Solar power, derived from the Sun's heat and light, is also being widely developed.

Desert Expansion

Global warming may cause less rainfall in some areas already prone to drought. A place particularly at risk is the Sahel region of Africa, on the southern fringes of the Sahara Desert. The amount of rain falling there each year has dropped by a quarter over the past four decades. Further reductions might make it uninhabitable. People who live there may have to seek new homes elsewhere, and this may cause conflict with local people.

Wind turbines capture the natural energy of the wind and use it to generate electricity.

Global warming is causing deserts to expand. People living on their fringes risk starvation.

Reducing Carbon Emissions

Carbon dioxide (CO_2) is released into the atmosphere by human activities, and this is a major cause of global warming. CO_2 and other "greenhouse gases" hold heat in the atmosphere that would otherwise vanish into space. To curb global warming, people need to reduce the amount of CO_2 that they release —their "carbon footprint". CO_2 that has already been released can be captured and stored deep in the earth or under the sea.

Left: This recycling symbol is used worldwide. Recycling can help to limit climate change.

Below: The Sleipner project off the coast of Norway was the world's first commercial CO_2 capture and storage facility. Captured CO_2 is stored in depleted gas reservoirs under the sea.

Recycling Waste

Obtaining the raw materials needed to manufacture goods uses up energy that adds to global warming. Recycling waste can help to reduce the amount of energy we use. Some materials are easier to reuse than others— aluminum, used to make cans, is particularly effective, plastics generally less so. Everyone can help by using recycling facilities and taking glass to bottle banks—always provided that the journey to the recycling center does not use up more energy than it saves.

Aluminium cans are 100 percent recyclable. Each one recycled saves enough energy to power a television set for three hours.

Male, capital of the Maldive Islands, is one of the low-lying cities threatened if sea levels rise.

At Risk from Rising Sea Levels

Global warming is already melting glaciers in Greenland as well as parts of the Antarctic ice sheet. The water released is expected to raise the level of the world's oceans. Estimates of the rise range from 7 to 23 inches (18 to 59 cm). Any sizeable rise could threaten low-lying islands and their inhabitants. It could also cause problems for people living in coastal regions—and many of the world's great cities are located on the oceans' shores.

Industrial Pollution

Industry adds to global warming by spewing greenhouse gases into the atmosphere. A map of the main sources of emissions shows that the heaviest polluter is the United States. Africa and Oceania, which pollute the least, are the places most at risk from climate change.

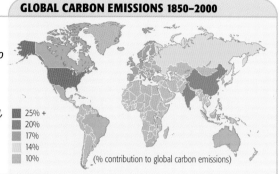

GLOBAL CARBON EMISSIONS 1850–2000

25% +
20%
17%
14%
10%

(% contribution to global carbon emissions)

CLIMATE CHANGE PROJECTIONS

2017
Global temperatures will have risen by 0.2°.

2027
Global temperatures are expected to rise by 0.4°. They will rise by 0.2° even if greenhouse gas emissions remain at year 2000 levels. If greenhouse gas emissions were to stop altogether, the temperature would still rise, as the impact of emissions endures for years after emission.

2100
Temperatures are likely to have risen at best by between 1.1° and 2.9°, at worst by between 2.4° and 6.4°. Sea levels are predicted to rise over the same period at best by between 7–15 inches (18–38 cm), at worst by between 10–23 inches (26 26–59 cm).

Projections are based on findings of the Fourth Assessment Report of the United Nations Intergovernmental Panel on Climate Change, published in 2007. The range of figures reflects different scenarios for climate change fed through computer models.

No creature has more to lose from global warming than the polar bear, the Arctic's top animal predator.

The Natural World at Risk

As people spread across the globe, moving into the last wilderness areas and cultivating ever more land, the space available for animals is shrinking. Forests are cut down, the seas are fished on an industrial scale, and previously marginal lands are used for farming. The result is a growing threat to biodiversity—the huge variety of life forms living on the planet. In future years, climate change may provide a new threat by disturbing traditional patterns of birth, growth and feeding.

Observers survey the Greenland coast for signs of melting ice. Global warming threatens the natural habitat of Arctic species.

Global Warming

The natural world of animals and plants can adapt to gradual climate change, but is likely to have serious difficulty in keeping up with the speed of human-made global warming. Scientists are already seeing changes in animals' behavior as a result of the climate change experienced in the last 10 years. If temperatures rise by significant amounts in the future, some species will be driven from their traditional homes by the altered conditions and may face extinction as a result.

Intrusion into Wild Places

Many wild animals need empty wilderness regions in which to survive. These regions are becoming smaller, however, as the human population increases. Habitats are being lost to farmland and housing developments, and miners and loggers are finding their way into even the most remote areas, such as the Arctic. Both Canada and Russia are claiming Arctic land and sea rights—in 2007 Russia planted its flag on the sea bed under the North Pole. Larger animals are at risk, too, from hunters with high-powered rifles. As new roads cut through the wilderness, animal populations become cut off from one another, further reducing their chances of survival.

Property development along the shoreline, as seen here on Spain's Costa Dorada, threatens coastal species on the shore and at sea.

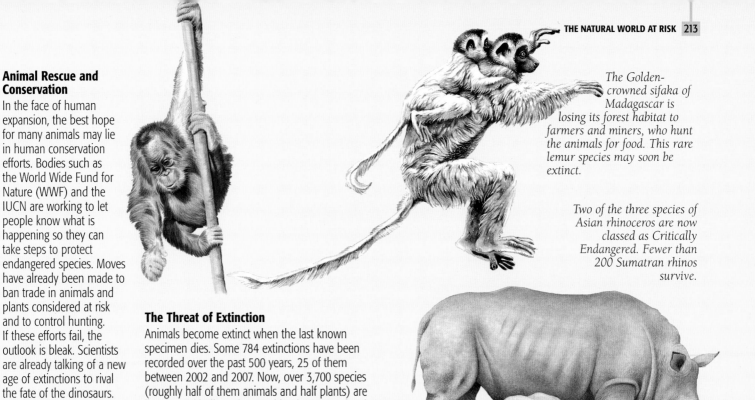

Animal Rescue and Conservation

In the face of human expansion, the best hope for many animals may lie in human conservation efforts. Bodies such as the World Wide Fund for Nature (WWF) and the IUCN are working to let people know what is happening so they can take steps to protect endangered species. Moves have already been made to ban trade in animals and plants considered at risk and to control hunting. If these efforts fail, the outlook is bleak. Scientists are already talking of a new age of extinctions to rival the fate of the dinosaurs.

The Golden-crowned sifaka of Madagascar is losing its forest habitat to farmers and miners, who hunt the animals for food. This rare lemur species may soon be extinct.

Two of the three species of Asian rhinoceros are now classed as Critically Endangered. Fewer than 200 Sumatran rhinos survive.

The Threat of Extinction

Animals become extinct when the last known specimen dies. Some 784 extinctions have been recorded over the past 500 years, 25 of them between 2002 and 2007. Now, over 3,700 species (roughly half of them animals and half plants) are listed as Critically Endangered by the International Union for the Conservation of Nature (IUCN). As human numbers increase, some experts predict that half of the world's existing animal species could die out during this century.

Destroying the Rain Forest

Rain forest is one of the richest habitats for wildlife on the planet. In particular, South America's Amazon Basin is home to a larger number of animal, plant and insect species than any other region of comparable size on Earth; one in five of all the world's bird species are thought to live there. Yet the area is now under threat from people seeking to put the land to commercial use. To make matters worse, the soil itself rapidly becomes unproductive once the protective tree cover is removed. Land that was home to thousands of species soon turns to scrubby desert.

Brush fires light up the Amazon rain forest as cultivators use slash-and-burn tactics to clear land for farming plots or cattle ranches. About 7,720 square miles (20,000 sq km) of forest are lost each year.

Breakthroughs in Medicine

Over the next decades, medicine will probably be transformed by a scientific revolution in genetics—the study of genes, the building-blocks of life. Genes are controlled by a chemical code called DNA. By manipulating combinations of genes, researchers can now help to shape living things, from plants and insects to human beings. The new knowledge promises dramatic progress in treating illnesses. Yet it also gives scientists previously undreamed-of powers—even to play God, their critics claim.

Mapping our Genes

Before the genetic revolution could properly get under way, it was necessary to map out all the 20,000 to 25,000 genes that, in different combinations, make up the 100 million cells in the human body. This huge task was undertaken by the Human Genome Project, which started work in 1990. The sequencing of the final chromosome—the rod-like structures that contain the genes in DNA—was published in 2006.

Gene Therapy

Millions of people around the world suffer from hereditary conditions such as sickle-cell anaemia and haemophilia. These conditions are passed on from parents to their children by defective genes. Now, doctors are finding new ways to combat them. They can replace faulty genes with healthy ones. In time, gene therapy techniques may put an end to such conditions forever.

The genetic revolution really got under way after 1953, when Francis Crick and James Watson discovered the double helix (spiral) shape of DNA.

A man's sperm cells approach a woman's egg in the first stage of making a baby. Inside the head of the sperm are 23 chromosomes (half the DNA found in a normal body cell). These will merge with the egg's 23 chromosomes and begin mapping out the baby's body.

Stem Cell Research

Stem cells are cells that do not have a single, fixed function; instead, they have the ability to develop into any kind of tissue or organ. Exciting new research shows that these cells may be used to help damaged tissue to regrow. For example, a person with a diseased liver who would now need a transplant, may be cured in the future by using their own stem cells to replace the damaged parts of the liver.

Stem cells can be used to "grow" corneas or parts of corneas that can then be transplanted into damaged eyes.

Whose Baby?

Science has transformed human reproduction. Fertility clinics help infertile couples to have children, and the number of babies who die at birth has been cut dramatically. Now genetic advances are opening up the possibility of altering the genes of babies in the womb, in effect creating "designer babies". If any country were to allow this to take place (they don't at present), parents would be able to choose the sex of their child, and could also seek to boost the child's intelligence or looks.

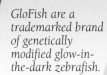

This tiny baby is in the early stages of development in the womb. Genetic research gives scientists the ability to screen babies in the womb for birth defects and inheritable diseases.

GloFish are a trademarked brand of genetically modified glow-in-the-dark zebrafish.

THE GENETIC REVOLUTION

1990
The Human Genome Project gets under way.

1994
The first commercially grown genetically modified food—the Flavr Savr tomato—goes on sale in the USA.

1996
Dolly the sheep is born. She is the first mammal cloned from an adult cell.

2002
Researchers decode the DNA of rice.

2003
Glofish, the first bio-engineered pet, goes on the market. It glows red in polluted water.

2005
The Human Genome Project and a private firm, Celera Genomics, both claim to have produced a 92-percent complete version of the human genome sequence.

The Obesity Crisis

Obesity is a vital health issue today in most developed countries. In the USA more than one-third of all adults are now classed as obese, while in Britain experts say 60% of men and 50% of women could be obese by 2050. Some people hope that new drugs will help solve the problem, while stomach stapling and other forms of surgery can also sometimes be used in extreme cases. However, the basic medical advice on obesity remains unchanged: eat healthy foods and exercise more.

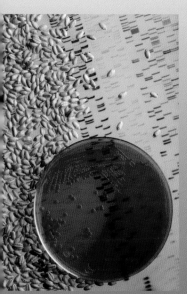

Dolly the sheep was revealed to the press in 1997 as the first mammal to be cloned from a cell taken from an adult animal—in her case a six-year-old ewe.

Mission to Mercury

One of the most ambitious planetary probes of recent years was NASA's Messenger mission. Launched in 2004, the craft flew past Venus in 2006 and two years later reached Mercury, the innermost planet of the Solar System, which was last visited by a spacecraft in 1975. The probe made three flybys before finally going into orbit around Mercury in 2011, sending back information on its composition and on its magnetic fields.

Next Steps in Space

In the new millennium, space research is literally rocketing ahead on many different fronts. Information from satellites orbiting the Earth increasingly affects our daily lives. Scientists from many countries are collaborating on the International Space Station, which has been in operation since 2000 and is due for completion in 2010. Meanwhile, unmanned craft beam back vital new information on the planets —at a cost of millions of dollars. Some people think the money could be better spent in other ways.

International Space Station

The world has come together to build the International Space Station (ISS), which circles the Earth every 92 minutes. Its main backers include the USA, Russia, the European Space Agency, Canada, and Japan, but scientists from many other countries have also visited it to carry out research. It has been continuously occupied since November 2000. It has been visited by astronauts and cosmonauts from 15 different nations.

An artist's impression of the Messenger probe shows it as it may have looked when it first flies by Mercury in 2008. Mercury has the oldest surface and is the least explored of the four rocky planets (Mercury, Venus, Earth, and Mars).

The ISS is a multi-billion dollar project. Some of the experiments conducted in the space station seek to find out if it would ever be safe for humans to live on Mars.

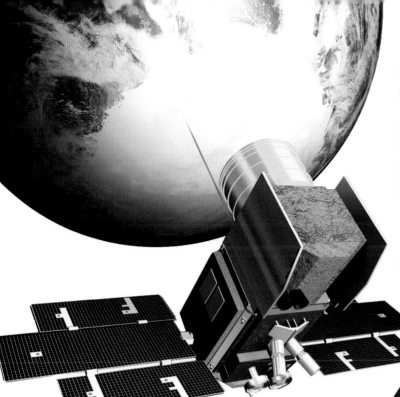

Unmanned Satellites

One of the unmanned satellites used by NASA to study Earth is called ICESat. ICESat-1 circled the globe from 2003 to 2010, gathering information on Earth's atmosphere, weather patterns, and the state of its land and ocean ecosystems. ICESat-2 is scheduled for launch in 2016. Many other robot laboratories have been launched in recent years.

NASA's Ice, Cloud and Land Elevation Satellite (ICESat) probes the growth and retreat of ice sheets, providing vital information for the study of global warming.

Climate Research

Some of the most important research enabling scientists to monitor global warming is now coming from space. Researchers use data from unmanned craft to work out the temperature in the troposphere—the lowest part of the Earth's atmosphere—and to survey changes in vegetation patterns and ice cover. Meanwhile weather satellites track the hole in the ozone layer—a part of the atmosphere that protects against harmful radiation from the Sun.

Satellite instruments monitor the ozone layer and record the size of the ozone hole above the Antarctic. In 2000, the hole was three times larger than the land mass of the United States.

Space Tourism

Seeking a way to recoup the high cost of space travel, the Russian Space Agency in 2001 began offering wealthy individuals the chance to visit space. The first to take a trip to the International Space Station was an American businessman. Now the program is booked up more than two years in advance, even at a cost of $20 million a ticket. Plans are also afoot to vastly expand space tourism: Virgin Galactic hopes to launch regular commercial sub-orbital spaceflights in the near future.

Anousheh Ansari became the first woman space tourist when she visited the International Space Station in 2006.

Global Positioning System (GPS) maps make navigating faster and easier.

Spies in the Sky

Although peaceful satellites made a vital contribution to the quality of life on Earth, most of the hardware now circling the planet is military. Information on such craft is mostly top secret, but it is known that spy satellites can provide detailed pictures of objects just a few meters across. The GPS in-car satellite navigation system relies on data from US Department of Defense satellites.

SPACEFLIGHT MISSIONS

1986
On January 28, the Space Shuttle Challenger explodes over the Atlantic Ocean just 73 seconds into its flight. All seven crew members die.

2003
NASA lands two rovers—unmanned robot vehicles—to explore the surface of Mars. China launches its first manned spaceflight.

2005
The European Space Agency launches Venus Express, which is currently orbiting Venus.

2008
The Phoenix mission lands on Mars.

2011
NASA launches the Juno mission to Jupiter. It will arrive in 2016.

2020
The USA plans a fresh manned mission to the Moon by this date.

2030
The European Space Agency plans a manned mission to Mars.

USA Superpower

With the collapse of the Soviet Union in 1991 (see page 172–173), the USA became the world's only superpower. US power is based above all on its military might, particularly its huge arsenal of nuclear weapons—which nobody wants to use. So America faces a dilemma: how best to use its military muscle to improve US citizens' lives and, hopefully, also make the world a better place.

World's Only Superpower

The USA became a superpower after the First World War. During the Cold War, its military strength was rivalled by that of the USSR, but the Soviet collapse at the end of the Cold War left the US position unchallenged. The US military military has more than 2,000 nuclear warheads in operational readiness–enough to destroy the world many times over. Since 2005, US policy has been, on occasions, to use its non-nuclear missiles as first-strike weapons against enemies thought to pose an overwhelming threat.

The F22 Raptor, used by the US air force, is a stealth fighter designed to be hard to spot on radar screens. It can fly at over twice the speed of sound.

US flags flutter on Wall Street, heart of New York's financial district.

WALL ST
←22-51

Economic Strength

The USA is an economic giant, as well as a military one. In 2010, its Gross Domestic Product (GDP)–the value of its goods and services–was more than twice that of its nearest rival, China. Its wealthiest state, California, on its own earned more than all but eight of the world's other nations. Even so, the USA borrows more than it earns abroad, leading to worries about soaring debts.

Airport security is now a US priority.

A memorial to the victims of 9/11 stands at Ground Zero in New York.

The Terrorist Threat

Protected to the west and east by vast oceans, US citizens felt safe on their home ground. But on September 11, 2001, that suddenly changed. Al Qa'eda terrorists hijacked four civilian airliners and flew them into the World Trade Center in New York, and the Pentagon, in Washington, DC. (see page 192). Since then several other terrorist plots on US soil have been been foiled, although in 2013 two Chechen brothers killed three and injured 264 others with homemade bombs at the Boston marathon.

US soldiers on duty in Iraq, supported by a UH-60 Black Hawk helicopter.

Co-operation or Confrontation?

The USA is so powerful that the country's politicians are faced with a problem: should they work for their goals in co-operation with international bodies like the United Nations, or should they act alone? America chose to act without the UN's support when it invaded Iraq, preferring instead to call on willing partners, like Britain. Some US politicians argue that the USA should not intervene in other countries' affairs at all; others suggest it should impose its own values, such as democracy and free markets, if necessary by force.

George W. Bush (US President 2001–09) with Ban Ki Moon, the South Korean diplomat appointed Secretary General of the United Nations in January 2007.

US Defense Bases

The US military has defense bases all over the world. The air force currently has over 100 facilities in 28 countries, stretching from Greenland to the South Pacific. Missile defense relies on early-warning data from the US mainland and from Fylingdales in the UK. In the future it is hoping also to operate from Greenland and eastern Europe.

EARLY WARNING BASES

US MILITARY DEFENSE

GREENLAND

BOSTON

ALASKA

CALIFORNIA

FYLINGDALES

U.K. POLAND

CZECH REP.

■ Actual (2007) ◄ Launch Platform
■ Planned ⟵ Ground-based interceptors

The Limits of US Power

Despite its military superiority, there are limits to what the USA can achieve in practice. In Iraq, US forces were unable to restore peace because much of the country's population did not want them to be there and one part of the country wants to conquer the rest. Troops went in to Iraq to find weapons of mass destruction, but none were found, which suggests that US intelligence is not always reliable. At home, US wealth and precautions cannot always protect against extreme weather, such as tornadoes and, in 2005, Hurricane Katrina.

Challenges Ahead

Since the end of the Cold War, the United States and Russia are no longer deadly enemies. In the long run, though, a greater threat to American supremacy may come from challenges to its economic might. Although it remains the world's richest nation, China, Russia, and India are starting to catch up. Policymakers have to decide whether to treat the rising powers as allies or rivals.

USA SUPERPOWER

2000
Republican George W. Bush beats Democrat Al Gore in one of the closest-ever presidential elections.

2001
On September 11, Al Qa'eda terrorists crash airliners into the World Trade Center and the Pentagon. A month later, US-led forces invade Afghanistan, where Al Qaeda operates training camps, driving out the ruling Taliban regime.

2002
The USA withdraws from the Anti-Ballistic Missile Treaty with Russia.

2003
US-led forces invade Iraq, toppling its dictator Saddam Hussein.

2004
George Bush is re-elected for another four years with an increased majority.

2005
Hurricane Katrina devastates New Orleans.

2007
President Bush authorizes a troop surge to combat the continuing insurgency in Iraq.

2008
Investment bank Lehman Brothers in New York is allowed to fail; resulting panic almost brings down world banking system and causes worst economic slump in decades.

2011
US credit rating is cut from AAA to AA+ and share values fall worldwide.

2014
Withdrawal of US troops from Afghanistan. Signs of economic recovery.

SOUTH AMERICA AT THE CROSSROADS

1999
Panama Canal is transferred from US to Panamanian control.

2000
Vicente Fox (b.1942) becomes the first opposition leader to win a Mexican presidential election since 1911.

2001
Protests after financial crisis in Argentina, cause a change of government.

2002
Venezuelan President Hugo Chavez survives a coup attempt.

2005
Evo Morales (b.1959) is the first Native American president of Bolivia.

2006
Morales nationalizes Bolivia's natural gas fields.

2012
Bolivia becomes sixth full member of Mercosur.

2014
Brazil hosts World Cup.

2016
Rio de Janiero in Brazil to host summer Olympics.

The Move to the Cities

In Brazil, deforestation is driving forest peoples from their homes. Elsewhere, more and more poor farming families are choosing to move to the cities in the hope that they will be able to earn more money there. But many new arrivals find themselves worse off, living in slums without electricity or plumbing.

A logger in the Amazon rain forest.

A migrant family seeks a new life in the city.

A Matsés boy from Brazil. The tribe's home is threatened by logging.

Medicinal Plants Lost

One problem associated with the deforestation of the Amazon rain forest (see page 213) is that it threatens medicinal plants. The forest is a natural storehouse of drugs, many of them still unknown to science; by some estimates, barely 1 in 100 species have so far been tested for their potential use as medicines. The danger is that some may be lost before the benefits they could bring have been discovered.

Native peoples use the lipstick tree to treat many conditions, including snakebites.

Argentina has its own Silicon Valley in Cordoba. Foreign firms there include US mobile phone producer Motorola.

The Importance of Oil

The country in South America with the richest resources of oil is Venezuela, the eighth largest oil exporter in the world and the fourth largest supplier of oil to the United States. Hugo Chavez, Venezuela's left-wing president from 1999, used the country's oil wealth to help the poor and introduce social reforms. But the oil is proving a mixed blessing, as mining operations also endanger the rain forest and its peoples. The native Indians are now working closely with environmentalists to make their protests heard.

Oil workers drill a new well near Maracaibo in Venezuela. The nation's oil wealth has given it increased political influence in the region.

South America at the Crossroads

South America is a dynamic continent whose dozen countries are linked by the Spanish language (plus Portuguese in Brazil) and the Roman Catholic faith. The continent is best known for carnival, dances such as salsa, tango, and samba, and for its football teams— Brazil and Argentina have between them won the football World Cup seven times. Yet despite rapid economic growth, the gap between rich and poor remains wide.

Meeting Brazil's Energy Needs

Brazil is South America's biggest country, and its energy needs are correspondingly great. Even though it has substantial oil and gas reserves of its own, it still needs more fuel to support its booming economy. One solution has been to grow its own fuel supply: sugar beet, a major local crop, is refined into ethanol, which can be used to power cars. Another solution has been to import supplies, notably via a pipeline bringing natural gas from Bolivia.

The GASBOL pipeline carrying Bolivian natural gas to Brazil is the longest in South America, stretching for 2,000 miles (3,150 km). Bolivia has objected to the low price Brazil pays for the gas, while Brazil is concerned that it has to pay for gas it doesn't always use.

The War on Drugs

A few South Americans have tried to grow rich by exporting illegal drugs—especially the leaves of the coca plant, which are used to make cocaine. As a result, the region has been a focus of the US government's ongoing War on Drugs. Since 1999, American and Colombian authorities have worked together, with limited success, to try to stop coca cultivation in Colombia. Critics complain, though, that not enough has been done to provide growers with other ways of earning a living when their crops are destroyed.

A woman gathers coca leaves in Colombia, where the plant has been used for thousands of years to relieve the effects of high altitude.

A Mighty Neighbor

The shadow of the USA looms large across South America, and its leaders respond in very different ways. Some think that economic cooperation with America —and increased international trade—is the best route to helping their countries develop. Others are suspicious of US motives, and remember that in the past the US has intervened to remove political regimes considered unfriendly to US interests. The relationship remains an uneasy one.

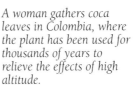

Three times elected president of Venezuela, Hugo Chavez was South America's most vocal critic of US policy. He survived a coup attempt in 2002, but died of cancer in March 2013.

MEMBERS OF MERCOSUR

Trading Links
Originally set up in 1991, Mercosur is a free-trade association linking some of South America's major nations. Some countries have signed up as associates. The accord removes customs dues and other barriers to the exchange of goods. The name is short for the Spanish term for "Common Market of the South."

■ Member states ▨ Associate states ▨ Observer state

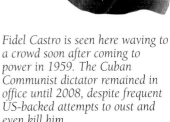

Fidel Castro is seen here waving to a crowd soon after coming to power in 1959. The Cuban Communist dictator remained in office until 2008, despite frequent US-backed attempts to oust and even kill him.

Divided Britain

Britain is divided on Europe. The Channel Tunnel opened a direct link with the continent, and children now learn the metric system in school. But the country retains its traditional measures (pints and miles), and few people want to give these up. Britain has also kept the pound, unlike neighboring Ireland, which has adopted the Euro.

Pounds sterling.

Both inches and centimeters are commonly used.

A road sign displaying miles.

The Houses of Parliament.

A pint of beer.

THE EUROPEAN UNION

1957
Six nations sign the Treaty of Rome to found the European Economic Community (EEC).

1967
The European Community (EC) is formed.

1973
Britain, Ireland and Denmark join the EC.

1981
Greece joins the EC.

1986
Spain and Portugal join.

1992
Maastricht Treaty: the EC becomes the European Union (EU).

1995
Austria, Finland, and Sweden join the EU.

2004
Ten new member states, mostly from Eastern Europe joi EU.

2007
Romania and Bulgaria become members.

2012
EU wins Nobel Peace prize.

2013
Croatia joins the EU.

The blue flag of the European Union.

A United Europe?

In the course of the 20th century, Europe was torn apart by two world wars. By 1945 it was bankrupt and many of its cities were in ruins. Then, in 1957, old enemies came together to found the Common Market, predecessor of today's European Union (EU). Since then, change has been dramatic. The EU is now the world's largest economic bloc, with more people and more wealth even than the USA.

Eurosceptics and the Loss of National Identity

People who fear the growing power of the European Union are known as Eurosceptics. They are concerned that the different member states risk losing their national identities. They also worry about the transfer of powers from the various national parliaments to the EU headquarters in Brussels, and prefer the idea of local control. Eurosceptics tend to view closer political integration as a threat, not an opportunity. Starting in 2009, the so-called Eurozone crises, made many people think the EU would fall apart. It has not done so.

Euro Enthusiasts

Supporters of the EU point out that integration encourages member states to work together rather than against one another, promoting peace and prosperity. They remind doubters that Europe is now wealthier than it has ever been and that democracy is firmly established in all EU nations. They also point to the many countries waiting to join as proof of the success of the European project.

Euro currency.

A young girl from Switzerland (which is not a member of the EU) celebrates a national holiday in traditional folk dress.

A Tight or Loose Union?

Euro enthusiasts and sceptics clash over the nature of the EU and the extent of its powers. Supporters of a closer union, generally including the governments of France and Germany, want common rules to apply across the organization, even if that means EU decisions override the wishes of national parliaments. They also want the EU to have a united voice in foreign policy, and possibly even a joint defense force. Opponents, often led by Britain, want the union to limit itself to encouraging economic co-operation.

EUROPEAN UNION MEMBERS

Member States
With the entry of Bulgaria and Romania in 2007 and Croatia in 2013, the EU now covers most of Europe. In 2014 the EU counted 28 member states. Switzerland, Norway, and Iceland have all chosen to opt out. A cluster of Balkan countries, plus Belarus, Ukraine, and Moldova on the Russian border, might one day join. Turkey's membership is currently under consideration.

◼ MEMBER STATES
◻ NON-MEMBERS

Shoppers in Italy are largely enthusiastic about the Euro, which replaced the lire in 2002.

The European Parliament building rises above the waters of the River Ill in Strasbourg, France. The parliament also meets in a second seat in the Belgian capital, Brussels.

Representatives of EFTA meet at the World Economic Forum in Switzerland in 2007.

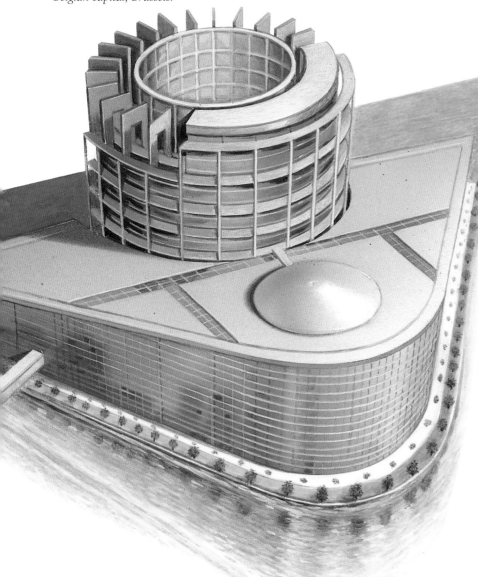

The EU's Rival

Countries that do not want the political commitments involved in joining the EU have the alternative of signing up to the European Free Trade Association (EFTA). Founded in 1960, EFTA limits its activities to removing barriers to trade among its constituent states. It has, however, lost ground to the EU over the past few decades, and now has only four members: Switzerland, Norway, Iceland, and Liechtenstein.

A Greener Future

The EU has taken various environmental initiatives, including signing the Kyoto Treaty to combat climate change and establishing its own carbon trading scheme in 2005, although so far this has had little effect. It is currently committed to cutting carbon emissions by 20 percent from 1990 levels by the year 2020.

Europe is cutting its carbon footprint through the use of energy-saving devices such as dryballs, which shorten the drying cycle in spin dryers. But the footprint has simply moved to China, where the dryballs are made.

1991
The Soviet Union is dissolved. Russia becomes an independent nation.

1992
Liberal reformers introduce "shock therapy" measures to create a market economy.

1993
President Yeltsin suspends the Supreme Soviet. He sends troops in to Russia's parliament building to put down a revolt, and 197 people are killed.

1994
The First Chechen War breaks out in the south.

1998
An International Monetary Fund loan saves Russia from financial ruin.

2000
Vladimir Putin succeeds Yeltsin as president.

2008
*Dmitry Medvedev is sworn in as president of Russia. Putin becomes prime minister.
Russia–Georgia War fought in August 2008.*

2012
On 2 March Putin becomes president once more and Dmitry Medvedev returns to his role as prime minister.

Reshaping Russia

After losing the Cold War, Russia not only gave up its Communist ideology, but also its empire. The many republics that had made up the Soviet Union gained their independence, and Russia found itself alone, a vast country committed to economic reform. The change to a market economy caused hardship for millions of people, and life expectancy for Russian men fell to 57 years (the European Union average is 78). Russia is only now finding its feet again. It seeks political and financial stability and a new role to play in global politics.

The president governs Russia from the Kremlin in Moscow, once an imperial palace and later the Communist Party headquarters.

Local women sell fresh produce at a farmers' market in the Kamchatka region of the Russian far east. Private enterprise is now encouraged throughout the economy.

Introducing Free Markets

In the 1990s, reformers used shock tactics to turn Russia from a state-controlled economy to a market economy. Subsidies were cut, loss-making firms were closed down, and private ownership of firms was introduced. A few people (billionaire Roman Abramovich among them) grew hugely rich from the changes, but others such as teachers and pensioners were reduced to poverty. Millions of people found themselves without a job. Ten years passed before the benefits of a market economy began to show.

Putin Power

During his first term in office (2000–08), President Vladimir Putin sought to boost the power of the state. He brought much of Russia's vast resources of oil and gas back under government control, and Russia grew wealthy as world prices for both rose. His attack on the "oligarchs" who took control of much of Russian industry in the 1990s proved hugely popular, helping him to win approval ratings of more than 70 percent from the public.

Left: In 2008 Dimitri Medvedev became the new president of Russia. Former president Vladimir Putin became prime minister. In 2012, Putin returned as President and Medvedev as prime minister.

Opposition Suppressed

As part of his drive to reassert central authority, Vladimir Putin restricted the freedom of the media. He took back control of leading newspapers and television channels from the wealthy businessmen who had bought them in the 1990s. Today, editors who are critical of the government fear they may get the sack. Their self-censorship makes it hard for opposition views to be heard.

Workers remove a statue of Bolshevik leader Vladimir Lenin in the wake of the revolution that overthrew Communist rule in 1991.

Moscow's GUM—in Russian the letters stand for State Universal Store—is Russia's most famous retail outlet. Usually described as a department store, it is actually a mall with more than 200 separate shops, many selling expensive Western brand-name goods.

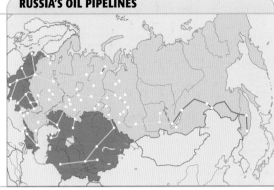

Energy Superpower
The oil pipelines of Russia form the largest pipeline system in the world, extending almost 31,000 miles (50,000 km), with more planned. Europe is heavily dependent on oil supplied by Russia. Much of it comes through Kazakhstan.

RUSSIA'S OIL PIPELINES

— Existing　— Planned

More Money to Spend
When world oil and gas prices started to rise in about 2000, Russia found itself becoming wealthy. Eastern Russia (in Asia) has not profited as much as European Russia, where more cash has found its way into the pockets of many ordinary people. The result has been a boom in retail spending and an increase in car ownership. By 2010, Russia's economy was nearly half the size of Europe's leading economic power, Germany.

A Nostalgia for Past Times
It may seem strange that any Russians should wish back what they now call "the Soviet times," but some do say that they would be glad if Stalin returned. Many students wish for a return to the days when Russia was a widely feared superpower, and the old and poor recall a time when manual workers had highly paid jobs for life, and the state subsidized rents, fuel bills, even food. They have forgotten the darker side of those times. Such nostalgia signals the limits to the success of the free market.

In 2007, former world chess champion Garry Kasparov addressed anti-government demonstrators from behind a cordon of watchful riot police in St. Petersburg.

The Chinese Dragon Awakes

Chinese symbol of power and wealth.

For the early part of the 20th century China was in turmoil, riven by civil war and invaded by Japanese troops. Then, in 1949, the Communists seized power under Mao Zedong, who imposed strict dictatorial rule. After Mao's death in 1976, the Communist Party retained control, but introduced free-market economic reforms. The world's most populous nation, which had been poor, began to grow rich. The dragon had finally awoken.

Private Enterprise

Until Mao's death, China's government controlled the growing, distribution, and sale of agricultural produce. After his death, China's rulers relaxed their hold on the economy, allowing people to trade in their own name and keep the profits. Productivity soon increased and small businesses flourished. By 2005 over 70 percent of the economy was in private hands. Foreigners were also invited to invest in Chinese firms. The result has been an economic boom that continues today.

A Chinese farmer transports vegetables to market in a homemade cart. The prosperity of the cities has still not fed through to the hundreds of millions of people living off the land.

Shoppers jostle one another at a street market in Beijing. The economic boom is putting more cash in people's pockets than ever before.

Smoke from a factory chimney spreads out across Guilin, one of China's most picturesquely sited cities. Industrial pollution remains a huge problem in China's booming, largely coal-fed economy.

1.39 Billion People!

China is the world's most populous country, with over 1.39 billion people. This figure would have been even higher if the government had not decided, in 1979, to adopt a one-child policy. Couples in cities were required to pay a fine if they had more than one child, and abortion was encouraged. (A modified version of the policy is still used.) The aim was to improve living standards, and the poverty rate fell from 53 percent in 1981 to 8 percent in 2007.

Environmental Pollution

The results of the economic reforms in China have been spectacular. China's economy is one of the fastest-growing in the world, and is now reckoned to be second only to that of the USA in size. Millions of people are better off, but the economic growth has come at a price. Environmental pollution is a major problem. Rivers are being polluted by factory chemicals, and sulphur dioxide from coal burning fills the air (China produces twice as much sulphur dioxide as the USA). Health problems are rising fast as a result.

PEOPLE ON THE MOVE

Provincial Migration

The growing inequality between the rich cities and the poor countryside is causing discontent in China. Many poor people from the provinces are migrating to the more prosperous central and eastern regions to find work in the cities. Modern farming methods have reduced the need for a large agricultural workforce.

Migration from these provinces | Immigration to these provinces | No great population movement

The World Trade Center in Hong Kong is a showpiece of the territory's booming consumer economy.

Made in China

China's economic turnaround was at first based on cheap industrial goods produced for export markets. Manufacturers have since turned their attention to higher-value goods, knowing that soon other emerging nations will be making their own cheap goods, rather than buying those made in China.

Electronics

Plastic toys

Clothes

THE CHINESE DRAGON AWAKES

2001
China joins the World Trade Organization.

2002
China launches a $15 billion project to divert water from the Yangtze River region to the very dry areas around Beijing.

2007
It is announced that people living in China's cities who have more than one child will get a black mark on their credit record.

2008
Beijing hosts the Summer Olympic Games.

2014
One-Child policy is updated to allow a family to have two children if one of the parents is an only child.

2025
Unless trends change, in 2025 China is set to overtake the USA as the biggest producer of greenhouse gases.

A Tibetan monk hangs up prayer flags, a survival of the ancient Bon religion.

Occupation of Tibet

Chinese forces invaded the mountainous land of Tibet in 1950, claiming it as a historic part of their nation. Many Tibetans protested, and have since waged a lengthy struggle for independence, headed by the exiled religious leader known as the Dalai Lama. Although all foreign governments now recognize Chinese rule, human rights organizations continue to draw attention to ongoing abuses by the Chinese authorities.

China and the Rest of the World

In China, as in Russia, there were protests against Communism as the government introduced its free-market economic reforms. Pro-democracy supporters were brutally repressed in 1989 in Tiananmen Square. Mostly, however, China has presented a peaceful face to the world in its boom years and has avoided policies that could cause conflict and so risk harming its path to prosperity. Yet its new wealth is starting to cause problems. In a world of limited natural resources, the nation finds itself competing with other powers for the raw materials needed for further growth. Chinese industrial pollution is also contributing to global warming, causing international concern.

India on the Rise

Until recently, India was underdeveloped. It lacked modern industry, transportation, and health care, and seemed unable to get out of this situation. In the 1970s, over half the population lived below the poverty line. The situation changed with the introduction of reforms aimed at opening up the economy. The result has been a boom, especially since the 1990s, that has brought new prosperity to middle class Indians. Today India still has a huge gap between rich and poor, but most people sense that the nation is on the rise.

A barber shaves a baby's head in the Hindu mundan *ceremony. Some 77.5 percent of India's population are Hindus.*

In Bangalore, one of India's high-tech cities, homeless families have pitched temporary shelters beneath an advertisement promoting a rich lifestyle.

Rich and poor

India is now a leader in many high-tech fields of computer software and engineering. The wealth this generates is found mostly in the cities among educated middle class people, particularly those who speak English. However, over 200 million Indians (20 percent of the total) still live in poverty. The pressing task facing India's government is how to spread the prosperity more evenly.

Workers in a call center in India respond to queries from customers in Britain or America about their bank balances and utility bills. India's economic rise has been partly fuelled by outsourcing—the relocation of office jobs from the West.

INDIA ON THE RISE

1991
Narasimha Rao becomes prime minister and introduces economic reforms. He encourages foreign investment, which grows from US $132 million in 1991–92 to $5.3 billion in 1995–96.

1990s
Greater emphasis is placed on educating women, raising their status and providing better health care. Non-governmental agencies tour rural areas to discuss birth control.

2000
It is estimated that 42,000 babies are born in India every day.

2003
There is worldwide recognition of India's status as a "tiger economy."

2014
The metropolitan area of Mumbai (formerly Bombay) has an estimated population of more than 20 million people.

Over One Billion People

In 2000, Indian government officials decided that a baby who was born in a Delhi hospital in May that year would symbolically represent India's billionth baby. With a population now totalling over 1.27 billion people, India supports more than one in six of the world's population. The huge and growing number of people is overstretching India's natural resources, and it is feared the country will struggle to provide enough food and water to support them.

Nuclear Issues

India became a nuclear power in 1974, when it conducted its first underground test in the Rajasthan desert. Its neighbor and rival Pakistan responded 24 years later with a test of its own, raising fears of an arms race that could threaten the safety of the subcontinent. India also has a nuclear program that supplies 4 percent of the nation's electricity—a figure projected to rise to 25 percent by the year 2050.

In 2006 India signed a co-operation pact with the USA, guaranteeing India access to US nuclear technology and fuel so that it can meet its energy needs.

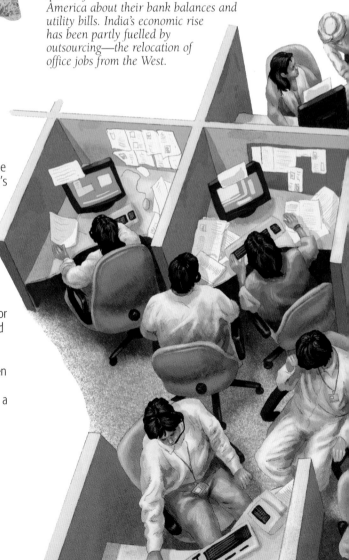

Slow Change in the Villages

India's new wealth has yet to reach the countryside, where more than half the population lives. Almost 7 out of 10 people still scrape a living in the countryside. But as the standard of living for the 700 million people living in India's villages slowly rises, more people will want to start buying more foreign goods. Buying may become a more important part of the Indian economy than selling "outsourced" skills (see The Boom Years below).

Two Indian villagers with their cows, which are venerated by Hindus. In India, the income gap between town and country is narrowing, unlike in China, where it is widening.

Women's Issues

India upholds equal opportunities for women. It became one of the first countries to have a female leader when Indira Gandhi came to power in 1966, and there are now female judges, airline pilots and astronauts. But the literacy rate remains lower for women than for men. And even though the dowry system—which requires a bride's family to make a payment to her in-laws—was banned in 1961, cases of dowry-related violence continue to be reported in the media.

A woman displays an ankle bracelet and henna designs on her feet. Such adornments are typically worn by a Hindu bride.

The Boom Years

One of India's boom industries of the 21st century has been the "outsourcing" industry—companies in Europe and America "outsource" part of their work to Indian companies, because the Indian companies can do the work more cheaply, allowing the Western companies to cut their costs. Each year, about 2.5 million mostly English-speaking graduates enter the workforce of India. However, a number of emerging countries are starting to challenge India's leadership in outsourcing. They include the Philippines, Malaysia, Vietnam, Hungary, and Poland.

CENTERS OF POPULATION

NEW DELHI
GANGES VALLEY
KOLKATA
KERALA

PEOPLE PER SQUARE KM *

- Less than 100
- 100-250
- 250-500
- 500-1000
- 1000-2000
- More than 2000

Uneven Distribution

This map of India shows densely populated areas (darker colors) and less crowded areas (lighter colors). The main centers of population are the Ganges Valley region in the north and the Kerala region on the southwest coast. The capital, New Delhi, and the city of Bangalore, a high-technology center in south-central India, are also highly populated.

The Muslim World in Turmoil

No part of the world has seen more political turmoil in recent years than the Muslim countries of the Middle East. Foreign powers, led by the United States and Britain, have regularly intervened to assert their own influence. They sent armies to Afghanistan to put an end to five years of fundamentalist Muslim rule by the Taliban, who they believed were harboring Al Qa'eda terrorists. They also invaded Iraq and toppled its ruler, Saddam Hussein, who was viewed as being a threat to the West. The result has been a growing resentment of the West, voiced by powerful Muslim clerics and their followers.

A Muslim religious leader addresses a congregation from a mosque pulpit. Islam is divided between Sunni and Shia sects.

Conflict in Afghanistan

Afghanistan is a troubled land. The mountainous terrain and the religious, ethnic, and regional conflicts of its tribal people make it difficult to rule. For a decade, from 1979 to 1989, Soviet and Afghan forces fought for control of the country. Then in the 1990s, the Islamic Taliban gained control, enforcing a strict version of Sharia law. The West intervened in 2001 and launched a bombing campaign against the Taliban. Now, the country—one of the poorest in the world—is in ruins, and the fighting continues between the Islamic militants,

In 2006, some five hundred Afghan refugee families in Pakistan prepared to return home to Afghanistan. United Nations officials gave each family a small cash sum, six bags of wheat and a plastic sheet.

THE MUSLIM WORLD

Muslim Majority Countries

There are an estimated 1.6 billion followers of Islam. Muslims form a majority of the population in a band of countries stretching from Africa's west coast to Pakistan and Afghanistan, including the Horn of Africa. Further east, Bangladesh, Malaysia, and Indonesia are mainly Muslim.

■ Countries with Muslim majorities

■ Countries evenly split

■ Countries with Muslim minorities or few Muslims

In Lebanon, a nation that has been torn apart by civil war and invasion, children play on an abandoned tank.

A Problem for Israel's Neighbors

The creation of the state of Israel has created special problems for Israel's neighbors: Jordan, Syria, Lebanon, Saudi Arabia, and Egypt. They have become home to hundreds of thousands of Palestinian refugees who have been unable to return to their original homes. The refugees remain a disruptive presence, not fully part of the countries in which they settled and resentful of the cramped and poor conditions of the camps in which many are forced to live.

Muslim women scientists at work in a laboratory. Muslim fundamentalists such as the Taliban believe girls should not be allowed to go to school to be educated.

Women's Roles

Muslim women feel sharply the clash between old and new ways in the Islamic world. In many countries, new career opportunities have opened up for women. But traditionalists insist that the proper place for women is in the home, wearing veils or head-to-toe coverings in the presence of men, as required by Sharia law.

Discontented Youth

Many Muslim countries in the Middle East and North Africa have rapidly growing populations, and there are not enough jobs to go round. Lots of young Muslims in these regions are out of work and resent the lack of opportunities. They want the situation to change. This makes them willing to listen to people with extreme political and religious views.

Youth unemployment is a serious issue in many Islamic countries, and can trigger discontent.

Hostility to the West

Muslim hostility to the West has various causes. Some people resent the history of foreign intervention in their countries, tending to blame it on outsiders' greed for oil. Others point the finger at the creation of Israel (which was backed by the Western powers), and the consequent uprooting of Muslim Palestinians from their ancestral lands. Much of the tension, though, comes from the fact that people with very different outlooks are forced to rub shoulders in a world made smaller by modern mass communications and air travel.

Right: An anti-American slogan in Teheran, Iran.

THE MUSLIM WORLD IN TURMOIL

1996
The Taliban come to power in Afghanistan, capturing the capital Kabul. Their hardline policies include amputating the hands of people charged with theft; banning television, music and cinema; forbidding girls aged 10 and above to go to school; ordering working women to stay at home; and requiring men to grow beards and women to wear the burqa (full head-to-foot veils).

2001
In the wake of 9/11, US forces invade Afghanistan to root out Al Qa'eda terrorist training camps and remove their Taliban sponsors from power. The Taliban destroy the priceless Bamiyan Buddha statues carved out of a mountain cliff in central Afghanistan.

2003
The USA leads a coalition to invade Iraq.

2011
The Arab Spring rebellion begins with revolutions in Tunisia and Egypt. There is civil war in Libya, with a NATO military intervention supporting the overthrow of dictator Muammar Gaddafi. Major uprisings also affect Syria, and other Middle Eastern and North African countries.

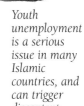

DOWN WITH THE U.S.A

مرگ برام

Mahmoud Ahmadinejad was elected 6th president of the Islamic Republic of Iran in 2005, aged 48. He quickly won a reputation for his fiery anti-Western speeches.

The Challenge to Africa

Africa has a young, fast-expanding population and some of the world's richest natural resources, including oil, gold, and copper. Its footballers, athletes, and musicians have won fame around the world. Yet it remains the least developed continent, with the highest rates of illiteracy and poverty. As recently as 2003, over a third of its people were living on less than US$1 a day. Its 54 nations face huge challenges if they are to improve the standard of living for the next generation.

Political Instability

Since gaining independence, many African countries have struggled to achieve political stability. The artificial boundaries established by the colonizing powers did little to help. Corruption and the tribal loyalties shown by many of the new ruling bodies have added to the problem. In many countries, the army has been seen as the only body able to impose order. Democracy has struggled to establish itself, and the most common form of government is still army-backed presidential rule.

This mother and her three children are malnourished because of a famine. The UN lists 17 African countries in which a third or more of the population suffers from malnutrition.

Greatest Poverty

Poverty remains an overriding problem. Surveys show that Africa is on average worse off today than it was 25 years ago. When the United Nations (UN) issued a Human Development Report in 2003, the 25 lowest-ranked nations were all in Africa. International attempts to address the problem through debt relief have so far had only limited success.

Nelson Mandela led the battle against minority white rule in South Africa and the apartheid system that enforced separation of Blacks and Whites. Now the country has a multi-ethnic government and a booming economy.

Thieves escape with oil taken from a pipeline near Port Harcourt in the Niger Delta. The resulting oil spill explodes, endangering the lives of the local villagers.

Darfur Civil War and Famine

A civil war is raging in the Darfur region of Sudan. Poverty and drought led rebel groups to take up arms against the Sudanese government. They accused it of neglect and of favoring the Arab people in the north of the country. The government sent bands of armed men (militias) against the rebels, and these militias have been responsible for a campaign of mass rape and murder, forcing hundreds of thousands of people to seek shelter in refugee camps.

Refugees shelter in a camp in the Darfur region of Sudan. Over a million people have been driven from their homes by terror attacks launched by armed militias.

Lack of Clean Water

According to the World Health Organization, almost half the population of Africa still lacks access to safe drinking water. The problem is particularly severe in rural areas and urban slums. Typically, the job of fetching water falls to the women and girls, who sometimes walk miles every day to get supplies from wells or standpipes. Unclean water can spread diseases such as cholera and dysentery.

These women in Mozambique, like millions of others in Africa, spend hours each day fetching water, which they carry on their heads (often while also carrying children).

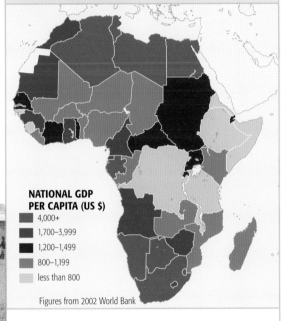

RICHEST AND POOREST REGIONS

NATIONAL GDP PER CAPITA (US $)
- 4,000+
- 1,700–3,999
- 1,200–1,499
- 800–1,199
- less than 800

Figures from 2002 World Bank

Africa's Rich and Poor

This map shows the countries of Africa graded by the amount of money earned per person each year. The richest countries are in the north and south. In general, the countries south of the Sahara Desert are poorer than those to the north, which benefit from closer trading links with Europe and the oil-rich Middle East.

AIDS

The AIDS disease is a worldwide problem, but the situation in Africa is particularly severe. More than 60 percent of people with AIDS are thought to live in Africa, and 2 million of the 2.8 million AIDS-related deaths in 2005 occurred there. Victims rarely have access to drugs that could help them to keep the condition in check. How governments respond also plays a part; Uganda has been particularly successful in cutting infection rates.

The red ribbon is the international symbol of the fight against AIDS. It was devised by a group of US artists in 1991 to raise awareness of the condition.

THE CHALLENGE TO AFRICA

1960
Nigeria and other states win independence as the colonial era nears its end.

1990
Namibia is the last African nation to win its freedom.

1994
South Africa comes under Black majority rule; the apartheid system ends. Genocide in Rwanda claims more than 1 million victims.

1999
Democracy returns to Nigeria after 16 years of military rule.

2002
Fighting flares in Uganda between government forces and the rebel Lord's Resistance Army.

2005
The Sudanese government signs a peace treaty with rebel groups, but violence continues in Darfur.

2006
Twenty-two countries south of the Sahara are still contaminated by landmines.

2010
South Africa hosts the football World Cup.

Fighting for a Fair Share of the Wealth

In several African states that have good natural resources—for example, South Africa and Botswana – the standard of living is rising rapidly. But other African countries that are mineral-rich continue to battle poverty. Nigeria—Africa's most populous nation—has vast oil reserves in the Niger Delta, and is one of the world's top 10 oil exporters. Yet the Delta region remains under-developed, and the people who live there are poor. Oil could have made Nigeria wealthy, but it has mainly enriched large oil corporations and corrupt local officials. As a result, some people have turned to violent guerrilla tactics to try and obtain a share of the oil wealth. Oil workers have been kidnapped and held for ransom, and oil is regularly syphoned off illegally from pipelines to sell for local use.

Glossary

Abdication To abdicate is to give up one's responsibilities.

Abolitionists People who believed strongly that slavery and the laws that permitted it should be abolished.

AIDS Short for Acquired Immune Deficiency Syndrome. A serious illness caused by becoming infected with a virus called HIV (Human Immunodeficiency Virus).

Analog A continuous transmission of data (as used in early computers and VCRs). Analog devices have been almost entirely replaced by digital ones.

Anarchist Somebody who rejects the need for a system of government, authority, or control in society, and favors political disorder.

Apartheid A policy of the South African government for most of the 20th century. It involved keeping black people strictly separate from white people.

Appease To calm someone down by giving in to their demands.

Aviation Operating and flying aircraft.

Axis Powers The Fascist allies fighting on Germany's side in World War II.

Balkans The mountainous peninsula region of south-eastern Europe between the Adriatic and Ionian Seas in the west and the Aegean and Black Seas in the east.

Ballistic missile Long-range, rocket-powered missile carrying a nuclear warhead.

Barbary pirates Sea robbers from North Africa led by the Bey (ruler) of Tripoli.

Battalion A large military unit, especially of infantry, ready for battle.

Big Brother society A society in which everyone is constantly under surveillance by cameras, police, and spies working for the head of the government.

Bio-weapons Weapons of terror containing some living component, for instance a virus that could spread disease among people or plants.

Black Codes Laws passed in the Southern states in 1865–66 that gave freed slaves a few civil rights, but denied them many others, including education.

Bolshevik In Russian, "a member of the majority." Bolsheviks were followers of Lenin, who in 1918 changed their name to the Russian Communist Party.

Bootleg liquor Alcohol illegally sold during Prohibition.

Bounty hunters Men who made a living from hunting down runaway slaves and claiming the reward money offered by their owners.

Brinkmanship A brink is the edge of a cliff. Leaders who practise brinkmanship take their nations to the edge of war; if they are lucky, their opponent gives way at the last minute.

Boycott To boycott someone is to have nothing further to do with that person; if a meeting is boycotted, nobody attends it.

Bureaucrats Government officials, especially those who apply rules rigidly.

Capitalism An economic system in which individuals or corporations provide the money ("capital") to set up businesses that employ people who are paid a wage. When all costs have been met, any profits from the sale of the goods produced are paid back to the people who provided the capital.

Carbon footprint The amount of carbon dioxide that each person releases into the atmosphere by burning coal, using a car, taking a plane, etc.

Cartel A group, either of firms or of countries, that tries to fix the price of the goods that its members produce.

Chlorofluorocarbons (CFCs) Colorless gases widely used to cool refrigerators since the 1930s, and also to propel out liquids in aerosol sprays. Because of their damaging effect on the ozone layer, their use is forbidden in many countries.

Civil rights The rights to which a country's citizens are entitled: they include education and the vote.

Clones Clones are organisms or cells made by scientists in laboratories. They are produced without a male and a female cell joining together.

Collectivization In Communist countries, the taking over of privately owned farms by the state.

Colony An area that is ruled by another country and occupied by settlers (colonials).

Communist A supporter of a classless society in which all property is owned by the community of people and everyone contributes and receives according to their abilities and needs.

Communist bloc A term describing the Soviet Union plus its allies, the Communist-led countries of Eastern Europe.

Confederate States The 11 Southern states that seceded from the Union in 1860–61.

Congress The body of the US government responsible for making laws, producing a budget, and passing bills. It is divided into the House of Representatives and the Senate.

Conscription Compulsory enrolment into the armed forces.

Constitution A written statement or guide to the government of a country.

Coup The sudden overthrow of a country's government, especially by its army officers.

Democracy A system of government representing all its citizens equally through elected representatives and based on majority decision-making.

Depression A time of world economic crisis, particularly the Great Depression of the 1930s.

Détente In French, "relaxation:" the easing of tense relationships, especially between states.

Diphtheria A serious, contagious bacterial disease that affects breathing and damages the heart and nervous system.

DNA Short for deoxyribonucleic acid. Molecules of DNA are found in the nucleus (center) of cells.

Economic sanctions Strong measures taken by one country (or more) against another to force that country to change its policy on some important matter.

Ecosystem A term invented in 1934 to describe the community of plants, animals, and humans as it relates to its surrounding environment.

E-learning Short for "electronic learning," or learning by using a computer to communicate with a teacher who may be many miles away.

Emancipation Setting free from social restrictions; liberation, especially the improvement of women's rights.

Espionage Spying on one country while working for the intelligence service of another.

Feminists Women who campaigned from the 1840s onward for all women to have equal rights with men.

Fabian Society An organization founded in London in 1884 to promote gradual socialist reform.

Fascism A political belief holding that people should obey the will of the state, which itself should be controlled by a strong leader. Mussolini, Hitler, and Franco were all Fascists.

Falange From the Spanish for "phalanx"—a line of troops ready to fight. The name of the Fascist Party in Spain in the 1930s.

Founding Fathers The 55 men from the 13 original states who in 1787 drew up the Constitution of the US.

Free markets In a free market, buying and selling can be carried out under whatever rules the buyers and sellers decide, without interference from national governments.

Frontier The borders of the US states settled by Whites. On the other side were Native American lands and wilderness.

Futuristic Used of designs that do not follow traditional forms, but invent new styles, inspired by science fiction and the latest technology.

Genes The factors that control how characteristics—height, hair color, musical ability, for example—pass from parents to children. The study of genes is called genetics.

Gestapo The Nazi secret police.

Gin/ginning cotton The gin (its name comes from "engine") was a machine that made it possible for the first time to process a type of short-fibered cotton grown easily in the South.

Glasnost In Russian, "openness." A keyword used by Soviet leader Mikhail Gorbachev in his drive during the late 1980s to make the Soviet system more efficient–and more Western in style.

Globalization The expansion of businesses across the globe. Goods may be made in one country, from raw materials shipped in from another country, and then be sold on to people living in yet other countries.

Guerrilla tactics Warfare carried out by small unofficial units, usually against a larger army.

Gulag A labor camp in the USSR.

Hippies A movement of young people that began in the late 1960s in California. They sought a life of freedom, peace, and pleasure. Many took drugs.

Immigrants People from one country who choose to live and work in another country.

Intifada Arabic for "uprising," this is the name given to the campaign of violence carried on since 1987 by Palestinian fighters against Israel's occupation of the West Bank and the Gaza Strip.

In vitro fertilization A technique for helping infertile couples to conceive, where egg and sperm are brought together in a laboratory.

Jim Crow laws Named after a "minstrel show" of 1828, these state laws were passed between 1881 and the 1950s to prevent Blacks and Whites from mixing in public places.

Kamikaze Japanese for "divine wind," this was the name given to a plane loaded with explosives that was deliberately crashed into an enemy ship. The pilot had no hope of survival.

Ku Klux Klan A secret society founded in the South in 1866 to prevent Blacks from owning land or using their right to vote.

Lawn jockey A hitching post carved and painted to look like a Black jockey. Escaping slaves could recognize a safe house by such a feature.

Merchant ships Ships with few or no guns, built and used for carrying goods to other countries for trade.

Mandate An order from the League of Nations to a country, giving it power to administer another country or territory (large piece of land).

Mantra A word or phrase thought to be holy and repeated over and over as a prayer or aid to meditation.

Mobilize To prepare and organize troops for active service.

Munitions Military ammunition, weapons, equipment and stores.

Nationalists People with strong patriotic feelings who want political independence for their country.

Nationalization The takeover by the state of an industry previously run by its owners or managers for its shareholders.

NATO The North Atlantic Treaty Organization, an alliance of European states and the US, formed in 1949 for defense against possible Soviet aggression.

Newspaper magnate The influential owner of many of a country's newspapers.

Oceanographer Someone who studies the seas: their climates and everything that lives in them.

Offensive A military attack.

Oligarchs People who hold power without being born to it or elected to it.

Ozone layer A layer of ozone gas between the Earth and the Sun. It acts as a sunscreen, preventing harmful ultra-violet rays from reaching the Earth.

Pioneers People who "go where no-one has gone before." The explorers and settler families who in the 1800s left the safety of the eastern US for the West. Early settlers in Canada, too, were pioneers.

"Phoney war" Time from the outbreak of war until spring 1940, when little seemed to happen.

Pocket battleship Small battleships.

Poverty line A relative measure of income inequalities. People whose income is a certain proportion (normally as much as 50 percent) below that of the average income in their country are said to be living below the "poverty line."

Plutonium A chemical element (Pu) produced in nuclear reactors that can give off immense energy if exploded.

Proletarian An expression from Marxist Communism, meaning people who work with their hands and do not own or manage businesses.

Propaganda Information, often one-sided or untrue, given out by a government or party to influence people in their favor, particularly through articles, radio broadcasts, and films.

Referendum When a government wants to know the opinion of voters on a single important issue, it can hold a referendum. This is like an election except that the voting paper contains only one question, to which people are asked to answer Yes or No.

Reparations Compensation paid by a losing side in a war for the damage it caused to the land and population of the winning side.

Republic A state in which people elect representatives to exercise power. A republic is headed by an elected or nominated president, instead of a monarch.

Reservation An area of land set aside by the US government for Native Americans, who were forced by law to settle there.

Secular Concerned only with this world's affairs; having nothing to do with religion.

Segregated "Kept apart"–a term used for the official separation of people according to their race or skin color, so that by law they must go to different schools, live in different areas, etc.

Sharia law Sharia means 'the way'. It is the way of life set out for Muslims in the Qur'an. A legal system worked out by Islamic religious leaders, based on those principles.

Slavs A group of peoples in central and Eastern Europe who speak Slavic languages (such as Polish or Russian).

Slump A sudden heavy and serious fall in the value of a country's economy, when business and the stock market are affected and people are thrown out of work.

Socialists Those supporting the political system by which the means of production and distribution are owned and controlled by the community as a whole.

Soviet In Russian, originally "a council of workers' delegates." Refers to the Union of Soviet Socialist Republics, a Communist state in eastern Europe and northern Asia made up of Russia and 14 republics.

Speculate To invest money in stocks and shares in the hope of making a lot more money as they increase in value and can be sold at a profit.

Subconscious The area of people's thought that lies in the mind below the thoughts of which they are fully aware. Subconscious thoughts may surface in dreams.

Supremacist A person who believed that White Americans should be "supreme" (in top place) and Black citizens should be denied their rights under the law.

Sustainable Those who practise sustainable living supply their needs, as far as they can, in such a way that they can renew whatever they use from their own resources.

Transcendentalism A way of thinking important in New England in the 1840s. It holds that humans should rely less on material possessions and more on the life of ideas.

UN Short for United Nations, the international organization set up in 1945 at the end of World War II to promote world peace.

USSR The Union of Soviet Socialist Republics, created after the revolution of 1917. It was dissolved in 1991.

Women's Lib Short for "women's liberation." Arising in the late 1960s, it rejected the dominance of men in the workplace and the home, and demanded improvement of women's place in society.

Workhouse An institution in which the poor were given food and accommodation in return for unpaid work.

Index

PICTURE CREDITS

All efforts have been made to obtain and provide compensation for the copyright to the photos and illustrations in this book in accordance with legal provisions. Persons who may nevertheless still have claims are requested to contact the copyright owners.

MAIN ILLUSTRATIONS: Leonello Calvetti 91; Lorenzo Cecchi 116-117, Francesca D'Ottavi pp. 11, 13, 22-23, 93, 95, 106-107, 122-123, 146-147, 153, 160-161, 168-169; Michela Gaudenzi pp. 44-45; GB Project 222-223b; MM comunicazione (Manuela Cappon, Monica Favilli, Gianni Sbragi, Cecilia Scutti) pp. 17, 20–21, 24-25, 27, 60-61, 64-65, 75, 150-151, 186-187, 188, 206-207, 224-225, 232-233; Antonella Pastorelli; pp. 42-43; Paola Ravaglia: 144-145, 158; Andrea Ricciardi di Gaudesi pp. 39; Studio Stalio (Alessandro Cantucci, Fabiano Fabbrucci, Margherita Salvadori): 136-137; 172-173, 185, 200-201, 204-205, 210-211, 220-221, 228-229..

OTHER ILLUSTRATIONS: Lorenzo Cecchi, Michela Gaudenzi, MM Comunicazione (Manuela Cappon, Monica Favilli, Gianni Sbragi, Cecilia Scutti), Paola Ravaglia, Studio Stalio (Alessandro Cantucci, Fabiano Fabbrucci, Margherita Salvadori), Starry Dog Books

MAPS: Julian Baker, Paola Baldanzi

PHOTOS: © 2007 by Olivier Blondeau: 167tl. © Chepe 166tr. © Jacques Descloitres, MODIS Land Rapid Response Team at NASA GSFC. 192tl. © Eurovision TV/Indrek Galetin (EBU) 195bc. © Chiyacat 8ad. © Michel de Nijs 166cr. © 2006 by Infrogmation 167cr. © Rpernell 166tr. © 2009 by Pete Souza: 163tr. © 2006 by Tomasz Szymanski: 166-167b. © 2007 by Vesilvio 10bl. © Haider Yousuf 195c. © WOMAD (Taranaki, New Zealand) 190tl.

BRIDGEMAN ART LIBRARY pp. 8-9b, 16a, 19, 24tl, 27tr, 29, 30-31b, 31tl, 32tr, 33b, 34cl, 35b, 36tl, 38br, 36-37c, 38br 38rl, 39tr, 40–41b, 40cl, 41, 43tc, 48tr, 48cl, 49tr, 49cr, 51cl, 52c, 56tl, 56tr, 56cl, 57b, 58-59b, 59tl, 61tr, 62cl, 65cl, 66cr, 66tr, 67cr, 68-69c, 72br, 74tl, 75tl, 76br, 77bl, 78cl, 80-81b, 81l, 83l; © Caroline Townsend by SIAE 2009/Beatrice Webb House, Dorking, Surrey, UK 59cd; © Canadian War Museum, Ottawa, Canada/ The Bridgeman Art Library 76cd e 79; 86bl, 87tl, 87tr, 88bc, 90cl, 91bl, 94ar, 94cr, 98ar, 102cl, 109cr, 112bl, 113br, 121al; © Antonio Petrucelli/ Bibliotheque des Arts Décoratifs, Paris / Archives Charmet / The Bridgeman Art Library 92al; © British Library Board / The Bridgeman Art Library 90cr; © Dorothea Lange / Library of Congress, Washington D.C., USA / The Bridgeman Art Library 95al; © Fontsere / Private Collection / Archives Charmet / The Bridgeman Art Library 30cl; © Gignoux / Private Collection / Archives Charmet / The Bridgeman Art Library 100bl; © John Held Junior, Collection of the New-York Historical Society, USA / The Bridgeman Art Library 88-89l; © Pablo Picasso by SIAE 2009 / Museo Nacional Centro de Arte Reina Sofia, Madrid, Spain / The Bridgeman Art Library 110-111ac; © Paul Maeyaert / The Bridgeman Art Library 86-87b; © R. Vepkhvadze / Bibliotheque des Arts Décoratifs, Paris, France / Archives Charmet / The Bridgeman Art Library 100ar; © Royal Mail Group Ltd. / The Bridgeman Art Library 119ar; © Wang Sheng Lie / Private Collection / Archives Charmet / The Bridgeman Art Library 108-109; © Y. Romas / Private Collection / RIA Novosti / The Bridgeman Art Library 100-101c. 137br, 138b, 154bl. CTESIPHON BOOKS: 104-105b. © Dedda71: 157cr. DK IMAGES p. 40b; Getty Images p. 28tc; p. 9t; © Imperial War Museum, London, UK / The Bridgeman Art Library 70-71c; © Look and Learn/ The Bridgeman Art Library / Private Collection 48-49b: © Marc Chagall by SIAE 2009 82cl; © Pablo Picasso by SIAE 2009 83ar. FOTOLIA: © Matthew Cole 214-215c, © Mario Bruno 8as (popolazione), © Vitaliy Pakhnyushchyy 220cs. GETTY IMAGES: 54b, 54br. 102ad; Imagno/Getty Images 114ad; Keystone Features/Getty Images 118cl, 122cl; Popperfoto/Getty Images 120c; Reg Speller/Fox Photos/Getty Images 118-119b. 163cr, 171br, 25cr, 194b; © 2007 by Christian Holst / Getty Images 190-191b. THE ART ARCHIVE: 48bl, The Art Archive/ Culver Pictures 50tr, The Art Archive / Eileen Tweedy 74cr, The Art Archive / Imperial War Museum 66cl, The Art Archive / Private Collection / Marc Charmet 81bl, The Art Archive / Private Collection London 68cl ; © The Art Archive / Ocean Memorabilia Collection: 61cr; The Art Archive / Alfredo Dagli Orti 103; The Art Archive / Central Bank Teheran / Gianni Dagli Orti 104cr; The Art Archive / Domenica del Corriere / Gianni Dagli Orti 120bl; The Art Archive / Eileen Tweedy 106c; The Art Archive / John Meek 107cb, 114-115, 118cr; The Art Archive: The Art Archive / Culver Pictures 87b, 98-99c; 128-129b; The Art Archive / Gianni Dagli Orti: 140br; The Art Archive / Imperial War Museum: 129al; The Art Archive / National Archives Washington, DC 130c, 134ar, 160al. THE IMAGE WORKS, INC.: Bill Bachmann / The Image Works: 152ar; Françoise de Mulder / Roger-Viollet / The Image works: 158-159a; DoD / Roger-Viollet / The Image works:

156-157b; Mark Godfrey / The Image works: 147al; Andrew Lichtenstein / The Image Works: 157cl; Manchester Daily Express / SSPL / The Image Works: 126bl, 141b; Mary Evans Picture Library / Eddie Bairstow / The Image works: 156bl; John Nordell / The Image Works: 143al, 161br; RIA / Topham / The Image Works: 155cr, 40ar; Science Museum / SSPL / The Image Works: 10-11b; SV-Bilderdienst / The Image Works: 6-7cb, 32cbl, 36-37b; Topham / The Image Works: 132bl, 140cl, 143b, 144cl, 146cl, 156c; US National Archives / Roger-Viollet / The Image works: 126al, 134-135b, 140ar. © Bill Bachmann / The Image Works 184br; © Wesley Bocxe / The Image Works 176-177b, 182-183b, © Craig Brough / Professional Sport / The Image Works 191tl; © Patricio Crooker / Drik / MajorityWorld / The Image Works 188-189b; © Julia Cumes / The Image Works 181cl; © Françoise De Mulder /Roger-Viollet / The Image Works 170-171b; © Ilyas Dean / The Image Works 20-21b, 29tl; © Lynne Fernandes / The Image Works 17t; © Zoriah Fernandes / The Image Works 17br; © Jock Fistick / Imapress / The Image Works 174b; © Monika Graff / The Image Works 167br; © Jeff Greenberg / The Image Works 165tl; © Justin Guariglia / The Image Works 27cr; © Louise Gubb / The Image Works 22b, 23tl; © Kirsten Haarmann /VISUM / The Image Works 171tl; © Fritz Hoffmann / The Image Works 184tr; © Marilyn Humphries / The Image Works 193tl; © Peter Hvizdak / The Image Works 192cl; © Stephen Jaffe / The Image Works 164-165b; © Rajesh Jantila / africanpictures.net / The Image Works 181br; © Journal-Courier / Valérie Berta / The Image Works 188c; © Saeed Khan / Dean Pictures / The Image Works 166br; © Jason Laure / The Image Works 181cr; © John Maier / The Image Works 188cr; © John Moore / The Image Works 178cr; © Shehzad Noorani / MajorityWorld / The Image Works 164tl, 176bs; © Novosti / Topham / The Image Works 164tr, 173tl; © Photo News / Topham / The Image Works 192-193b; © Edy Purnomo / The Image Works 191br; © Renk / Fujifotos / The Image Works 191tr; © Timothy Ross / The Image Works 30tl; © Steven Rubin / The Image Works 37tl; © Tony Savino / The Image Works 19tr, 31tl; © Norbert Schwerin / The Image Works 166bl; © Akhtar Soomro / Dean pictures / The Image Works 178cl; © Sean Spraque / The Image Works 172bl, 187cr; © Michel Szulc-Krzyzanowski / The Image Works 182tr; © Allan Tannenbaum / The Image Works 168tl; © Topham / PA / The Image Works 169tr, 170tr; © UPPA / Topham / The Image Works 176cr; © US Navy / Lightroom / Topham / The Image Works 175bl; © Ariadne Van Zandbergen / africanpictures.net / The Image Works 183tl; © Graeme Williams / africanpictures.net / The Image Works 180tr, © David Wells 228ad, © Ilyas Dean 230b. ISTOCKPHOTO: © Robert Reid / Istockphoto: 153ar; © Wojciech Zwierzynski / Istockphoto: 133ac; © Anna Yu / Istockphoto: 157al; © Brasil2 212-213b, © Steven Lewarne 212cd, © John Pitcher 212as; © Narvikk 211as, © Luca di Filippo 209bd, © Fajean 208-209, © Oktay Otrtakcioglu 208c, © Lise Gagne198as, 202as, © Claudia Dewald 201c; © Adam Korzekwa 204ad, © Konkrete 207cd, © Andyd 208a, © Tom Grill 208bs, © Robert Kohlhuber 214bd, © Paul Mckeown 217bd, © istockphoto 218c, © Craig DeBourbon 218-219c, 218-219b, © Jorik Blom 218bs, © Philip Dyer 222ac, Adrian Dracup 222ad, © Paul Cowan 222as, © Pamela Hodson 224as, © Franky De Meyer 224cd, © David Iliff 224ad, © Denis Babenko 226cs, © Stefan Klein 227ac, © sami Suni 227as.THE KOBAL COLLECTION: Di Novi / Columbia / The Kobal Collection / Joseph Lederer p. 41b; Edison / The Kobal Collection 53tl/ Epoch/The Kobal Collection 53r, Keystone/The Kobal Collection 53b, Mèliès/The Kobal Collection 52bl; © Yanco/Tao/ Recorded Picture Co/ The Kobal Collection 63b; 20th Century Fox / The Kobal Collection 94bc, RKO / The Kobal Collection / Longet, Gaston 96-97c; RKO / The Kobal Collection 97bs; Touchstone/Jerry Bruckmeyer Inc / The Kobal Collection / Cooper, Andrew 120-121b; Walt Disney / The Kobal Collection 96cs; Warner Bros / The Kobal Collection 96ar. LONELY PLANET IMAGES: Jonathan Smith / Lonely Planet Images 99al, 99c. Columbia / Goldcrest / The Kobal Collection: 132-133b. © NBC TV / The Kobal Collection / Lee, Leah 195cl; UGC / Studio Canal+ / The Kobal Collection 195tr. LONELY PLANET IMAGES: © Jonathan Smith 164bs; © Martin Moos 223ad, © Graham Bell 224ad, © Jonathan Smith 225as, © Ray Laskowitz 226cs, © Richard l'Anson 226-227c, © Bruce Bi 227as. MARCO LANZA (FLORENCE): 137al. NASA: 150br, 151, 151al, 152cl. COURTESY RONALD REAGAN LIBRARY: 141ar, 156ar.SCIENCE MUSEUM/SSPL: 90BS. NASA: 197cs, 199ad, 8as(Terra), 217c, Pat Rawlings (SAIC) 197cc, 198b; Johns Hopkins University Applied Physics Laboratory 197, 216s; International Space Station 216bd, ICESat 217as. © Worldwide Aeros Corp. 198b. SHUTTERSTOCK IMAGES: © Jonathan Feinstein 202b. © 2005 by Ben Bloker 2186tl, © 2006 by Josè Cruz 221c, © 2008 by Jack Dykinga 215bl, © Shankbone 199tl, © 2006 by Christian Wagner 210c, © www.glofish.com 215c, © Alexander Zemlianichenko 224c.